Dual Innovation Systems

Smart Innovation Set

coordinated by
Dimitri Uzunidis

Volume 31

Dual Innovation Systems

Concepts, Tools and Methods

François-Xavier Meunier

iSTE

WILEY

First published 2020 in Great Britain and the United States by ISTE Ltd and John Wiley & Sons, Inc.

ISTE Ltd
27-37 St George's Road
London SW19 4EU
UK

www.iste.co.uk

John Wiley & Sons, Inc.
111 River Street
Hoboken, NJ 07030
USA

www.wiley.com

Library of Congress Control Number: 2020942147

British Library Cataloguing-in-Publication Data
A CIP record for this book is available from the British Library
ISBN 978-1-78630-612-8

Contents

Introduction

Technical superiority is essential for successful military operations: "a small edge in performance can mean survival" (Alic *et al.* 1992). This is why the defense industry continues to propose increasingly high performance systems, and from the Manhattan Project to combat aircraft, passing through communication systems, it has significantly contributed to technical progress, especially after World War II.

Beyond the security aspect, contribution to technical progress is one of the arguments advanced by the industry to highlight the positive effect of arms expenditure. Indeed, due to tight budget constraints in developed countries and increasing costs of defense materials, the impact of defense on the overall economic performance of a country has come under scrutiny; the driving role played by defense technological innovation within national innovation systems seems to be an argument for maintaining this expenditure.

On the other hand, since the late 1980s, the technologically pioneering role attributed to the defense industry has been challenged; this marked the end of the spin-off paradigm (Alic *et al.* 1992). In pure economic terms, it was more difficult to justify military expenditure, and the relation between military and civilian domains appeared under a new light. Consequently, a long-term view was proposed of how military technological spin-offs to the civilian domain alternate with civilian technological absorptions in the military field (Dombrowski *et al.* 2002).

At this point, a duality emerged and captured the interest of the scientific community. The simplest definition of this concept is undoubtedly the one proposed by the French Ministry of Armed Forces, according to which it "must make possible military and civilian applications" (Ministre de la défense 2006). Nevertheless, this definition does not cover the full complexity of the concept of duality, which today retains several senses, none of which gathers consensus, both from academic and operational perspectives.

Upon its emergence in the 1980s, duality was presented (notably in the United States) as a means enabling civilian sectors to benefit from military Research and Development (R&D) expenditure (Quenzer 2001; Uzunidis and Bailly 2005). Duality is then to a certain extent an argument that goes against the existence of a crowding-out effect associated with defense expenditures compared to civilian expenditure in R&D. From then on, the relations between defense production and civilian production became a major field of analysis for defense economists, and duality a widely employed concept. It is the focus of many works (Gummett and Reppy 1988; Alic *et al.* 1992; Cowan and Foray 1995; Molas-Gallart 1997; Kulve and Smit 2003; Mérindol and Versailles 2010) and facilitates the understanding of connections between the Defense Industrial and Technological Base (DITB) and the rest of the economic sectors. The development of underlying principles of duality would be an opportunity to improve the economic and technological performance of military expenditure and justify its economic legitimacy. Indeed, by supporting the synergies between civilian and military innovation, duality is a means to reduce the cost of defense policy and improve the innovation capacity of a country.

Nevertheless, an opposing view on duality has progressively emerged and has taken a parallel development path. Its supporters perceive the rapprochement between defense innovation and civilian innovation as a risk of disseminating military technologies in general, and weaponry systems in particular (Alic 1994; Tucker 1994; Bonomo *et al.* 1998; Meier and Hunger 2014). According to this paradigm, on the one hand, duality weakens the capacities of States to control defense technology dissemination, making it easier for enemy or unallied powers to acquire it. On the other hand, military technologies are this way made available to non-State groups, which would then pose a new threat for the States. From this perspective, duality would lower the performance of military expenditure as a guarantee for peace and would pose a risk for global security and economic stability.

Besides these two macroeconomic approaches, there is a later microeconomic perspective on duality, which is seen as an opportunity for defense companies to diversify their activity. Although the aeronautics sector is a pioneer in this field, today almost no industrial sector involved in the military field is free from a dualization of the market, and duality is now key to the strategy of defense companies (Depeyre 2013; Mérindol and Versailles 2015a).

System integrators in particular are leading this rapprochement between civilian and defense fields (Prencipe 1997, 2000; Gholz 2002; Sapolsky 2003; Hobday *et al.* 2005; Lazaric *et al.* 2011). Given their specificity, they have to aggregate an increasing number of technologies that are not always exclusively owned by defense manufacturers (for example, semiconductors or telecommunications) and must be able to appropriate or "absorb" technologies that are nowadays not necessarily intended for military application. Conversely, while system integrator skills were originally developed within the defense industry, they are now widespread in many large civilian companies. Due to this competence, such manufacturers, particularly those with access to high technologies, can integrate in their production a broad technological spectrum, which partly originates in the military field. Therefore, due to technology transfers, companies in both defense and civilian sectors benefit from technical advances in various sectors.

From a broader perspective, this dualization can be interpreted as a rapprochement of civilian and military production systems (Guichard 2004a, 2004b; Guichard and Heisbourg 2004; Serfati 2005, 2008; Bellais and Guichard 2006). In 1995, the U.S. Congressional Office for Technological Assessment defined duality as a process through which the Defense Technology and Industrial Base (DTIB) and the broader Commercial Technology and Industrial Base (CTIB) merged into a single National Technology and Industrial Base (NTIB) (US Congress 1990). In its most integrated sense, duality is then defined as an organization aimed at joint defense-civilian technological and industrial production. In the absence of a border between defense technology and civilian technology (if it never existed), the two sectors have an opportunity to cooperate in the research and development of technologies in order to take maximum advantage of overall competences and knowledge previously divided between two environments.

According to this approach, situations such as civilian material being used in a military context, off-the-shelf purchases by the Defense Ministry or, conversely, a technology initially intended for defense being appropriated by an industry, no longer fall under the umbrella of duality. The latter is only defined in terms of commonality, synergies and technological coherence between technological systems and "meso-sectors", according to the approach proposed by Guichard (2004a, 2004b). The challenge is then to classify technologies in order to evaluate duality. If uses are no longer considered key factors for duality, then it is possible to reduce the bias of the analysis linked to fluctuations in the acquisition policies of Defense Ministries. Moreover, while uses are essential in assessing the criticality of a technology for defense operations, they provide no explanation for a potential technological transversality. How a technology is used gives no indication on its technological characteristics. In this case, an essential distinction lies at the basis of this analysis. The dual use of a technology (market-related duality) should be distinguished from dual innovation (production-related duality).

A second theme approached in addition to duality, and deriving from it, is that of technological innovation as such. When studying innovation, the definition proposed by the second edition of the *Oslo Manual* can be used, namely: "Technological product and process innovations (TPP) comprise implemented technologically new products and processes and significant technological improvements in products and processes. A TPP innovation has been implemented if it has been introduced on the market (product innovation) or used within a production process (process innovation)" (OECD 2005). By this definition, it is the very essence of innovation to provide companies with a competitive edge. This definition resumes the position supported by Porter (1985), who presents it as key to company competitiveness. Companies willing to maintain sustainable competiveness on a constantly evolving market must have innovation at the core of their strategies.

Moreover, companies are at the center of the innovation process: seizing technological opportunities is a first step that must be followed by protecting the advantage thus obtained, which is key to capitalizing on it (Teece 1986). A company can implement several protection regimes, with various performance levels in terms of degrees of appropriability (Dosi 1988). Six appropriation instruments are commonly identified (Levin *et al.* 1985): patents, secrecy, lead time, effects of the learning curve, duplication cost and time and the efforts involved in sales and high-quality services. While patents are acknowledged as an efficient product innovation appropriation mechanism, secrecy, lead time and the effects of the learning curve are considered as efficient for process innovation protection. The latter are nevertheless difficult, if not impossible, to understand, at least as far as secrecy, a very significant concept in defense industry, is concerned.

Technology draws particular attention from economists, who, among others, attempt to formulate a precise definition of this term. There are many approaches according to which technology – sometimes referred to as "technique" – is not considered as a simple artifact. It is obviously composed of one or several artifacts, but it may also include technical systems, knowledge, a social environment or uses (Pinch and Bijker 1984; MacKenzie 1993; MacKenzie and Wajcman 1999; Bijker 2010; Bijker *et al.* 2012).

Knowledge plays an essential role in these approaches, similar to that described by Carlsson and Stankiewicz (1991), according to whom technology is a "flow of knowledge and competences". Knowledge is the basis of technological systems and operates as a means to differentiate them. On this subject, the economists make a fundamental distinction between codified knowledge and tacit knowledge (Polanyi 1983). Codified knowledge is explicit, and can easily be the object of transactions through a medium (for example, a patent) which carries it. Tacit knowledge comprises know-how that is often associated with an individual or an organization, which renders commodification more difficult.

Even codified, technological knowledge is not transferred as simple information. There are costs involved in the acquisition of unformalized knowledge and organizational competences required for its use (Mansfield 1998). While the study of knowledge is instrumental to understanding technological systems structuring, the analysis is expected to capture, beyond its formal part, the informal aspects that are necessarily associated with it.

A rich economic literature explores the dissemination of knowledge and, following the above presentation, that of technology. Examining this literature in order to analyze dual technological innovation seems worthwhile. The majority of empirical studies on this subject involve patent data. These data related to knowledge flow identification are validated by a wide diversity of application fields. They were notably used to identify geographical transfers of knowledge (Jaffe *et al.* 1993; Autant-Bernard and Massard 2000; Autant-Bernard *et al.* 2014) and knowledge flows within research (Ham *et al.* 1998). Some used them to capitalize on innovation spin-offs (Trajtenberg 1990) or to study the role played by inventors in knowledge transfers (Jaffe 2000). Finally, many works utilizing patent quotations as analysis instruments examine knowledge or economic spin-offs from public research (Jaffe and Trajtenberg 1996; Henderson *et al.* 1998).

The analysis of technological dissemination between the defense sector and the civilian sector, either within the well-defined framework of duality or within the broader one of technology transfers, involves patent data only to a limited extent. When employed by defense economists, patent data are mainly used to describe the situation within the field itself (Gallié and Mérindol 2015). The works of Chinworth on duality in Japan (2000a, 2000b) are worth mentioning. Using a more thorough and regular approach, the works of d'Acosta *et al.* (2011, 2013, 2017) deal with duality, and more broadly with technological innovation in the field of defense, using patent data and an approach based on technological classes.

Less directly related to duality, other works using patent data take into account the defense theme in their analyses to show, for example, that technology transfers from public R&D to the market sectors are influenced by the defense character of innovations (Chakrabarti *et al.* 1993; Chakrabarti and Anyanwu 1993).

In this book, in order to study dual technological innovation through knowledge, two theoretical frameworks are employed. The first is the coherence framework. It was introduced in the 1990s by the works of Teece *et al.* (1994), who studied company diversification strategies. Coherence analyses originally dealt with the connection between production operations within a company. They were subsequently adapted and enhanced in order to assess the technological coherence of diversified companies (Piscitello 2005), industrial sectors (Krafft *et al.* 2011) and technological programs (Avadikyan and Cohendet 2005). These studies facilitate the understanding of how knowledge gets structured.

The second framework is the dominance framework. Economic dominance theory (EDT) is used to explore asymmetric relations between various entities interacting in a network. EDT originates in the works conducted by Perroux (1948) on the power between regions and nations in international exchanges. EDT employs a tool, namely influence graph theory

(IGT; Lantner 1974), which identifies the dependences and interdependences between entities.

According to Lantner, IGT facilitates the assessment, within any structure that can be represented by a linear system, of the "global" influence that an entity A exerts on an entity B. But the study of this global influence requires consideration of what happens in the rest of the structure. The connections between A and C, D, etc., impact and amplify the direct influence on B (Lantner and Lebert 2015). In this study, IGT is applied to technological knowledge flows in order to better understand their dissemination between civilian and defense sectors.

Adopting a systemic approach, this work reconciles a global analysis framework centered on the concept of duality (Guichard and Heisbourg 2004; Mérindol 2004; Bellais and Guichard 2006; Serfati 2008) with an approach of technologies (Pinch and Bijker 1984; Carlsson and Stankiewicz 1991; Carlsson *et al.* 2002; Bijker 2010) facilitating the evaluation of their dual potential. The empirical work relies on the systematic analysis of knowledge production (Jaffe 1986; Jaffe and Trajtenberg 2002; Verspagen 2004; Hall *et al.* 2005) within large defense companies. It employs tools originating in the theory of technological coherence (Teece *et al.* 1994; Cohen 1997; Piscitello 2005; Krafft *et al.* 2011; Nasiriyar *et al.* 2013) and also those resulting from EDT (Perroux 1948, 1973, 1994; Defourny and Thorbecke 1984; Lantner 1972, 1974; Lantner and Lebert 2015; Lebert 2016; Lebert and Meunier 2017).

This leads to a reflection on the role that knowledge and its dissemination plays in dual potential measurement and the characterization of the modes of interaction between the civilian sector and the defense sector in an innovation process.

Endeavoring to understand the mechanisms for dual technological innovation dissemination, this works addresses three main challenges. The first challenge is to define dual technological innovation and propose an analysis framework for its study. To address this challenge, the first essential step is to understand that duality is a relatively fuzzy notion, taking on many characteristics depending on the interpretation (Cowanand Foray 1995; Kulve and Smit 2003; Guichard and Heisbourg 2004; Mérindol and Versailles 2015b). Defense manufacturers assimilate duality to a form of market diversification, while public powers perceive it as a means to relax a budget constraint (Gutman 2001) and at the same time take advantage of new innovation relays; these two examples show that duality is a multifaceted concept. In order to deal with its technological component, while keeping in mind this complexity, the proposed analysis framework relies on a precise meaning of the concept based on the principle of joint military–civilian technological production. In the context of this work, duality differs from technology transfers (Molas-Gallart 1997), and the proximities between civilian and military sectors in technological production play an essential role in dual innovation structuring (Guichard 2004b; Fiott 2014).

The second challenge relates to methodology. It involves designing a set of tools aimed at evaluating the dual potential of technologies. According to the above-mentioned analysis framework, this requires the determination of the joint military–civilian technological production potential. Traditionally, economics defines a technology based on the knowledge it comprises (Carlsson and Stankiewicz 1991). It is to this knowledge, either considered as individual units or as an articulated set, that a technology owes its characteristics. Therefore, the study of knowledge production in civilian and defense sectors makes it possible to measure their capacities to jointly produce technologies that, if not identical, are at least compatible. Moreover, a knowledge-based assessment of this matter has the advantage that it avoids *a priori* judgment on the potential use of technologies, thus enabling an approach that is both independent from and complementary to that of the expert. It is consequently possible to define a set of tools that measure the dual potential of any technology employing original theoretical frameworks in duality analysis, namely the theory of technological coherence (Teece *et al.* 1994; Piscitello 2005) and EDT.

The last challenge is to understand the influence of duality on knowledge production. This leads to a repositioning of dual technological innovation in its global environment. Indeed, besides measuring the dual potential of a technology, the challenge is in this case to better understand the roles played by the defense sector, on the one hand, and by the civilian sector, on the other hand, in structuring dual innovation-related knowledge. In fact, designing a technology does not rely only on the production of its internal knowledge, but also on the production of external knowledge. According to Fleming and Sorenson (2001), knowledge production is correlational. Therefore, studying how dual innovation-related knowledge is structured requires an analysis of the knowledge specific to the respective innovation.

Furthermore, knowledge that may be useful either upstream of technological development or downstream of knowledge dissemination should be considered. Hence, the definition of the technological environment in which a dual innovation emerges facilitates the understanding of complementarities between civilian and defense sectors, and the description of dual potential depending on the interactions between the studied technology and its technological environment.

Consequently, the added value of this study is threefold: first, a duality analysis framework rooted in the principles of industrial economics and innovation economics, because of which duality is no longer considered a defense particularism; second, a set of tools that make possible, in addition to the traditional case studies, the measurement of the dual potential of various knowledge systems and their comparison; finally, an analysis of the dual potential of knowledge systems that are representative of the innovation activity of the world's largest innovative companies in the field of defense between 2010 and 2012.

PART 1

Presentation of Dual Innovation System

Introduction to Part 1

Technological production is partly driven by the intended uses of the developed technology. This does not exclude the possibility that certain technologies simultaneously have multiple uses. Putting together defense innovation and civilian innovation for the joint production of technologies that are useful to both civilian and defense domains is a challenge that can be addressed by gaining a certain understanding of technology production and dissemination mechanisms.

This first part of the book aims to build the theoretical framework for studying various modes of interaction between the defense innovation sector and the civilian innovation sector. Starting in the 1980s, technological duality has been dealt with in many works (Gummett and Reppy 1988; Alic 1994; Cowan and Foray 1995; Molas-Gallart 1997; Kulve and Smit 2003; Mérindol and Versailles 2015b), but the manner in which it is defined often varies from one author to another. It is nevertheless easy to get a sense of dual innovation, whose common and prosaic definition is the search for synergies between defense and civilian sectors in the innovation process. However, distinguishing it from related and sometimes amalgamated notions, such as dual-use items, technology transfers, spin-offs and spillovers, is not always an easy task. Whatever the case, the most recent works seem to agree on the systemic nature of dual innovation (Guichard 2004a; Mérindol and Versailles 2010; Acosta *et al.* 2013) and in order to integrate all the dimensions of duality, this is the path followed in building the theoretical framework proposed here.

The analysis will however focus on the purely technological dimension and the perspective adopted for this purpose is that of the technological system, as defined by Carlsson and Stankiewicz (1991) as a flow of knowledge and competences. Due to this approach to technology, the specific role of knowledge flows can be pointed out. As will be shown further on, these differ from other flows of goods or services and have an essential role in the definition of dual potential. In this context, the way knowledge dissemination is dealt with is crucial. In line with the above, a systemic perspective will be adopted here.

This first part of the book aims to propose a "universal" framework of analysis of duality, which facilitates an analysis focused on one of its components and its integration in the broader perspective of innovation systems. In terms of knowledge dissemination, this proposal opens up the way to creating a set of tools that will enable, in addition to the case studies, the measurement of the dual potential of various technological systems. The first step is to understand how knowledge production is a vector of technological proximity between the civilian sector and the defense sector and how this proximity can be measured.

This part is composed of three chapters that successively present the concept of duality, the method used for the study of knowledge dissemination and the definition of an original framework of analysis for the subsequent study of duality.

Conclusion to Part 1

This first part enabled the connection of an approach of technological duality whose analysis includes all the characteristics of this complex technological expression with an analysis of the process of knowledge dissemination highlighting the role of knowledge and its characteristics in its potential of dissemination within technological systems.

The initial added value of this part is to propose a consistent framework of analysis going from the general (dual system of innovation) to the particular (dual process of knowledge dissemination). Consequently, the next empirical analysis can focus on a specific aspect of technological duality, while preserving a more general perspective. The objective is to extend the analysis by gradually integrating the other DIS characteristics.

The further added value of this approach is that it goes beyond the defense specificity of the generally proposed analyses of technological duality and addresses the subject in a more traditional manner. Duality is addressed here by means of knowledge and is presented in line with the previous chapter, as a matter of joint technological production relying on more or less significant cognitive proximities.

This perspective is seldom favored as it does not proceed from defense-related specificities, but from a generic reflection on the processes of knowledge dissemination, before adapting them to duality. Similar to other technological fields involving other specificities, the methodological tools that will be presented in the next part are adapted to the general framework, enabling a consideration of the specificities of the defense industries.

1

Definitions of Technological Duality

1.1. Introduction

The relationship between civilian production and military production has evolved throughout the centuries. However, it was after World War II that this relationship developed considerably, and also became more complex. The period prior to the 1970s abounds in "spontaneous" technological spin-offs resulting from military innovations produced during World War II. Then, during the 1980s, the technological initiative attributed to the defense industry was called into question; it was the end of the spin-offs paradigm (Alic 1994). From a pure economic perspective, military expenditure became more difficult to justify.

In the transition period between the 1970s and 1980s, the term "dual use" was introduced in the United States to justify civilian R&D expenses on defense budgets, and thus bypass WTO rules (Uzunidis and Bailly 2005). Many authors have since then studied this notion, approaching it from various angles (Gummett and Reppy 1988; Alic *et al.* 1992; Alic 1994; Cowan and Foray 1995; Molas-Gallart 1997; Kulve and Smit 2003; Guichard 2004a; Mérindol and Versailles 2010). While duality between civilian and military sectors obviously suggests a rapprochement between these two sectors, no consensual definition has been reached. There are two major lines of research in the literature. The first one focuses on the object supporting duality, while the second deals with the actors and the objectives they are trying to reach through duality.

This chapter presents a review of the theoretical and empirical literature on duality and related concepts, aiming to highlight the key characteristics of this phenomenon.

1.2. Duality

1.2.1. *From spin-offs to duality*

The debate on the role of defense innovation in a dual technological universe is marked by extremely clear-cut positions. The first states that, due to military R&D specificities, public expenditure is less productive in this sector than in the civilian sector (Mowery and Rosenberg 1991; Lichtenberg 1995); it opposes the idea that due to these (financial, technical or organizational) specificities, defense innovation can generate technological breakthroughs that the market would not be able to bring (Alic 1994; Mowery 2009). Moreover, it adopts a position according to which civilian or military technical specificities limit technological transferability (Chesnais and Serfati 1992; Serfati 2005, 2008), or that it is first of all the civilian sector that stimulates innovation (Braddon 1999; Stowsky 2004). In reality, all these perspectives strongly depend on how defense innovation is perceived and on the authors' understanding of the relationship between civilian and military sectors.

The first works employing the concept of dual-use technologies referred to specific technologies, which, given their characteristics, led to applications in the civilian and military fields. The direction of this dissemination ran particularly from defense to the civilian world; this was named the "spin-off paradigm" by Alic *et al.* (1992). They referred to technologies developed within large military programs and subsequently used for new opportunities (most of which were not expected). The orientation of these spin-offs from the defense sector toward the civilian sector dominated the perception on the civilian–defense relation until the end of 1980s. It is worth noting that this perception of duality highlights the fact that, given their nature, only certain technologies can be the object of a transfer from one sector to another.

Such an understanding of this relation focuses on the result rather than on the technological rapprochement between the military and civilian sectors (Gummett and Reppy 1988). This assessment relies on many case studies, conducted in particular in the United States at the end of the 1980s, which identify technologies that can be transferred, most often from the military to the civilian sector, but also in the reverse direction in certain cases. Industrial sectors such as data processing, electronics or aeronautics in particular have been cited in many works, such as those of Flamm (1988), Gansler (1989) and Alic (1994) or in OTA (Office of Technology Assessment) publications, such as the 1990 report entitled "Arming our allies: Cooperation and competition in defense technology".

These studies reveal all the difficulties faced by researchers and experts in their efforts to identify technologies that pass from one sector to another and to draw a list of the industrial sectors in which they are used. Albrecht (in Gummett and Reppy 1988) points out the difficulty in measuring these spin-offs. He highlights the fact that this concept involves two dimensions whose differentiation is important: an intrasector dimension and an intersector dimension, the latter being rarely mentioned at that time, which further complicated the identification of these dual-use technologies.

Centered on dual-use technologies, this conception does not appear precise enough to account for the complexity of interactions between civilian and defense sectors. Indeed, merging the two terms – dual and use – together does not yield a concept that accounts for all the differences in how the defense world and the civilian world interact in the development of a technology (Fiott 2014).

Few authors presently believe that this dual use is intrinsically related to the nature of technology. The proposed idea is that this duality depends above all on the process of appropriation by a particular social environment (Stowsky 2004). Hence, transfer modalities in particular are studied.

This understanding of duality "relates to the ways in which objects (products and artifacts) used in a field can be adapted to others" (Molas-Gallart 1997). This raises the question of mechanisms for technology transfers from civilian to defense sectors (spin-in) and from defense to civilian sectors (spin-off). In this approach, the mutual nature of duality is more often highlighted. This leads to the idea of a long-term relation between civilian and military innovation and can generate trend reversals (Galbraith *et al.* 2004).

1.2.2. *Technological duality*

Dual technology transfer is a particular case of transfer occurring when a technology developed for military (or civilian) purposes is transferred toward a civilian (or military) application (Molas-Gallart 1998). Rooted in technology transfers, duality reinforces the hypothesis according to which technologies, strictly speaking, are the object of duality, but no longer highlights the intrinsically dual nature of certain technologies.

By differentiating between direct transfers and transfers requiring an adaptation of technology, as well as between transfers operating within the same unit and those involving two units, Molas-Gallart differentiates four main types of transfers (see Table 1.1). This typology makes it possible to specify the most efficient mechanisms depending on the type of transfer studied. This approach has the advantage of highlighting the prominent role that certain actors or institutions can play, depending on the type of transfer (technology broker, scientific journals, mixed research laboratory, service provider, consulting and outsourcing, etc.).

Mode / Actors	**No adaptation**	**Adaptation**
Transfer internal to a single unit	Internal straight transfer	Internal adaptational transfer
Transfer between two or more units	External straight transfer	External adaptational transfer

Table 1.1. *The four main types of transfer (source: Molas-Gallart 1997)*

However, from a methodological perspective, this does not solve the question of recognizing technologies that can be the object of a dual transfer. Several identification methods are thus considered in various research works.

The most commonly used method employs case studies. In defense economics, the interest of this method is in bypassing the reliability problems of available data on technologies. Many case studies have been conducted on various sectors or on various technologies, such as machine-tools, civilian aeronautics, information technologies with semiconductors, data processing and the Internet, to name just a few (Mowery

2010); for a full summary see the prospective strategy study conducted by IRIS[1]. These case studies show the diversity of situations and the dual transfer methods, but do not offer an overall view on the subject.

A further solution enabling the identification of a technology passing from the military sector to the civilian sector involves the study of the financing source and can be an identification solution. Indeed, it is at least possible to formulate the hypothesis that the research programs of a defense ministry *a priori* assign a military nature to innovations that could result from the program. It marks these technologies as military or at least dual. It is on this principle that certain analyses rely for the study of technology transfers from the public R&D to market sectors, and for stressing the influence of the military nature of the innovations on these transfers (Chakrabarti *et al.* 1993; Chakrabarti and Anyanwu 1993). It is however difficult to maintain a clear distinction: what falls within the defense budgetary perimeter varies from one country to another, depending on its history, on the size of its Defense Industrial and Technological Base (DITB), on its defense strategy choices, etc.

The actors can also play the role of technology markers. One technology developed by actors of the DITB would be qualified as defense technology, unlike others. This is, among others, one of the approaches chosen by Chinworth (2000a) to analyze duality in Japan. This method makes it possible to approach the question from a global perspective, but involves the risk of considering, in the analysis, technologies developed by manufacturers that are partly active in the civilian field, and hence not necessarily intended for defense purposes.

Finally, the most clear-cut approach is to consider that certain technologies are intrinsically associated with defense activity. This is, for example, the approach of Acosta *et al.* (2013, 2017), which assume that certain technological classes of the International Patent Classification (IPC) are by hypothesis technological classes in the defense field. Hence, studying

1 "The origin of critical technologies in the defense industry in France: spin-ins or spin-offs between defense and civilian sectors? Qualitative and quantitative processing for the case studies recently conducted in France". IRIS stands for Institut de relations internationales et stratégiques (The French Institute for International and Strategic Affairs). Established in 1991 as a public interest association, IRIS is a French think tank dedicated to geopolitical and strategic issues, the only international think tank established by a fully private initiative, with an independent approach.

the sectors of application of these technologies, which extend beyond the defense perimeter, these authors measure their level of duality. Methods can complement each other and thus contribute to refining the identification of technologies that are relevant for study (Chinworth 2000b).

The analysis of technologies, and notably that of the knowledge composing them, is an interesting approach. Indeed, beyond the technological object itself, technology can be defined through the set of knowledge it encompasses (Carlsson and Stankiewicz 1991). Duality is then related to knowledge dissemination between civilian and defense sectors. This reinforces the idea that it is difficult to *a priori* determine if a technology is dual or not (Mérindol 2005). Defense programs are knowledge-intensive projects, with varied sources and unpredictable final results. Consequently, knowledge duality may cause know-how transformation and generate opportunities, both for civilian manufacturers and for those active in the defense sector (Guillou *et al.* 2009).

From this perspective, the existence of either civilian or military prevalence in the duality process is more difficult to interpret than in the spin-off paradigm, as defined by Alic *et al.* (1992). In order to benefit from duality, "the whole challenge resides [...] in the equilibrium between specialization and building a joint knowledge base by the actors" (Mérindol 2005, p. 52).

This analysis in terms of knowledge leads to two opposite conceptions:

– the first would be to consider knowledge duality as a spillover, strictly speaking (a term that is more relevant than spin-off and spin-in in knowledge economics). Then duality would be the result of spillovers (knowledge transfers) between civilian and military fields, without premeditation on behalf of any of them. Duality is then perceived as a process of translation from one field of application to another. This view is finally quite close to that proposed by Chinworth (2000a) and Acosta *et al.* (2013, 2017);

– the second involves the simple consideration of the presence of spillovers as a corollary of the absence of duality:

> Particular research is done exclusively in one domain and adapted more or less without change in others. The existence of spillovers, therefore, is not evidence of duality, and might in fact be evidence of its absence. Thus, promotion of spillovers can be viewed as a policy designed to correct the 'duality' failure of a program of R&D. (Cowan and Foray 1995, p. 852)

According to this perspective, duality resides in the joint civilian–military design of knowledge. In this case, duality is an input data of technological change; it involves an evolution, if not identical, at least compatible with the technical characteristics of civilian and military applications.

This being said, a certain number of works have been conducted which indicate that the border between the two sectors is highly porous to knowledge. Three key stages in the research enable the progress toward a method for systematic knowledge analysis in duality. The first stage is that of studies conducted at the company level, according to which the sources of knowledge employed by defense companies are both defense and civilian companies (Chakrabarti *et al.* 1993). The second is that of studies at the technology level, which try to track all the links between knowledge produced in the defense field and that produced in the military field (Acosta *et al.* 2011, 2013, 2017). They pay particular attention to spillovers, as is the case for Japan, in the work of Chinworth (2000a). Finally, one article proposes to lay the bases for a systematic study of knowledge by means of patents. This study does not rely on a view of knowledge duality in terms of spillovers, but in terms of similarity in knowledge production, otherwise put, a cognitive proximity between the civilian field and the defense field. In that respect, it is in agreement with case studies that try to identify similarities and differences between civilian research and defense research in various technological domains (Lapierre 2001). Hence, this analysis is close to the above-mentioned second perspective, according to which, instead of being characterized by transfers, duality is characterized by a potential joint production of knowledge and it advances a shared foundation used by both parts (Meunier and Zyla 2016).

In addition to knowledge composing defense technologies, the complexity of these systems contributes to obscuring the link between civilian innovation and defense innovation. During World War II and in the decades after it, arms programs grew in complexity. The hydrogen bomb, fighter jets and ballistic missiles are examples that prove this dynamics. In order to develop these complex technologies, those who designed these programs needed to develop new system engineering knowledge for a better integration of these technologies in a homogeneous system (Sapolsky 2003).

Defense systems lost none of their complexity. They combine many components that are hierarchically organized to produce an integrated operational system. They are often referred to as Complex Product Systems (CoPS) (Prencipe 1997; Hobday *et al.* 2000, 2005) because of the significant number of components, knowledge depth and competences to be implemented, as well as the production of new knowledge required by their development (Hobday 1998).

In the face of this complexity, two types of knowledge can be distinguished: one related to system architecture and the other to components (Henderson and Clark 1990). This distinction is essential when studying duality (Mérindol 2010). Indeed, while complex systems emerged in the military field, they then spread to civilian sectors, driving the development of competences in the field of system integration. From then, it was possible for the civilian and military sectors to share knowledge on the technological components as well as system engineering. Consequently, the observation of duality became even more difficult and subtle.

Nevertheless, this way of assessing whether duality between two knowledge systems is related to one of the knowledge components shared by two systems, or to two systems relying on the same knowledge architecture, is not trivial. On this subject, contemporary literature points out that the specificity of knowledge in the defense field is more often at the system architecture level than at the component level (Lazaric *et al.* 2011). In other terms, defense systems combine technologies that, taken individually, are used by both defense and civilian sectors, but associate them in an original manner.

This distribution of knowledge between defense and civilian sectors obviously evolves depending on the various technical systems developed and on the innovations they generate. A proper understanding of duality requires the consideration of temporal dynamics. Duality should be considered at the very beginning of a product life, namely during the research phase, and should obviously stop during the development phase (Gagnepain 2001).

Given that duality is not a constant phenomenon, then the period, phase and moment during which it is manifest should be identified. Alic *et al.* (1992) offer a first macrolevel approach of this dynamics explaining, for semiconductors, the reversal of the direction of spin-offs between the civilian and military sectors by the domination of military demand in the 1980s and, afterwards, by a domination of civilian demand. This made the military sector dependent on civilian innovation, as it is the latter that mainly directs R&D efforts in this field.

In the 1990s, Foray (1990) and Chesnais (1993) noted a transformation in the relation between civilian R&D and military R&D. Foray highlighted the weakening of the role of military R&D in the increase of industrial productivity and pointed out the following two factors:

– the distortion of the scientific and technical system related to the technical specificities of the military material. As such, they highlighted the operational nature of R&D programs financed by defense, which favors the development expenditure as well as a strong product instead of process orientation of these programs;

– the end of the four types of spin-offs identified by Mowery and Rosenberg (1991): direct effects (commercial application of technologies directly issued from defense), second-order effects (only one part of technology is embedded, either in a material form or as knowledge), effects related to research (reflected in knowledge dissemination) and organizational effects (for example, through a community of researchers); these disappear with the end of the generic nature of technologies.

Based on this observation, Foray recommends two organizational transformations: on the one hand, organizing the increasing dependence of military technology on civilian R&D and, on the other hand, promoting the idea of defense financing for civilian programs, as a guarantee for their development. In the particular case of France, the upstream study programs are presented as one of the means of "insertion of defense R&D policies in global technological policies" (Foray and Guichard 2001). It is the interaction of these programs with the other devices that should be considered, in view of its role as an instrument of duality.

Besides these long-term dynamics, a microanalysis facilitates the understanding of short-term dynamics. From an evolutionary perspective, the dual potential of a technology varies in time, and also depends on the type of R&D program (Cowan and Foray 1995).

First, the time variation: the notion of a technology lifecycle (Utterback and Abernathy 1975; Abernathy 1978) highlights two phases (experimentation then standardization) during which the dual potential evolves. The experimentation phase has the highest potential, while standardization brings down dual potential. Indeed, during the experimentation phase, potential applications of technology are not yet clearly identified, and therefore they may appear interesting to both civilians and militaries. But jointly conducted research may speed up the timetable; this means that actors in the defense sector and those in the civilian sector conduct tests together and thus accelerate the technology maturing process. They can also save time in terms of the "event", by conducting a higher number of tests before the standardization phase. Thus they reach a higher level of technology maturity within the same lapse of time (Cowan and Foray 1997).

During the standardization phase, the application domains require specific adaptation to the defense case or to the civilian case (norms, regulations, etc.). Each application caries on developments that lead to technological trajectories diverging between the two domains, and reduce the number of potential collaborations.

Then, things depend on the type of project: once more, according to Cowan and Foray, the potential of a product-oriented project is not the same and does not evolve at the same pace as the potential of a process-oriented project. A product-oriented project has a lower dual potential, as it is limited by demands specific to the application domain. Moreover, the standardization phase strongly reduces this potential even further. A process-oriented project is, on the other hand, less limited by the civilian or military specificities and the standardization phase can be at least in part jointly conducted, leading to civilian and military convergence on the implementation of the technology.

In this approach, duality is perceived as a mechanism for the joint production of technology. Organizing R&D according to duality principles would then enable a larger number of potential applications, the delay of standardization-related technology lock-in and consequent preservation of technology variety.

On the other hand, other research according to the technology lifecycle has proved that defense may show renewed interest in technologies after their standardization in the civilian sector, and thus revive their dual potential (Sachwald 1999). Duality is perceived here as a spin-in getting close to the off-the-shelf purchase practice within a cost reduction policy.

A last note on temporality is worth making in relation to the life time of a defense program, and particularly to its maintenance in operational conditions (MOC). This characteristic of defense programs increases the complexity of the civilian–defense relation. Indeed, even if, as underlined by Droff (2013), in MOC duality facilitates the proximity between civilian and military activities, the fact remains that, due to regulatory and operational constraints of military MOC, manufacturers have to maintain competences and technologies for a very long time after their development. In these types of activities, duality is related to transfers or to the provision of equipment adequate for a given territory.

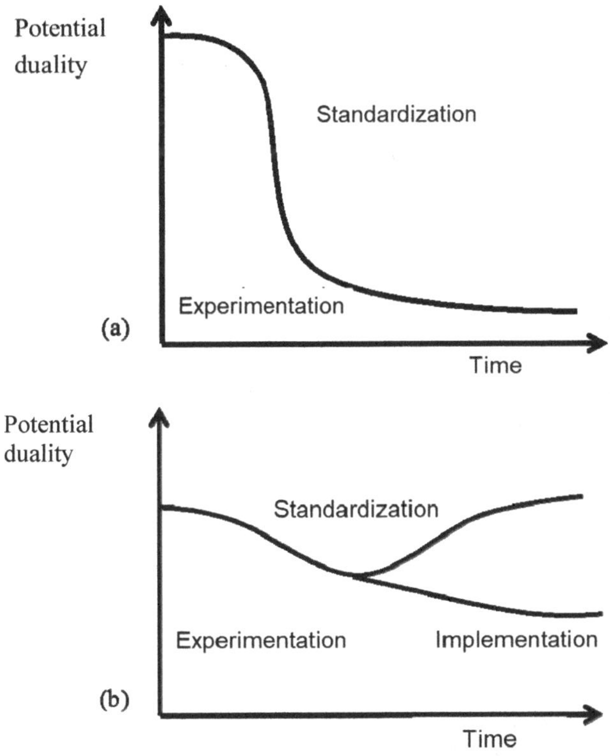

Figure 1.1. *Technology cycle and dual potential. (a) Product-oriented; (b) process-oriented (source: Cowan and Foray 1995, p. 858)*

Given these considerations on the temporal dimension, *a priori* knowledge on the applications of a technology in the future seems unlikely, as the majority of them have multiple uses (Sachwald 1999). In addition to temporality, some consider that future applications of a technology depend in particular on the social network in which it is developed or used (Cowan and Foray 1995; Kulve and Smit 2003). In innovation sociology, the notion of collaboration between network actors is essential for the economic dynamics. The concepts of techno-economic networks (Callon 1991) or sociotechnical networks (STN) (Elzen *et al.* 1996) point out this aspect; they are also the source of inspiration for the approaches of duality that place the collaborations between actors at the core of the analysis (Kulve and Smit 2003). Their main contribution is that the study of duality is no longer focused on technologies, but on the networks in which they emerge. The characteristics of these networks are susceptible to facilitating dual development. The idea of a temporality in the dual potential, as advanced by Cowan and Foray, is preserved, together with the idea of transfer mechanisms specific to each situation.

This approach inspires the most recent works on duality and the innovation system perspective is nowadays often preferred for the integration of these network effects in the analysis (Guichard 2004a; Guichard and Heisbourg 2004; Mérindol 2004; Serfati 2008; Bellais 2014). The system set-up, animation and organization are presented in this context as essential challenges of dual technological innovation.

The approaches in terms of innovation system do not fit the "outdated perspective of technical change that is taking place quasi-autonomously from the rest of economy" (Amable 2003). In defense economics, it is the multidimensional nature of this approach that renders it particularly interesting for addressing matters of organization, governance or strategy of duality.

1.3. Actors and objectives of duality

Duality organization refers directly to expected (economic, technological, strategic) performance, which varies depending on the actor and influences their behavior (Lu *et al.* 2015). Its implementation associates sometimes conflicting challenges, from knowledge management to public policy challenges (Daguzan 2001). Moreover, there are different ways to consider duality, and therefore various objectives and different strategies. Similar to the definition of a dual object, there is no general agreement on the principles that should guide duality implementation.

For a proper consideration of this diversity in the implementation of duality, this section studies the matter from the most microeconomic perspective (company strategy) to the macroeconomic level (international relations).

1.3.1. *Dual strategies of companies*

At the end of the Cold War, given the decrease in defense expenditure, the production of systems for military purposes was gradually privatized and consolidated around large groups. These companies can then consider duality as a means to reach a balance and stabilize results in a contracting or at least very cyclical market (Depeyre 2013).

From then on, from a company perspective, dual strategy involves addressing both civilian and military markets. Duality is intuitively represented as a means to achieve economies of scale or scope. This however requires many adjustments within such a company, which must reconcile more or less diverging regulatory, technical, financial and commercial constraints. The analysis proposed by Mérindol and Versailles for Thales company is particularly instructive. In this article, Thales strategy is referred to as "global duality". "The company is trying to benefit from its technological advantage by developing synergies between the solutions proposed for a set of products on adjacent markets (defense, aeronautics, land transport, etc.)" (Mérindol and Versailles 2015b, p. 10). The analysis indicates the influence that such a strategy has on the competences and technological developments of a company.

In reality, there are various ways to consider a dual strategy. One case may involve market diversification without diversification of competences; this amounts to capitalizing on its competences by adapting its offer to new clients. A reverse approach to dual strategy may involve proposing new products to the same (military or civilian) clients using new competences coming from the other sector, in completion to those already existing in the company. Duality is then the result of strategic reflection for the company whose objective is, in one case, to shift specific resources to a new market (market diversification), while in the other case the objective is to take advantage of new resources for the same market (product diversification). Less often, it involves both simultaneously.

Whatever the situation, this dual diversification requires reaching a compromise between two sometimes distant universes. Literature stresses three challenges that the companies should address; they refer to the role of demand, financing needs, and management of competences.

Let us first consider the role of demand: besides the specificity of military demand, for which performance criteria are essential and strategic superiority or sustainable supply are high priority, a "small edge in performance can mean survival" (Alic *et al.* 1992, p. 114). Already in 1988, Albrecht (Gummett and Reppy 1988) raised the question of the role of final users in the dynamics of technology transfer, both in relation with the army and with civilian users. This proves essential in the dominance of one sector or another in the development of technology. The dominance (in terms of value) of a (civilian or military) demand with respect to the other drives the manufacturers to address this demand as a priority, which leads to structuring the products depending on the expectations of the dominant client. The other one is secondary and must do with the technology such as developed, though it may not exactly meet its needs.

Due to consumer computing emergence, the civilian sector has progressively become the main engine of this industry, while the military sector became a follower engaging in off-the-shelf purchase in the semiconductors field (for example, Alic et *al.* 1992). Moreover, users do not have the same understanding of technology as manufacturers, and are not necessarily concerned by its origin. Therefore, a technology that best meets their need is preferred to the one originally developed to meet that need. Taking their expectation into account is an important element in the dissemination and development of duality, initiating transfers from one sector to another (similar to the example of lead users).

Next, financing constraints should be considered: the financing structure of defense companies is characterized by specific constraints marked by the state's dominant role, fluctuating financial markets, less involved banks, etc. (Goyal *et al.* 2002; Besancenot and Vranceanu 2006). Nevertheless, due to the dualization of defense, financing structures seem to converge. One question formulated in the literature is how this technological duality can modify the financing structure of defense industries and bring them closer to the civilian sector. The works conducted by Jean Belin seem to show that, for a defense company, duality appears to facilitate its access to private capital and therefore improve its financing capacity (Belin and Guille 2008).

Finally, constraints related to the management of competences: the more or less efficient use of this knowledge depends on the competences within organizations; knowledge management becomes a key competence in the implementation of duality (Versailles and Mérindol 2014). Companies active in the defense sector rethink the limits within which they draw and use their knowledge. Consequently, the limits of a secrecy-based knowledge management strategy, formerly prevailing in this sector, become obvious. Some studies even indicate a stronger tendency for patent filing in the companies active in defense (Guillou *et al.* 2009). According to innovation economics, there is an interest in new strategies for knowledge management and more widely for the management of competences (Lazaric *et al.* 2011).

Depending on the type of company, these constraints weigh differently on the strategies. Nowadays, more than in the past, following the large-scale privatization taking place in the 1990s in the major arms producing countries (Bellais 2005; Lazaric *et al.* 2011), top manufacturers play the role of Lead System Integrators (LSI), and the dual potential of armament systems depends on their capacity to integrate a wide variety of subsystems from various horizons (Mérindol 2010). It is worth noting that the integrator role can also be assumed by a public organization. As such, the French National Aerospace Research Center (Office national d'études et de recherches aérospatiales (ONERA)), which absorbs and develops technologies from both civilian and military sectors to the benefit of both, is a good example (Lafon 2001). Unlike large organizations, entrepreneurship or spin-off strategies can also be platforms that facilitate the dissemination of technologies between civilian and defense sectors (Azulay *et al.* 2002).

Referring to innovation in general and dual innovation in particular, one part of the literature points out the importance of knowledge networks and learning processes. On this subject, innovation sociology enables the significant expansion of the analysis framework by studying innovation networks. They show that their organization plays a role in the use of technological potentialities, and in particular in the use of dual potential.

Guichard (2004a) recalls the interest of sociological approaches that understand the encounter between different social worlds in terms of processes. Her analysis relies particularly on "technoeconomic networks". These are defined as "a set of heterogeneous actors – public laboratories, technical research centers, industrial firms, financial organizations, users, and public authorities – which participate collectively in the development and the diffusion of innovation and which via numerous interactions organize the relationships between scientifico-technical research and the marketplace" (Callon 1991, p. 220). Guichard points out the role of an actor who "shifts and transforms ideas, means, objects, roles and their links and maintains various interests in alignment until a single solution emerges" (Guichard and Heisbourg 2004, p. 97). According to this solution, Guichard refers to this role as that of "translator" within "dual networks".

According to this approach, network construction is a collective challenge centered on this translator. She recalls that these networks have variable geometry and go beyond the set of actors composing them, and are also composed of a set of intermediaries such as written documents (scientific articles, reports, patents, etc.), embedded competences (mobile researchers, engineers moving from one company to another, etc.), money (cooperation agreements between a research center and a company, financial loans, a client purchasing a good or a service, etc.) and more or less elaborated technical objects (prototypes, machines, end-user products, etc.). They are structured around three poles, each of which has its role: the scientific pole (knowledge production), the technical pole (design of a coherent object able to provide services) and the market pole (groups the users and defines the demand). Therefore, the dual network is a specific case of a technico-economic network (TEN). According to this approach, technology is not *a priori* defined as dual. Its development at the core of a network grouping two different social worlds, the defense and civilian worlds, through the interactions it generates, confers technology a dual nature.

Assuming that the duality of a technology is defined by the network in which it is developed, this analysis of duality comes close to the framework of analysis developed by Kulve and Smit (2003). They reworked the TEN and proposed the concept of STN, which they apply to the specific case of duality. They developed the idea that the social network within which technologies are developed determines the dual nature of a technology, unlike other approaches that focus on uses or financing, for example. It is a network of dual actors working together around the same technology that makes it possible to qualify the respective technology as "dual" (Guichard 2004a, 2004b; Guichard and Heisbourg 2004). Within this theoretical framework, the way to understand duality resumes the principles established by Cowan and Foray (1995, 1997), which stipulate that the transfer of a technology developed in an innovation network entirely dedicated to defense toward the civilian sector (or vice versa) is rather a proof of the absence of duality.

Duality no longer involves the organization of transfers, but the use of possible synergies between civilian and defense sectors during the innovation process. It is perceived as a window of opportunities. Such a network is a set of social interactions, whose stability generates high resilience. Therefore, the nature of these relations is essential for maintaining success; this relies particularly on the involvement of actors dedicated to the construction of the dual network, whose role is particularly pointed out. Furthermore, Kulve and Smit mention the set of other factors leading to the success or failure of such a network (Table 1.2). They point out the policies aiming to develop certain competences associated with the construction of such networks as key factor of the successful integration of civilian and military industrial and technological bases (Kulve and Smit 2003).

Success factors	Failure factors
Actors dedicated to network construction Mixed network of civilian, military and dual actors Significant technological overlapping of various applications	No dual financing possibility No common "dual" purpose of the participants Differences between lifecycles of the applications

Table 1.2. *Success or failure factors of duality (source: Guichard and Heisbourg 2004, p. 102)*

Moreover, many authors underline the fact that the elaboration of complex systems (also referred to as CoPS) involves mastering wider knowledge. Such knowledge is rarely concentrated within a single actor, consequently mechanisms for knowledge management throughout networks are required. New possibilities of interactions between actors emerged in order to create fully or partially dual technologies. In this context, the protection of innovations and their valorization are essential. New practices are established in the defense industry and they modify the organization of companies given the fact that the management of intellectual property rights (IPR) requires new competences (Ayerbe *et al.* 2012, 2014).

Innovation networks are particularly dense (Cantner and Pyka 2001; Kuhlmann 2001). Duality led to the emergence of new actors within the innovation networks of the defense world. The complexity of knowledge management increased (Mérindol 2004). In the 1990s, the emergence of "systems of systems" (systems interconnected through information and communication systems) facilitated technology transfers between defense and civilian sectors. This was done jointly with the emergence of LSI, characterized by the role of evaluator, manager and architect of programs that certain companies had to assume (Lazaric *et al.* 2011). Consequently, LSI is a key actor of dual innovation network, as it is the one that, mastering the system architecture, is able to integrate knowledge coming from both civilian and military sector. Besides mastering the system-related knowledge architecture, integrating such a system requires knowledge associated with subsystems or other components (Prencipe 1997; Hobday *et al.* 2005).

In the case of a dual innovation network, LSI draws its knowledge from both civilian and defense worlds (which makes it a bridge between these two worlds) and develops organizational competences that cannot be dissociated from this activity in order to achieve it. Therefore, it plays a role in what some refer to as "coopetition" between the actors of a network (Depeyre and Dumez 2010).

Nevertheless, the consideration of duality through a network is not always satisfactory, as it focuses on coordination between actors. If systemic approaches are used, the analysis can include structural and institutional components, whose evolution can be assessed. This type of analysis relates to both defense and civilian sectors and stresses the governance problems in the implementation of duality.

1.3.2. *Dual policies of innovation*

Understanding duality from the systemic perspective amounts to studying the institutional, organizational, legal and financial arrangements. The problems raised vary in nature and often highlight the intangible aspect of the notion (knowledge, competences, informational proximities, etc.). This also points out the system governance problems and, consequently, the public policies associated with this form of coordination between civilian and military sectors. This is how the concept of "dual policy" or "duality policy" emerges. "It corresponds to the search for an organization of knowledge and information exchange in which the State is the facilitator. Public authorities must define the common research themes and initiate knowledge and information exchanges between the civilian and military research sectors" (Mérindol 2004, p. 102).

Although duality is not at the core of their analysis, Uzunidis and Bailly (2005) deal with the relation between military innovation and civilian innovation. They developed a framework of analysis as a system of systems at the national scale: "the organic square of the valorization or military research". This enables the system to be pure, easily regulated by mechanisms that control technology and information flows between countries in the military field and the application of Buy American, Buy French or Buy British principles. This valorization system relies on the interaction between regulation, technical progress, system strategy and economic environment. The American model serves as an example of application of this system that is "essentially characterized by massive financing of military technologies, which will later on (over an unpredictable time horizon) yield results in the civilian sector" (Uzunidis and Bailly 2005, p. 68).

From this perspective, technological duality is a potential that the system as a whole tends to valorize. This transversality of technologies between various products is essential in this model. Generic technologies must be rapidly disseminated within companies and knowledge sharing is consequently a key factor for system success. According to some authors, it may be interesting to shift from a market-based Smithian model, to a Schumpeterian model of "cognitive capitalism", based on a network organization facilitating "permanent innovation".

Serfati (2008) introduced the expression "French meso-system of armament" (FMSA) to study the specific case of France. This approach between the microeconomic and macroeconomic levels points out the interactions between three main actors: the General Directorate for Armament (Direction générale pour l'armement (DGA)), large contractors and technological agencies such as the French National Aerospace Research Center or the Atomic Energy Commission (Commissariat à l'énergie atomique (CEA)). It is possible to study the commercial and non-commercial interactions within FMSA and the rest of SNI. As far as duality is concerned, this approach enables an analysis of relations in the design of technologies, such as the relations between technology, economy and society. Due to the influence exerted by a country's history, its international relations, industrial sectors and technologies, entrepreneurial culture and the history of techniques, it is unlikely that a single optimal model for organizing technology transfers will be defined.

Moreover, the analysis made by Serfati (2008) notes that, despite the transferability of certain technologies between defense and civilian sectors, military innovation did not always play by the rules of duality. The case considered, commonly quoted as an example, is that of the development of the Internet in the United States, where the actors in the defense sectors did not support knowledge dissemination in the civilian sector. To deal with this type of behavior, she pointed out the positive role that IPR can play in an innovation system, particularly in the case of duality.

Indeed, according to Serfati, there are two advantages to using mechanisms for the protection of intellectual property in defense programs. First, this encourages civilian companies to participate in defense programs, as they see these mechanisms as a means to protect their interests. Second, by formalizing knowledge and rendering it accessible, mechanisms such as patents contribute to speeding up knowledge dissemination (anyone can study the patent and acquire the knowledge it contains), even if there is a cost to using this knowledge (Serfati 2005). Serfati adds however that the efficiency of IPR depends on how the rest of the system is organized, particularly by the development of public–private partnerships. The latter enable the management of competence transfers from a defense ministry to private companies, according to the PFI (Public–Private Finance Initiative) model (Bellais 2005). This offers a solution to problems related to information asymmetry and minimizes the systemic risk related to the financial power of the defense ministry, which can impose its demands on the contracting groups, particularly in terms of knowledge dissemination (Serfati 2005).

Within the framework of duality, the national scale is considered, as defense innovation problems are still mainly a national challenge to the present day. In the works of Guichard and Heisbourg (2004), duality is described as a "way to manage research, innovation and production of defense systems that aims to generate economies of scale, variety and externalities with the civilian sector" (p. 97). This management model places great emphasis on dual policy. It is a means to use a synergistic potential of defense innovation and civilian innovation by joint actions, coordination processes and incentive mechanisms (Guichard 2004a). This approach to duality management involves a governance that brings together public authorities, private companies and research centers.

Furthermore, Guichard (2004a) shows that this duality is managed by three different structures. They correspond to different levels of technological proximity, each entailing different recommendations in terms of governance of the innovation system:

– convergence: technical characteristics and performances involving the convergence of norms, and certification processes;

– integration: for disjoint products, requiring the implementation of common processes (within companies, to reduce the costs of varieties, and within the research system) by means of a collaboration structure;

– transposition: from a technological module or from a military product to a civilian product or vice versa. This involves passing from the preparation of defense systems to the insertion of civilian subsystems and the search for market opportunities for the defense subsystems.

This systemic approach indicates, among others, the complexity of civilian–military relations. Implementing public policies appears to be essential for organizing this relation. These public policies have two apparently contradictory objectives. The first is to continue mastering the technological flows in a more open world and the second is to take full advantage of the opportunities offered by this world.

Finally, in relation to the implementation of duality, Guichard underlines the role of dual policies. She develops the principles of action for the actual implementation of such policies. The first element highlighted deals with the norms and standards that must be harmonized between the two sectors, both at the national and supranational levels within international authorities. Then she underlines the importance of procurement agencies (DGA in France) in the organization of duality. In a dual system, these institutions are located at the interface between the actors of the civilian innovation system, on the one hand, and the actors of the defense innovation system, on the other hand[2]. To

2 For further details on the role of DGA in the French innovation system, see Lazaric *et al.* (2011). Their work discusses the competences that DGA must have depending on the evolutions of the national innovation system, from the project architect to the project manager.

facilitate interactions, they must structure the R&D programs in which cooperation is possible. For a dual actor, the success of such a procedure depends on its capacity to maintain and develop scientific and technical competences in order to be able to evaluate research and development programs. Finally, she notes that the integration of the production system depends on higher flexibility and coordination within it. This is accompanied by the implementation, consistently throughout the system, of dual research centers, such as the Dual Use Technology Center (DUTC) in Great Britain (aimed at the collaboration between universities, defense or civilian manufacturers on the same technological subjects; Molas-Gallart and Sinclair 1999), the technology broker, or to support a stronger involvement of defense in the civilian innovation networks. This was expected to facilitate technology and information transfers between the two worlds.

The systemic perspective facilitates the understanding of duality effects. They can be classified into several categories: direct, indirect, second order, informational and organizational effects, as defined by Cowan and Foray in 1995. This classification makes it possible to measure these effects and compare them depending on various objectives, for example convergence or divergence of economic and security effects (Chu and Lai 2012).

Public policy implications for duality go beyond the national innovation perspective. When public policy apprehends foreign trade from the perspective of duality, this intuitively raises the question of the risk involved by technology dissemination, which is higher due to their "trivialization". The impact of this risk depends on the type of technology (Alic 1994). The most obvious risk is that of nuclear proliferation (Meier and Hunger 2014), but there are studies related to many other fields. Evaluating this risk involved by all the technologies referred to as "dual" was a question raised very early on (Bonomo *et al.* 1998; Tucker 1994). Trajtenberg (2006) observed the effects of military R&D expenditure in counterterrorism. All this literature raises the question of the right balance between technical progress, growth and dissemination of military technologies, as indicated by the joint work of the National Academy of Sciences, National Academy of Engineering and Institute of Medicine of the United States (1987): "Balancing the National Interest: U.S. National Security Export Controls and Global Economic Competition". A large part of the literature dealing with this issue is intended to advise public authorities on their embargo policy and attempts more or less to draw a list of high-risk technologies. At the

European level, this is reflected by the EU Council regulation (EC) no. 428/2009, which states the control rules, a list of dual-use items as well as the methods for coordination and cooperation for its consistent application throughout European Union. In terms of international policy, the UN Security Council resolution 1540 against the proliferation of nuclear, chemical and biological arms integrates the risk related to the duality of certain technologies. At the same time, this gives rise to many cooperation actions (The Wassenaar Arrangement, the Nuclear Suppliers Group, the Missile Technology Control Regime, the Australia Group, etc.).

Appropriate behavior in relation with dual-use technologies is therefore a major challenge for the exporters. They need to prevent unauthorized sales, exports or transfers of dual-use items and the associated technologies. An error on their behalf may have financial and legal consequences. Some countries, such as the United States, have even drawn blacklists of companies with which any commercial relation is banned. This may destroy the reputation of the exporter and limit its opportunities, clearly affecting its growth. These issues related to the exportation of military or dual-use items are referred to as compliance. It is a matter of international cooperation, but it is also dealt with in a sovereign manner by each country.

Duality influences many public policies (defense policy, industrial policy in general or the budget policy) and can act both as a means and as a constraint in the pursuit of objectives by the governments. In this context, public authorities have various initiatives aimed at encouraging, accompanying or mitigating duality.

1.4. Conclusion

This chapter shows there is an abundance of studies dealing with duality, and consequently a wealth of analyses. It also shows the existence of wide disparities in the very definition of duality. As such, it is worth noting the following three points:

– dual "object" and its governance: "in some very important dual-use fields like advanced materials and chemicals it is exceedingly difficult to separate process from product technologies" (Molas-Gallart 1997, p. 374). Duality is "the search for an organization of knowledge and information exchanges in which the State acts as facilitator" (Mérindol 2004, p. 102). These two quotations show the difficulty encountered when trying to grasp what duality is. In one case, it concerns products, in another the technologies and knowledge they are composed of; this may or may not include the means of production. There are many ways in which these issues can be addressed, as presented above, and due to their wide diversity, a synthesis is a challenging exercise. Two axes of analysis are however prominent: the dual object and the governance of duality;

– spillovers: "when duality is seen as a relation that sits not in the technology itself, but rather in a network in which the technology is designed and used, one can distinguish between duality and spillovers" (Cowan and Foray 1995, p. 852). This determines the type of sought-for effects by the implementation of a dual organization. The point of view expressed by Cowan and Foray is not unanimously adopted. Certain analyses highlight the asymmetric nature of research and development and show the domination of one or the other sector in certain technological fields (Alic *et al.* 1992). This involves accepting a technological gap and being pulled by the other sector in order to benefit from spin-offs in one sense as in the other (Moura 2011). These are opposite approaches, since according to one of them the objective is to promote joint technological production, while according to the other, one of the sectors benefits from the progress achieved by the other. In this case, duality "refers to the methods through which objects (products and artifacts) used in one field can be adapted to other fields" (Molas-Gallart 1997, p. 370);

– dual potential: "often the dual-use potential of many technologies is not realized" (Molas-Gallart 1997, p. 370). This latter point shows that, besides a matter of nature, the difficulty in defining duality is also a matter of level. From identifying a potential up to its use under multiple forms, there is a broad range of examples of dual technologies at various levels, both in terms of intensity and in terms of stage in their lifecycle in which this duality is manifest (Mowery 2010).

2

The Knowledge System as Unit of Analysis

2.1. Introduction

As already noted, duality has many complementary facets, among which is technological duality. This chapter aims to build a framework of analysis enabling a departure from a commonly employed case study in order to empirically study this phenomenon. The method used for this purpose relies on the study of knowledge, which is a basic element of technological innovation (Carlsson and Stankiewicz 1991). While knowledge dissemination between civilian and defense sectors is only one part of technological duality, it is one of its essential elements. This is why the philosophy behind this method aims at universality.

Moreover, with the emergence of new information and communication technologies (NICT) and economic globalization, the framework of knowledge dissemination expands. In order to measure the opportunities and the risks associated with technological duality, the phenomenon should be analyzed at the scale of this knowledge dissemination, therefore beyond national borders. The patent enables a relatively uniform understanding of knowledge throughout the world and thus offers a dataset that is relevant for this objective.

The use of patent data has already proven its relevance in the study of knowledge (Jaffe 1986; Jaffe and Trajtenberg 2002; Verspagen 2004; Abrams *et al.* 2013). In order to get the most benefit from this data in an analysis of duality, it seemed essential not to depend on an *a priori* identification of dual technologies. This is why the concept of a technological knowledge system (TKS) is proposed. It enables the reconstruction of technological systems without depending on technological artifacts or uses that usually delimit the framework of dual technologies. Overall available knowledge is thus studied and reveals its dual potentials, even where experts would not have anticipated.

2.2. Technological knowledge systems and knowledge dissemination

2.2.1. *Unit of analysis*

In economics, there are at least two ways to deal with technology-related matters. One of them is the neoclassical approach, whose approach relies on the production process. Technology is the set of operational production means and is consequently related to lasting equipment. The second approach is that of economics of innovation, particularly dominated by the evolutionary trend originating in the works of Schumpeter (1911). It underlines the importance of innovation in wealth creation and describes the innovation process (particularly, but not limited to, the technological process) through a dynamic approach.

There are many taxonomies for the classification of innovation. In this study, which deals with technological innovation as opposed to non-technological innovation (services), it may refer to products or production processes and may be radical or incremental (see the Oslo Manual for a full presentation of the types of innovation; OECD 2005).

The approach retained in this work is closer to the second category of analysis and relies on a representation of technology that goes beyond the mere operational arrangement of the production factors.

According to evolutionary economists or sociologists of innovation, technique or technology is dealt with in interaction with society. In such a framework of analysis, similarly to the way in which MacKenzie and Wajcman (1999) approach technology, it can be defined as artifacts, technical systems, the knowledge that composes them and finally the control of these artifacts and technical systems in a social environment.

Consequently, studying technology amounts to analyzing these three components. This means understanding the technical choices materialized in the artifact, the organization of knowledge that enabled the development of technical solutions and finally the process of appropriation by a social environment that, in economic language, gets the artifact from the status of technical solution to that of innovation.

In particular, this work refers to evolutionary economic theory, notably to the idea that technical changes and innovation are closely related to differentiated specificities of knowledge accumulation, which open up many trajectories and technological regimes (Rosenberg 1976). The approach developed is centered on knowledge as essential factor of technological progress and innovation.

This seems a consistent choice in the study of duality, as it appears reasonable to estimate that a significant part of dual potential lies at the knowledge level. Indeed, technological artifacts with applications in both civilian and military sectors are rare. When they exist, most of them are generic technologies that are disseminated in society to such a degree that defense is only one use among many others (for example, light off-road vehicles). Although it may be close to the civilian solution, the military artifact has a certain number of characteristics, notably in terms of performance, which is a differentiating factor. This is due to the specification process, which progressively adapts technology to the final user (Mérindol and Versailles 2010), while the knowledge supporting the two solutions remains similar (for example, truck engines for an armored vehicle). Similarly, the appropriation processes in the military sector are completely different from those in the civilian sector. Hierarchy, conflict representation, geopolitical situation and the strategic choices of a country are some of the many key factors in the adoption of a technical solution for the actors in the defense sector, while their importance is minor for the rest of the population.

It is nevertheless obvious that this point of view can be contradicted by a certain number of counterexamples. Indeed, certain artifacts are perfectly dual (for example, satellites or space launch vehicles) while in the armies, the increasingly important role of the final user in the processes of appropriation of technical solutions bridges the gap between civilian and military modes of appropriation. This analysis was particularly stressed by Mérindol (2010) through the concept of the *lead user*.

Conducting an analysis of knowledge amounts to focusing on an essential, though not exclusive, component of duality, as underlined by most of the current approaches (Chinworth 2000a; Mérindol and Versailles 2010; Acosta *et al.* 2013; Meunier and Zyla 2016). Indeed, this enables the positioning of reflection upstream, the emergence of knowledge being observed before being allotted to the development of an artifact intended for a particular use, and downstream, which makes it possible to study the effect of appropriation processes on knowledge dissemination in society.

Technology is approached through a systemic perspective in order to better understand the multiple ways of technological interaction between the civilian and the military sectors. In fact, when the technological system is considered as a whole, we are able to measure the already existing proximities or those that should be encouraged between the two sectors.

The technological system was defined by Carlsson and Stankiewicz (1991): "A technological system may be defined as a network of agents interacting in a specific economic/industrial area under a particular institutional infrastructure or set of infra-structures and involved in the generation, diffusion, and utilization of technology. Technological systems are defined in terms of knowledge/competence flows rather than flows of ordinary goods and services" (p. 111). Technological systems are composed of four main elements:

– a hard core of technical and scientific knowledge;

– numerous technical systems;

– a market environment;

– an institutional interface.

This representation of the technological system (Figure 2.1) seems appropriate for the study of duality. Indeed, it shows that various products can address various consumers while relying on technologies built from a base (represented by the large gray rectangle) of similar technical and scientific knowledge. Hence, in the present case, one technology may lead to several distinct products, each of which is intended for the military sector or for the civilian sector, or a product relying on one or several technologies makes it possible to develop a product intended for both military and civilian sectors. In both cases, it is a set of knowledge that, combined in a certain manner, enables a bridge between the civilian and military sectors.

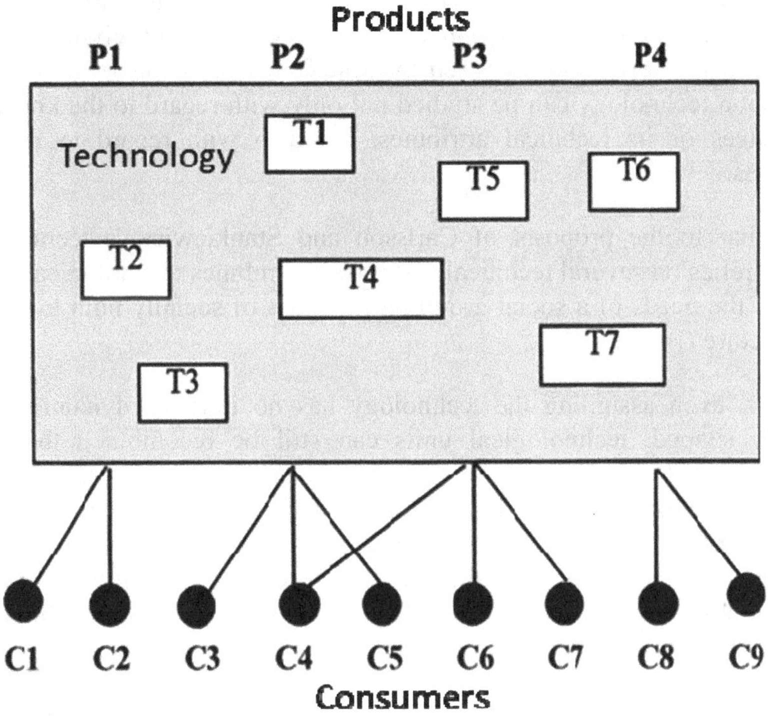

Figure 2.1. *The technological system (source: Carlsson* et al. *2002)*

A related but nevertheless distinct concept is that of technical system (Gille 1978). The author does not focus only on the technical characteristics or sectors having a link with the system, but tries more specifically to understand how the elements of a system (actors, organizations, knowledge, applications, uses) are organized. In his analysis, he puts forward the role of technologies referred to as "generic", also known as General Purpose Technologies (Bresnahan 2010), in the deployment of the respective system (De Bandt 2002). In the technical system, the set of knowledge elements and technological know-how are thus connected and consistent with an operational level (Bainée 2013).

To complete this systemic representation of technology and for a better understanding of what it involves in the study of duality, the theory of Social Construction of Technologies (SCOT) (Bijker *et al.* 2012) seems to be relevant and makes it possible to overcome the limits of the current approach of the technological interactions between defense and civilian sectors. Similar to the reflection proposed by MacKenzie, this theory relies on the idea that a technology can be studied not only with regard to the knowledge it involves or its technical attributes, but also with regard to its social attributes.

Similar to the proposal of Carlsson and Stankiewicz, a technological system relies on several technical systems. It combines technological units to address the needs of a social group on the basis of socially built knowledge architecture (Bijker 2010).

Thus, even assuming the technology has no intrinsic dynamics, being socially shaped, technological units can still be recombined throughout various complex systems. This is what SCOT defines as "interpretative flexibility": "Because the description of an artefact through the eyes of different relevant social groups produces different descriptions and thus different artefacts, this results in the researcher's demonstrating the 'interpretative flexibility' of the artefact. There is not one artefact, but many" (Bijker 2010, p. 68).

SCOT proposes a relativistic analysis of the technological systems that does not focus on the technological object, but stresses the importance of social groups in technology development and use. It considers a set of artifacts as a combination of knowledge units that are socially applied to address specific needs in a given context. Consequently, this approach makes it possible to overcome the previous deadlocks in the analysis of defense, particularly by avoiding a deterministic evaluation of technologies.

SCOT leads to analyzing the way in which technological systems are built. It stresses the importance of the technological dynamics determined by the manner in which knowledge is interconnected. It is then possible to consider the range of potential applications of knowledge beyond interpretative flexibility.

In these approaches, knowledge is the common basis of the technological system. For a proper understanding of what is referred to as knowledge, the latter should be first of all distinguished from information and then its characteristics should be studied.

The first thoughts on the economic nature of knowledge emerge in the neoclassical approaches, in which knowledge and information are interchangeable. This is notably the case of Arrow's (1962) work, which is the founding work on the subject. In this type of approach, knowledge (particularly the technological variety) has the characteristics of information: its use is non-rival; it is intrinsically indivisible; it involves high production costs, compared to the lower costs related to its repeated use; and finally, its use generates increasing returns (Dosi and Nelson 2010).

From this perspective, the economist perceives information as merchandise, which cannot be dissociated from knowledge and is supported by various media (books, journals, patents, etc.). In terms of analysis, there are two consequences. First, knowledge exchanges can be dealt with as economic transactions, using the traditional tools of microeconomics. This is, for example, the case for patent transactions. Then, as Arrow shows, to encourage innovation, there is a superiority of pure competition over monopoly, and also a superiority of the State over competition. This proof relies entirely on the existence of property rights (patents) that generate rarity and on the capacity of agents to have perfect information on the economic performances of knowledge/information.

Later on, the "Stanford-Yale-Sussex" (SYS) synthesis brings complementary elements, underlining the specific characteristics of technological or scientific knowledge (David 2004; Dosi *et al.* 2006). Compared to the previous approach, the major difference is that here the possibility of applying knowledge at any scale does not necessarily mean that its replication is easy or that it does not generate significant costs. This is explained by reasons specific to technological knowledge.

First, non-rivalry means that this knowledge is not exhausted when transferred or applied, but this does not mean that there is no cost involved by learning this knowledge. Second, the cumulative aspect of the production process constitutes a cost. Indeed, this means that in order to absorb knowledge (technological knowledge, in particular), an individual must first master the proper knowledge units and be able to combine them.

This necessity of mastering one piece of knowledge before being able to acquire another one has a more or less significant input cost. Hence, perceiving knowledge as a pure public good seems exaggerated since, even if its use is non-rival, producing and acquiring knowledge (including in the absence of property rights) often involves a non-negligible cost due to the costs of learning the respective knowledge or previous knowledge.

The costs and the modes of imitation or transfer of the technological knowledge differ from those associated with information (Mansfield *et al.* 1981). Even if codified, the transfer of technological information is not limited to this informational transfer and involves costs for the acquisition of non-formalized knowledge or organizational competences to use it. This involves uncertainty in the result of the knowledge flows, this result being imperceptible when these flows are assimilated to codified information flows.

It seems that knowledge, and in particular technological knowledge, can be distinguished from simple "commodity information". According to the proposal of Polanyi (1983), economists distinguish between codified knowledge and tacit knowledge. Codified knowledge is explicitly transcribed and can easily be the object of transactions; it is not attached to an individual, but to a support (for example, a patent); in this sense, it is close to information/knowledge such as defined by Arrow. As for tacit knowledge, it is difficult to translate. It comprises the know-how embedded in an individual or an organization.

Polanyi states further that all formalized knowledge relies at least partially on tacit comprehension. It can be assimilated to the capacity to understand, articulate and apply knowledge. All knowledge is therefore tacit or relies partially on tacit knowledge. Therefore, knowledge is never fully codified. The idea that there is always a tacit part in any knowledge is summarized by certain economists as follows: "The codified knowledge does not cover exactly the tacit knowledge base for which it tries to substitute" (Dosi 2009). Similarly, Winter (1998) proposes a classification of knowledge into several categories, from the most tacit to the most formalized. On the other hand, others see the passage from tacit knowledge to formalized knowledge as the result of an evolution of one into the other: "Typically, a piece of knowledge initially appears as purely tacit – a person has an idea. Often, though, as the new knowledge ages, it goes through a process whereby it becomes more codified" (Cowan and Foray 1995, p. 595). This process is an integral part of the life cycle of the technology.

The value of knowledge depends on the balance between tacit and formalized. Two opposed positions emerge. On the one hand, the capacity of a society to integrate new knowledge depends on this tacit knowledge – or "common knowledge" according to Gorz (2003). Hence, for the latter, the more a society formalizes knowledge, the more they are monopolized and therefore the society goes increasingly without common knowledge and becomes impoverished. On the other hand, the only means to preserve the exchange value of knowledge is to codify it; once codified, appropriated and embedded in products, it can be valorized. Instruments such as the patent help preserve this mechanism. In both cases, though the influence differs, knowledge dissemination depends on knowledge codification.

These clarifications on the manner in which the economists perceive technological knowledge contribute to a better understanding of why its study is conducted here by means of patents. In order to integrate in this work the distinction between tacit and codified knowledge, the perspective shared by Polanyi and Dosi was retained. Codified knowledge is directly carried by the patent, while tacit knowledge is embedded in the organizations, which, because of it, are able to articulate, understand and use formalized knowledge. It is this symbiotic organization of knowledge that is retained.

If a technological system is defined by a set of knowledge units, then there are two opposing ways to study it. The first involves the identification of systems based on the *output*, in the sense of technological artifacts associated with the system, and finding the knowledge that supports it. The second starts from knowledge, defines an interacting set and then identifies the artifacts relying on this set of knowledge.

The first method does not seem appropriate for dealing with duality. Indeed, analyzing dual technological innovation leads to the study of military innovations; but accessing the latter is often difficult, and even more so their technological characteristics. Data are by definition sensitive: detailed knowledge on the characteristics of a particular weaponry system, serving to connect it to a larger technical system, raises obvious security problems if information is disseminated (Buesa 2001). A possible way to solve this difficulty is to eliminate certain materials from the analysis, as they are considered too sensitive; nevertheless, this would prejudice the non-duality of these technologies. While the artifact in particular is sensitive and non-dual, these characteristics are not necessarily applicable to the knowledge it comprises. In this context, the development of an expert approach involving the study of military artifacts to understand the technological characteristics, in order to reconstruct the knowledge base and finally study duality, seems complex and risky for an economist.

Therefore, this analysis retains the second method. It relies on the analysis of knowledge in order to delimit technological systems. Consequently, exhaustive knowledge on military materials is not necessary; for an economist, it is easier to gather and analyze data related to knowledge, notably through patents. Therefore, the approach proposed here involves the study of interactions between knowledge in order to determine those constituting a system and enabling the production of technological innovations.

It is to this purpose that the TKS concept is proposed. It is defined similarly to a system of scientific knowledge, which corresponds to the set of closely interrelated knowledge, enabling the elaboration and comprehension of a scientific subject. For example, Cournot (1847) describes mathematics as a system of scientific knowledge "based on ideal notions that are present in all human minds".

With this in mind, TKS corresponds to the set of knowledge that, being closely interrelated, is the source of synergies in technological production. This consistent set of knowledge (whether or not based on scientific principles), associated with specific competences, makes it possible to propose technical solutions, which are then combined within one or more technological systems. According to the previously described approach, a TKS includes a formal part through patents and an informal part through relations and the interconnection between these patents (see Chapter 4).

2.2.2. *Knowledge dissemination*

Knowledge dissemination is essential in a dual innovation process. On the one hand, this knowledge sharing is the result of a strategic choice on behalf of the company; the latter may decide for or against the dissemination of a piece of knowledge depending on its competitive nature (Fauchart 2003). On the other hand, knowledge dissemination depends on the absorption capacities of other companies (Cohen and Levinthal 1990). Based on these elements, this section proposes a knowledge dissemination model.

First of all, it is worth recalling two properties of the knowledge production process: a cumulative process and a process based on a correlational structure (Krafft *et al.* 2011).

– A cumulative process: this can be readily understood by means of a famous metaphor: *nani gigantum humeris insidentes* ("dwarfs standing on the shoulders of giants") attributed to Bernard de Chartres. The knowledge accumulated and then transmitted by past generations makes it possible to see farther, serving as a foundation on which new knowledge is built. This metaphor shows that research and development depend on previously acquired knowledge. Two insights result from this. On the one hand, the higher a company's knowledge mastery, the stronger its ability to acquire and finally produce new knowledge; on the other hand, certain knowledge cannot be acquired without mastering the knowledge it relies on. These two elements, one of which is quantitative and the other qualitative, determine what Cohen and Levinthal (1990) refer to as "capacities of absorption" of the company. In other terms, the knowledge that a company can acquire depends on the knowledge it masters.

– A process relying on a correlational structure: the development of new pieces of knowledge enables the multiplication of their possible combinations and recombinations (Fleming and Sorenson 2001). Indeed, knowledge production depends on the environment in which it is inserted, particularly the technological environment. The relations existing between knowledge units also determine the production of future knowledge. Setting two pieces of knowledge in relation opens up two new fields of development that can only be reached by interconnecting knowledge. The structure of these relations (intensity, strength, hierarchy, etc.) determines its technological trajectory. Due to this structure, the concept of knowledge base, which is detailed further on, can be understood.

These two properties lead to considering, on the one hand, the precedence in the production of knowledge and, on the other hand, the combinations in which the production of new knowledge originates. For this, two categories of knowledge must be distinguished.

Using the typology proposed by Henderson and Clark (1990), two levels of knowledge are distinguished. On the one hand, the *component knowledge*, which corresponds to the unit of knowledge and can be more or less significant, and, on the other hand, the *architectural knowledge*, which reveals the relations between them.

This typology makes it possible to study the layout of knowledge in an organization. But this notion of architecture can be found at other levels. Indeed, according to Ulrich (1995), architecture is analyzed at the product level and in this case it is understood as the diagram that assigns to each component a function within a product. It is therefore this diagram that connects the components.

This distinction between architecture and component shows that understanding the manner in which knowledge is disseminated requires the study of the units of knowledge and of their articulation. To master a knowledge component, an organization should do more than appropriate it: it must be able to articulate it with other knowledge it has available.

Given the cumulative and correlational nature of knowledge, this shows that the way in which component knowledge and architectural knowledge are today dispersed within and among organizations determines the dissemination and production of future knowledge. Consequently, the environment and the interconnections established by economic agents are key factors for knowledge production.

In this respect, two approaches seem interesting. First, network approaches focus on the relations between actors. In recent decades, an increasing number of organizations and nations participated in knowledge production by multiplying the national or international collaborations (Powell and Giannella 2010). This is all the more true as far as patents are concerned. A report of the World Intellectual Property Organization (WIPO) dating from 2008 shows a strong increase in the number of patents registered throughout the world starting with the mid 1990s, especially in the five most important offices (United States, Japan, China, South Korea and Europe). Moreover, the number of authors per patent has also increased during these last years, an evolution that some interpret as a need to integrate a broader field of knowledge in order to be able to innovate (Powell and Giannella 2010). Finally, the knowledge sources and means of dissemination diversify (Dibiaggio and Meschi 2010). In such an environment, knowledge that is the source of technological opportunities is difficult to identify (Cohen *et al.* 2002).

In this context, innovation networks are developed and play an increasingly structuring role in the process of knowledge dissemination. The perspective of innovation is interesting, as the interactions between the actors of a network influence the characteristics of technologies, an idea shared by the previously presented theories (technological system and SCOT).

In the 1960s, approaches to knowledge networks that point out sources outside companies in their internal innovation processes emerge (Freeman 1991). These various studies made it possible to reveal the key role played by certain interactions in the success of an innovation. The definition proposed by Imai and Baba, summarized by Freeman (1991, p. 502), enables a simple presentation of these approaches: "Network organization is a basic institutional arrangement to cope with systemic innovation. Networks can be viewed as an interpenetrated form of market and organization. Empirically, they are loosely coupled organizations having a core with both weak and strong ties among constituent members... We emphasize the importance of cooperative relationships among firms as a key linkage mechanism of network configurations. They include joint ventures, licensing arrangements, management sub-contracting, production sharing collaboration". She signals in passing the interest of these approaches within a systemic approach. Moreover, similar to formal knowledge and tacit knowledge, some networks are formal, while others are not. In a work of synthesis, Freeman notes that the similarity can be further extended. Indeed, as informal knowledge often supports and completes formal knowledge, behind a formal network there is often an informal network.

One notable contribution is to point out the importance of sociological factors in the innovation process. This is, for example, the case of the relation between the final user and the producer of the innovation (Lundvall 1985). This relation was identified during SAPPHO project (Curnow and Moring 1968) as essential for understanding the expectations of future users and the circumstances in which the innovation could be used.

The concept of technico-economic network, which highlights the heterogeneity of actors, seems particularly interesting: "These long and heterogeneous networks introduce new and very different modalities of organization and of regulation from those of the preceding model centered on a single company" (Callon *et al.* 1992, p. 216).

Such a network comprises companies, research laboratories, financial organizations, users and public authorities. It enables the combination of a static analysis and a dynamic analysis. From a static point of view, it highlights the actors as well as the various intermediaries that put them in relation. From a dynamic point of view, it shows that the network transformation coincides with the evolution of the actors and of their relations.

The stability of these networks is a major challenge that depends on the elements composing them and on the role they play within them (Elzen *et al.* 2004). Two types of actors seem to be particularly useful. First, there are "actors dedicated to network building". They are also drivers alongside actors that are already engaged and involved in the search for new partners in order to feed the network. Then, there are "critical actors" who, without being directly involved in the technological development, have a role in directing it, such as financial actors.

From this perspective, Bouvier-Patron (2015) proposes a generic structure of alliances and partnerships between economic and institutional agents, as well as a typology of these agents pointing out their diversity and their position in the network. According to him, setting up a network relies on a high degree of "relational symmetry" between the actors. This means both an equivalent relative position and on both sides a low incentive to breakdown, guaranteeing a fair distribution of earnings.

Similar to Elzen, Bouvier-Patron (1994) shows the influence of "coordinating" agents in the structure of the network. In this case, the role of the coordinating agent is to build specific relations between the agents in order to guarantee a result specificity (processing the same generic knowledge within a specific relation leads to a single production). This proves to be advantageous for the actor providing a service. Indeed, if the relation is not specific, the result is more standard and, in this case, competition is stronger. On the other hand, for a specific product, the service provider has a higher negotiation power. For Bouvier-Patron, network stability therefore relies on microeconomic mechanisms. Once the agreement is negotiated, there is on both sides an incentive to fix the relation, which stabilizes the network. This mechanism relies on a free adherence to the network and on a possibility of exit if there are changes in the environment (irrecoverable low costs). It leads to the transformation of behaviors in the relation due to the specific nature of the knowledge generated during the interaction.

The network characteristic is therefore here a technological determinant. The analysis in network terms seems consequently adapted to the analysis of dual innovation. Indeed, the military field, and even more appropriately, dual innovation, often involves a set of heterogeneous actors within a wide network. The nature of these networks consequently influences the technological characteristics of duality (Guichard and Heisbourg 2004).

Moreover, the approaches making use of patent data focus on knowledge. Leydesdorff *et al.* (2015) point out that patents are a rich source of information on innovation activity and its context, as they specify the names of inventors and beneficiaries, the sources of their knowledge or the locations of the innovation activity. This type of information is particularly useful when observing knowledge production and dissemination, by mapping technological evolutions. Structural indicators are used for measuring the dissemination of technologies and knowledge composing them. Similar to many authors (Jaffe and Trajtenberg 2002; Verspagen 2004; Krafft *et al.* 2011), this work contributes to the necessary development of methodologies that account for this process. These methods are presented in the second part of this book.

As already explained, the absorption capacity of an organization relies on the knowledge it masters, in both formalized and tacit forms. Effectively, the formal part does not cover the entire knowledge mastered by an individual or a group of individuals. It readily reveals the mastered component knowledge; on the other hand, it does not fully reveal the knowledge enabling interconnections (architectural knowledge). This specific role is played by tacit knowledge. To analyze the capacities of absorption, tacit knowledge and formal knowledge must be both observed.

The formal part proves relatively easy to observe since, by definition, it leaves a trace; this is much less the case for the tacit part. Indeed, since it is not materialized as such and because there are individuals who carry this tacit knowledge, it is by observing implementations that this knowledge is revealed. Then by observing the organization of formalized knowledge, it is possible to reveal the underlying informal part, as it is partly because of it that formalized knowledge can be rendered consistent in order to produce a technology. This articulation of knowledge can be observed at various scales, at the level of a technological system, organization, industry, etc. Therefore, a better understanding of knowledge structuring is a challenge for companies themselves, but also for the set of actors that are trying to understand the knowledge dissemination process (public decision makers, economists, regulatory organizations, etc.), and more specifically in the context of duality. To conduct this work, patent analysis proves to be a source of relevant information.

First, it is worth undertaking a quick review of several characteristics of the patent (further details are provided in Part 2). A patent file is comparable to an academic article and contains two pieces of information. On the one hand, similar to an academic who must quote the articles underlying the development of his argument, a patent must quote the patents underlying its innovation proposal. On the other hand, the patent mentions the technological classes it belongs to or in other terms the type of knowledge it involves. As such, despite the fact that the study of patents shows that the development of knowledge in one field relies essentially on knowledge that was previously produced in the same field, a patent from one technological class can quote patents belonging to another technological class, establishing a relation between knowledge from various fields. In this case, whether the patent filer is able to acquire various knowledge on their own, or they use their environment, it is the correlational aspect of the innovation that can be analyzed through patent classification.

Moreover, the patents prove to be a useful source of information, as they compile an amount of information that is stable in time. The classification of technologies that is currently applied to patents certainly differs from that applied one century ago: it has adapted to technological evolutions. Nevertheless, this classification is backward compatible. It is therefore possible, for the patents of the main offices for the protection of intellectual property, to study the set of patents they registered with the current classification. This offers the possibility for studies over long periods of time.

Finally, there is worldwide dissemination of patents. It is the most broadly disseminated instrument for knowledge formalization. Moreover, WIPO shows, through its database (Fink *et al.* 2015) that its use has increased since the 1990s. Developing countries in particular are catching up, China being the top patent filer in the world. Moreover, patent filing tends to get unified, as an increasing share of patents are filed simultaneously with several offices, because of the Patent Cooperation Treaty (PCT), which simplifies the application system in several countries simultaneously. The data source is therefore huge.

It is nevertheless obvious that patent analysis does not provide exhaustive information, such an analysis having its limitations. In order to get the most out of the patent data while taking into account its limits, the empirical work relies on a classical representation of these data – the knowledge base (Nesta and Saviotti 2005; Nasiriyar *et al.* 2013) – to which a set of original tools is applied.

In order to study the dissemination of knowledge, the latter is represented as "landscape". In this network representation, the nodes correspond to component knowledge (identified by means of patent technological classes) and arcs between the nodes corresponding to the links between these pieces of knowledge (technological classes). These links can be of two types: either citation links, meaning that two technological classes are linked when a patent belonging to one technological class cites a patent belonging to another technological class; or co-occurrence links, meaning that two technological classes are linked when a patent belongs to these two classes simultaneously. This leads to two types of two-dimensional landscape, plus a third dimension related to the organizations in which these links are established; in other terms, the company that filed a patent.

For the representation of organizations, the concept of a knowledge base is used (Nesta and Saviotti 2005, 2006; Krafft *et al.* 2011; El Younsi *et al.* 2015). Hence, each organization has a corresponding knowledge network (identified by means of the technological classes of the patents it files), which are interconnected either through citations or through co-occurrences (the formal construction of these knowledge networks is detailed in the following part). The knowledge base (or technological network) of each organization is a fragment of the global technological network (technological landscape). Then each knowledge base can be studied, in the form of a graph, as a component of this global technological network. This approach offers several advantages.

First, it distinguishes the component knowledge corresponding to technological classes and the architectural knowledge, which is represented by the links between technological classes. But as previously mentioned, these two dimensions have to be taken into account in the study of knowledge transfers, as they determine the capacities of absorption of an organization. Second, it enables the visualization of motions at the level of nodes and links, and therefore at the level of component knowledge and architectural knowledge.

These two elements make it possible to define the current structure of knowledge. As already mentioned, the current structure determines the future motions. To understand this process, two components of the knowledge base are distinguished. The first is related to the concept of circuit; it corresponds to the use of combinations of existing production factors (in this case of knowledge). The second is related to its evolution; it corresponds to the replacement of current combinations by new combinations of production factors (Tremblay 2003). This makes it possible to measure opportunities in terms of knowledge dissemination, and therefore measure a dual dissemination potential.

Based on these theoretical elements, a description of the dissemination potential of technological knowledge is proposed. This general framework of analysis will be applied to the specific case of duality in the following section. Prior to this, a detailed presentation of the various stages of construction is recommended.

As already mentioned, knowledge is associated with technological systems. They are constituted of component knowledge that, being associated in a specific architecture, enables the proper operation of the technological system. The set of technological systems is therefore composed of various pieces of knowledge, which are either system specific or shared by several systems.

It is possible to consider a limit case in which two systems share exactly the same component knowledge. In such a case, the manner in which the component knowledge is combined (architectural knowledge) is what differentiates the two systems. Consequently, a component knowledge-based comparison between systems is not sufficient for measuring their proximity and their architecture. Moreover, this landscape is not fixed in time, particularly for specific knowledge that can be disseminated within other systems during their life cycle, and can even disappear from the system in which they emerged.

Once this representation accepted, the challenge is to measure those with the highest dissemination potential and identify the technological system they are intended for. On this matter, the idea advanced here is that two systems relying on common component knowledge and/or on close architectural knowledge require close, even common capacities of absorption. Hence, due to shared capacities of absorption, a piece of knowledge is more likely disseminated first between these systems. Hence, a piece of knowledge is more easily disseminated between two systems that are partly constituted of similar knowledge and/or rely on a close architectural knowledge.

This logic of analysis is applied to duality in the following section. When applied to duality, this approach makes it possible to build a theoretical representation of knowledge dissemination by focusing on the analysis of TKS. This representation is used to identify the weight of technological duality for a given TKS. Instead of technological artifacts as such, the study focuses on the knowledge associated with them. It is then a matter of measuring a dual potential that frees itself from various applications, which can be constrained by the users' perception on technologies.

2.3. Knowledge dissemination and duality

2.3.1. *Dual knowledge*

The TKS-based approach makes it possible to develop a single methodology that is applicable to all technological innovation cases, beyond the specific case of duality. Indeed, as already mentioned, knowledge is a constitutive element of all technologies. But studying the whole production of technological knowledge without bias related to the more or less real specificities of defense technological innovation makes it possible to compare without prior assumptions the overall knowledge to that which would be relevant to consider. This can be equally applied to a defense technological system as to any more or less strictly civilian system whose "spinoffs" should be measured in terms of knowledge beyond its field of origin. Finally, this makes it possible to go beyond the traditional case study whose coverage is necessarily limited. Nevertheless, this does not mean that the specificities of defense activity, notably in terms of knowledge protection, can be ignored, but only that they must be taken into account when using the results. This is the case in similar works conducted in other fields (Deyle and Grupp 2005; Nesta and Saviotti 2006; Cecere *et al.* 2014). The relevance of the analysis depends on the capacity to contextualize the results obtained.

Moreover, here it is a matter of knowledge, an input of the technological innovation process. As shown, for example, by the definition of Carlsson and Stankiewicz, knowledge is not one of the layers composing a technological system. The constraints related to the technical system itself, such as the artifact that materializes the technological system, the institutional interface or the market environment, also influence the structuring of the technological system. Therefore, the conclusions that can be drawn are only applicable to knowledge and are in no case related to the technological system in its entirety in the absence of a complementary work on these other aspects.

In other terms, the main contribution of this analysis is the evaluation of a dual potential related to a more or less significant knowledge proximity between various technological systems. Knowledge duality does not automatically mean dual technology. This potential can be measured with methodological tools, which are presented and used in the second part. Hence, it is possible to rank the dual potential of various systems while identifying the knowledge that serves as relay for its dissemination, locating them within certain technological systems or identifying the actors that master this knowledge.

Moreover, as already mentioned, the results of a study in terms of knowledge strongly depend on the context in which it is achieved. Consequently, one and the same result can have two different explanations. To put it simply, the dual potential of a technology referred to as "defense technology" can evolve in terms of knowledge either because the knowledge composing it is close to the knowledge used in the civilian fields, or because one or several civilian pieces of knowledge develop proximities with knowledge commonly used in defense innovation. In one case, it is the studied knowledge that evolves, while in the other case they remain constant, but their environment evolves. It is worth keeping this aspect in mind in what follows.

Considering the above-mentioned limits, the framework of analysis proposed in this work can be an efficient instrument for forward technology assessment. Identifying technologies that have a dual potential is a challenge: first, for the public authorities who are trying to reduce the cost of defense. In fact, if knowledge is not specific to military uses, it is reasonable to think that its development can be shared with others. On the other hand, the same public authorities try to maintain the technological superiority of the armies. This amounts to locating the knowledge that composes a defense system and thus organizing the R&D policy, considering the real need in terms of knowledge. Moreover, for the companies, understanding technological duality is nowadays a means to develop their activities beyond the spectrum of public defense demand, which is under increasing constraint, particularly in developed countries.

Considering these clarifications, using the term dual TKS instead of dual technology opens two possibilities. On the one hand, it highlights that it is exclusively the dual potential of knowledge that is measured, and, on the other hand, it shows that the duality of a technology does not relate only to knowledge and therefore concluding on the duality of a technological system requires additional analyses. Since it provides the possibility of studying the way in which knowledge is articulated in a technological system, the concept of TKS serves as an entry point for the study conducted here.

Within the framework of duality, TKS proves all the more useful given that, as already mentioned, it is difficult to start from the technological artifact. It is clear that an overly precise description of certain military materials would reduce the technological advantage of the armed forces using it, either by revealing the weaknesses, or by giving the opposing forces the possibility to develop the same type of technology. The TKS is not identified depending on the final artifact, but during the technology production process.

For this purpose, the methodology, which is further detailed in the following part, measures the strength of the links between pieces of knowledge. The objective is to determine the strong links or otherwise put the most commonly used associations in order to produce technological innovation. These links, which are measured by means of data contained in the patent filings, can be qualified as synergistic and help identify the limits of TKS.

Therefore, TKS depends to a large extent on how knowledge is articulated in the overall technological landscape. In this sense, it depends on two important notions: the technological paradigm and the technological trajectory (Dosi 1982). These are essential concepts in the evolutionary analysis of the innovation processes. They show that, given the current context, technological choices are not all considered in the same manner, which determines the innovation process.

First, the definition given by Dosi (1982) for technology is similar to the previous definitions, namely as a set of knowledge that is simultaneously directly "practical" (related to concrete problems and equipment) and "theoretical" (but applicable in practice, though not necessarily already implemented), know-how, methods, processes, successes and failures and also physical equipment and instruments. This definition points out knowledge once more as a constitutive element of technology.

Moreover, the concept of a technological paradigm aims to explain how technology evolves and is assimilated to a framework in which technical progress unfolds. "A "scientific paradigm" could be approximately defined as an "outlook" which defines the relevant problems, a "model" and a "pattern" of inquiry" (Dosi 1982). Technical progress is then defined by the technological paradigm. In other terms, the manner in which an individual seeks to produce technology depends on the technological paradigm they adopt. This paradigm determines the choices in terms of innovation.

This defines a technological trajectory. This notion is strongly associated with the cumulative nature of the innovation. It apprehends the innovation process through a set of possible directions (trajectories), delimited by past (individual and collective) choices, both in technological and economic terms.

In summary, the future opportunities related to innovation are constrained by our past choices, in other words, by the current technological paradigm (Dosi 1982). The trajectory defines to a certain extent the dynamics of the technological paradigm.

Therefore, TKS depend on the technological paradigm to which they belong and on the technological trajectories within which they evolve. There is no evidence of their absolute nature in the way of generating an evolution.

The third theoretical element that is worth pointing out in order to better understand the importance of TKS in the study of duality is the concept of selection environment (Nelson and Winter 1975). It shows that the environment in which an organization operates influences its technological choices. The authors highlight two categories of selection environments. On the one hand, the commercial selection environment, in which the technological choice is guided by the mechanism of profit expectation. On this matter, the role of the public military demand (single opportunity for the defense technology) distinguishes the environment for a company with defense activity; the influence of this parameter is all the more significant as this opportunity is essential for the company. On the other hand, there is the non-commercial selection environment, which puts forward the political regulatory or professional control processes, in the selection process. The specificity of defense activity is obvious in this case too, and it distinguishes the selection environment.

Therefore, when studying duality it is important to consider, in the formation of TKS, the selection environment to which they belong in order to capture the specificities generated in their technological paradigms. In this case, at least two selection environments can be distinguished: the first one in which the defense activity influences the technological selection process, and the second one in which the influence of defense activity is negligible. Hence, even if the technological problem is the same, the chances are that the manner in which it is approached within the defense sector differs from that in which it is approached in the civilian sector. This is why the TKS must be identified within a controlled selection environment, which makes it possible to interpret the results. The manner in which the TKS is structured in the defense environment is then compared with a reference structuring, and this comparison enables the measurement of their duality.

The object of the quantitative analysis is therefore first to identify the TKS, then to measure the duality of the knowledge composing them, by comparing them from one selection environment to another. Finally, the analysis of duality requires a differentiation of knowledge production in the defense sector from the rest of production. However, the difficulty is not the *a priori* classification of knowledge in one category or another. This is why, as detailed in Chapter 4, it is the analysis of knowledge synergies in the selection environments that enables TKS differentiation and, consequently, a positive analysis of duality.

2.3.2. *Dual process of knowledge dissemination*

Summarizing the already presented general framework of analysis of knowledge dissemination, an application to the specific case of knowledge duality is proposed. It relies on the identification of the TKS in a selection environment defined through companies active in the defense sector.

During the 1990s, the relation between state and defense industry was modified, particularly in Western countries. This period was marked by a wide privatization of knowledge (Mérindol 2014), which would redefine the role of companies in the innovation process. The developments in France and Great Britain were particularly representative for this change, while in the United States there was an evolution toward a new balance between the public and private sectors.

In France, this change is illustrated by the evolution of the role of the Directorate General for Armaments (Direction générale de l'armement (DGA)). In the 1960s, it managed the scientific choices *ex ante* and the technological options based on the needs of the military, having a significant role in the definition of technical properties of the defense industry. After two successive reforms, private companies gained higher responsibility (for a full overview, see Lazaric *et al.* 2011).

In 1997, a new division of labor between the DGA and companies was implemented. Most of the R&D activities were transferred to private companies, which engaged in horizontal and vertical integration, in order to benefit from their innovation activities. This marked the passage from a policy guided by technological research to a policy of best quality/price ratio acquisition and a significant wave of knowledge transfer from public authorities to the private sector.

The reform in 2003 restored the balance to a certain extent, notably in terms of preserving the technological know-how required by the future program. The DGA conducts fundamental research and takes on a role of financial and technological risk management, relying on public research centers (CEA, ONERA and CNES). Companies continue to have a prominent role in the execution of research and development programs.

Moreover, as shown by Guillou *et al.* (2009), this is accompanied by an increasing interest of companies in the management and protection of their knowledge. Hence, innovation conducted by companies active in the defense sector is developing and, though imperfect (secrecy is still practiced in this field, particularly for certain sensitive technologies), the indicator of this activity is the patent. These companies account for 10% of the patents filed in France in 2014, with an average of 20.2 patents compared to 4.4 for other companies (Belin 2015). This is reflected by the ranking of patents filed by companies. Hence in 2015, the following companies were among the top 10 organizations and companies filing with the National Institute for Intellectual Property (Institut national de la propriété intellectuelle (INPI)): Safran (no. 2), Airbus Group (no. 8) and Thales (no. 10). This disproves the stereotype of the defense company paralyzed by secrecy in order to protect its intellectual property.

The case of Great Britain shows a similar and even more abrupt evolution of the public–private balance. Indeed, in early 2000, the Defence Evaluation and Research Agency (DERA) left the State without most of its research capacities in the field of defense, a large part of which were transferred to a private company, Qinetiq. This privatization reinforced the market relations and supported the already ongoing strengthening of intellectual property in companies active in the defense sector (Molas-Gallart and Tang 2006).

In the United States, the balance between state, industry and public research was adjusted in a softer manner. Most of the works point out the integration of a wide diversity of actors within a network of innovation and show the central role of the Pentagon in its organization. Referring to this matter, Sapolsky (2003) and Gholz (2002) stress the competences of the Pentagon in assessing the behaviors of private system integrators that conduct most of the R&D programs. These competences rely particularly on the Defense Advanced Research Projects Agency (DARPA) and the universities because of which a large scientific and technological database can be maintained in the public domain, while the private sector provides a large part of the initiative in innovation.

The summary of the work prepared by Mérindol in the United States and in Europe at the end of the 20th Century seems to show that a new balance was reached between state, industry and research centers. It appears that, despite the disparities in the national models, knowledge privatization is their common characteristic (which actually extends beyond the defense sector). Knowledge creation and use are nowadays the drivers of competitiveness that companies are competing for (Freeman and Soete 1997), in both civilian and military sectors. The latter have a dominant position in the defense innovation process following the outsourcing of a part of public research and engineering capacities. The state has progressively moved to the position of architect of innovation networks, while preserving a part of the knowledge required for the proper exercise of this function, relying either on public scientific laboratories, or on personnel mobility between companies and public centers.

Hence, the companies active in the defense sector carry a large part of the knowledge related to this activity. The public sector keeps its knowledge updated, mainly in order to preserve its absorption capacities (Lazaric *et al.* 2011) or its competences in terms of cognitive architecture in an innovation network (Mérindol 2014). In this institutional context, companies have adapted to the technological change and, in particular, to the emergence of systems of systems in armament. The manufacturers have endorsed the role of systems integrator (Hobday *et al.* 2005) and must be capable of aggregating knowledge stemming from often very broad technological horizons. For these companies, knowledge flows are a major focus in order to preserve their innovation capacities and address the new demands of defense programs. For this reason, the emphasis is on company innovation.

"Defense company" is however an ambiguous designation. The reason is simple, namely the fact that the great majority of companies that manufacture defense material are nowadays diversified on other markets. In this sense, most of these companies are dual. This market duality of defense companies is more or less strong. Some of them continue to be extremely specialized, such as MBDA, manufacturer of missiles (100% of turnover in defense in 2014), or the manufacturers of land armaments Nexter and Krauss-Maffei Wegmann (recently merged, with 95% of turnover in defense in 2014). Others, such as Boeing or Airbus, are clearly more dual and, for them, the civilian market even accounts for the largest part of their turnover (respectively, 18% and 31% of the turnover in defense in 2014).

On average, in the top 100 largest companies in defense, the sales of arms accounts for around 57% of the yearly turnover since 2002 (SIPRI Arms Industry Database (China excluded), 2002–2014). But this distribution of activity does not correspond to the position (importance) that the companies have in the defense sector. Some highly diversified companies are actually key elements of defense production. Consequently, this criterion is not sufficient to distinguish between companies that are relevant to study and companies that can be left aside.

This market duality proves to be a constraint in the definition of industrial and, in the present case, technological perimeter, representative for the defense activity. It appears that, whatever the defined perimeter, it is more or less dual by definition. But the demarcation between defense and civilian sectors is a fundamental element of the method of analysis proposed here. Consequently, a solution for delimiting the sectors had to be found.

Following the example of Piscitello in his analyses on the diversification of companies, the retained solution is to weight the results of the analysis of the knowledge bases of companies by the part representing the defense activity in the company turnover (Piscitello 2000, 2005).

This method has two essential advantages. First, according to the concept of selection environment, it includes the idea that the market and the expected profits constrain the technological choices. Turnover being a means to approximate this constraint, it can be used to measure the defense aspect in the technological choices. But distinguishing the defense aspect is quite often a difficult task. For example, using financing in R&D projects proves to be random, due to the variety of ways in which defense financing is defined depending on the country in which the analysis is conducted. Therefore, this method addresses this difficulty. Moreover, with this method there is no *a priori* exclusion of technologies because their contribution to the defense industry would be considered too marginal. Each contribution is considered in relation to what it represents for the company. This offers an advantage in terms of completeness of the analysis itself, even though, as highlighted in the empirical part, a certain number of precautions are required in the interpretation of results.

Once this knowledge environment is defined and the TKS within it are identified (empirical method described in Chapter 4), it is possible to measure the dual potential of the dissemination of knowledge composing these TKS. For this purpose, besides the environment of defense knowledge as defined above, a global knowledge environment should be considered. The construction of a knowledge environment referred to as "global" is preferred to the construction of a knowledge environment referred to as "civilian", due to the porous border between the two sectors. Indeed, it would be excessive to think that the technologies identified in the defense knowledge environment are strictly dedicated to defense. And, as shown by the characteristics of companies used as empirical material in this study, most of them have a dual activity, which confirms that this binary distinction between civilian and defense is “virtual”. For these companies, the knowledge produced aims at both markets. Finally, it would be quite excessive, given the diversity of civilian companies, if the latter corresponded to a selection environment. The hypothesis is rather that defense knowledge production is a component of global knowledge production. It is therefore by comparing a TKS knowledge structuring in a defense knowledge environment with the knowledge structuring of this TKS in the global knowledge environment that dual potential will be measured in Part 2.

The proposal is to measure (component and architectural) knowledge proximities, as defined in the previous section, depending on more or less significant distortions in the way that knowledge is used (structured) in these two environments. This distortion gives some sort of measure of defense specificity. The stronger this distortion, the weaker the dual potential and vice versa. In other words, the more the knowledge of a TKS is used similarly in the defense specific environment and in the global knowledge environment, the stronger the dual potential of this TKS.

2.4. Conclusion

After having explained the choice of the knowledge system as unit of analysis, this chapter proposes an original analysis of knowledge dissemination in these systems. This makes it possible to distinguish the role of component knowledge from that of architectural knowledge in the evaluation of the dissemination potential of a technology. Comparing this framework of analysis with the characteristics of knowledge involved in a dual context, this chapter then describes a process of dual dissemination of knowledge. This is the process that is used as a basis for the empirical analysis proposed in Part 2. This point was already approached; knowledge dissemination is related to two components of TKS: component knowledge and architectural knowledge. The objective is therefore to understand the positions occupied by the elements related to architectural knowledge and to each component knowledge in the defense technological landscape and in the global landscape in order to be able to draw a comparison. The study of this position offers information on the potential of technological dissemination of TKS, and consequently on its duality.

3

Definition and Operation of Dual Innovation System

3.1. Introduction

Relying on the previous two chapters, this chapter proposes a definition of the dual innovation system (DIS), covering all the associated phenomena within a consistent framework. It is the general concept that circumscribes this work.

For this purpose, an in-depth presentation of the concept of an innovation system (IS) is offered. Various approaches are successively reviewed, before specifying the one that best fits the case considered here. Consequently, DIS is presented as an adaptation of these approaches to the specific case of duality, hence to a multisectorial context comprising many technological systems operating in a defense institutional framework.

3.2. Dual innovation system

3.2.1. *Approach in terms of IS*

Unlike neoclassical approach, a systemic approach to innovation is not a sequential process whose sole aim is to generate a new product (Smith 2000), strictly defined by economic constraints. It is the result of a more global process relying on three theoretical premises:

– institutionalist premise: institutions make economic choices. Therefore, institutional differences give rise to different economic behaviors and performances (Smith 2000);

– innovation is a cumulative process relying on constraints from inside and outside the company (Kline and Rosenberg 1986). These constraints are both technical and scientific, but also economic. Technological specializations thus generate self-sufficiency phenomena and system effects. From a related perspective, some authors point out the combinatorial nature of knowledge production as a correlational process (Olsson 2000; Fleming and Sorenson 2001);

– innovation is a social process that is typical of knowledge bases (Asheim and Coenen 2005). These knowledge bases differ in terms of interactive learning mechanisms that are specific to the agents of each system, which determines their future innovation capacities.

ISs are defined as "the network of institutions in the public and private sectors whose activities and interactions initiate, import, modify and diffuse new technologies" (Freeman 1988, p. 1). Several variants of the concept of IS are mentioned in the literature. Local ISs are forerunners and very widely represented. They are divided into national systems (Niosi 2002; Sharif 2006; Lundvall 2010) and, at a lower scale, into regional innovation systems (RISs) (Cooke *et al.* 1997; Asheim and Coenen 2005). Sectoral innovation systems (SISs) are built differently, as the borders of the system are no longer determined by the territory, but by the concerned industry (Malerba 2002). Finally, technological innovation systems (TISs) represent the last variant: they are centered on a specific technology, whose development, diffusion and use they enable (Bergek *et al.* 2008b; Markard and Truffer 2008; Markard *et al.* 2015).

These collective works are all the more interesting as these authors identify among the previously mentioned approaches the seven "key functions" of an IS: (1) knowledge development and dissemination, (2) entrepreneurial experimentation, (3) research orientation, (4) market creation, (5) development of positive externalities, (6) technology promotion or justification and (7) mobilization of required resources (Bergek *et al.* 2008b).

This type of approach emerged in the 1980s with the works of Freeman or those of Lunvall. The national innovation system (NIS) is defined as "a set of institutions whose interactions determine the innovative performance, in the sense above, of national firms" (Nelson 1992, p. 3). He summarizes the premises identified by Smith by considering them within the borders of a country. According to this approach, systemic interactions at the national scale are more significant than interactions between countries, while a smaller scale would not allow the understanding of the overall dynamics. This dimension is very interesting for the analysis of the armament industry, also referred to as the "sovereignty industry". Furthermore, in his work dating from 1993, Chesnais points out the role of the armament industry in the French national system.

Overall, Niosi *et al.* (2002) find four justifications for this hypothesis:

1) essential factors associated with markets (labor market included), resources and tastes, which are more uniform at the national level;

2) Lundvall (1985) and Von Hippel (1987) show that, compared to the international framework, the national framework is more supportive of informal relations;

3) interdependent technologies are rather developed within national economies (for example, in Japan, television technologies contributed to the development of video recorders, followed by cameras, broadcasting material and HD television);

4) national policies structure the interactions between the elements of the system.

Without denying the contributions of NIS-based approaches, RIS points out the importance of local actors. In France, according to the Notre law (2016), the role of economic development is nowadays exclusively assigned to regions, which are "from now on the only ones authorized to award aids and solely responsible for economic development guidance on their territory". Therefore, the region is a homogeneous framework for the definition of public policies and reinforces the legitimacy of these approaches. The idea advocated in the RISs is that the competitive advantages of nations depend on many innovation dynamics territorialized within "technological coalitions" (Storper 1995). The underlying hypothesis is that geographical proximities are the most essential in the innovation process, encouraging relations between innovative companies and thus supplying the required external contributions (externalities). These include the presence of a qualified workforce and production inputs, such as subcontractors for services needed for innovation and the reinjection of benefits back into the RIS (Doloreux and Bitard 2005).

When identifying system boundaries, administrative boundaries are not necessarily relevant. Their establishment must respect the consistency of the economic structure and a certain "inward" direction in the innovation process. This proves important when defining a policy aimed at supporting the development of RIS. If the territory is not coherent or sufficiently self-centered, the public policy will be less efficient (Edquist 2001).

In reality, there are many territorialized structures that make it possible to promote and use material or intangible externalities related to geographical proximities (Elidrissi and Hauch 2008). While the passage from national to local level can be limited to carrying the analysis to a different level, approaches such as technology clusters, science parks, innovative environments and industrial and technological districts "involve the development of a more dynamic view, in which the relevant space is no longer predefined, but can be created at several temporarily stabilized levels of coherence" (Massard *et al.* 2004). The concept of proximity is at the center of these approaches and its operationalization is a challenge for the economists dealing with territories.

In this field, the matter of accessibility to knowledge is a method for measuring this proximity (Massard and Mehier 2009; Autant-Bernard *et al.* 2014). The measurement of knowledge dissemination is therefore a common challenge between these approaches and duality.

SISs are a variant of the approach, not determined by the territory, but by a unit in the concerned sector, a similarity of techniques, demands and sometimes an interdependence in the actors' strategies. There are four elements that justify the SIS-based approach (Malerba 2002). They relate to:

– knowledge and learning processes: there are differences between sectors in terms of knowledge management mechanisms and learning regimes;

– technological base, inputs and demand: these elements that differ from one sector to another exert strong constraints on the behaviors of companies and organizations;

– institutions: this highlights the interactions between national and sectoral institutions. Moreover, there is a large sectoral variety in the structures of market and non-market interactions between companies and organizations;

– variety selection and generation: these fundamental processes, which are at the center of economic change for evolutionists, are greatly constrained by economic factors.

Based on these elements, Malerba proposes the following definition:

> a set of new and established products for specific uses and the set of agents carrying out market and non-market interactions for the creation, production and sale of those products. Sectoral systems have a knowledge base, technologies, inputs and demand. The agents are individuals and organizations at various levels of aggregation, with specific learning processes, competencies, organizational structure, beliefs, objectives and behaviors. They interact through processes of communication, exchange, co-operation, competition and command, and their interactions are shaped by institutions. A sectoral system undergoes processes of change and transformation through the co-evolution of its various elements. (Malerba 2002, p. 248)

The last category of approach, TIS, is very close to the previous one, to the point that it can be confused with it. There are two ways to perceive it. First, TIS can be seen as a subsystem of a SIS, when certain products or knowledge of a sector are highlighted; second, it is at the intersection of several SIS, which is the case when the product or technology is used in several sectors (Bergek *et al.* 2008a).

Whatever the TIS type, when conducting such an analysis, there are three fundamental choices that must be made beforehand (Bergek *et al.* 2008b). First, the choice of the unit that delimits the system: it can be either a product or a field of knowledge. Then, a choice of depth of analysis: should an in-depth study of TIS be conducted based on a specific case of technology application or, on the contrary, is the objective to understand all the possible applications of the technology in question? Finally, it is important to specify a spatial framework since, on this subject, TIS can be considered as a national or regional system.

The objective of this approach is to find the proper system level. On the one hand, a too high level of aggregation sometimes weakens the explanatory power of the system-based analysis. On the other hand, for optimal guidance of public policies implementation, some of them will sometimes be centered on a specific technology (Bergek *et al.* 2010). This approach has the advantage of being the most flexible in relation to the choice of the perimeter to be studied. This allows the closest possible proximity to a specific technology, but requires also high accuracy in the strict definition of the perimeter of the empirical analysis.

The IS eventually contributes to the understanding of the complexity of interactions involved in the development, diffusion and acceptance of a technology. The governance of such a system is at the center of the analysis (Edquist 1997, 2001) and makes it possible to consider the effects of this governance at various scales (national, regional or technological). Moreover, it offers the possibility of considering the objects of the analysis in all their dimensions, from design to use (Bergek *et al.* 2008b). For these reasons, it seems suitable for the study of duality. In the next section, a framework of analysis of duality is built based on these approaches.

3.2.2. *Definition of a DIS*

Based on the characteristics of duality presented in the first chapter, a framework of analysis covering the whole process is built. As many studies indicate, the approach in terms of IS shows, more or less centrally, the role of defense-civilian interactions in the process of innovation (Guichard 2004a; Mérindol and Versailles 2007; Serfati 2008; Lazaric *et al.* 2011).

The main characteristics of dual innovation determine the type of systemic approach to be adopted. As mentioned in this work, there are three such characteristics:

– the system depends on the dual innovation studied: a technology and its specific duality are studied. The institutions (government agencies, interest groups, companies, research centers and universities) involved in the development of a (particularly dual) technology vary widely from one technology to another. As an illustration, ONERA has an essential role in the dual development of aeronautic technologies, while CNES plays a more significant role in a study related to satellites;

– dual innovation is mainly a multisectoral phenomenon: the potential of a technology to be applied for various uses is central to duality. If a sector is characterized by a set of economic agents manufacturing similar products (Storper 1995), it is highly possible that duality relates to several sectors simultaneously, as it concerns a very wide variety of products;

– the national dimension is an important, but incomplete component: due to the strategic nature of the defense industry, the national framework is a relevant scale for the analysis of duality. Indeed, there are at least two reasons for technological duality to be considered a national defense challenge. On the one hand, from a positive perspective, it is one of the means to address the technological excellence required for the defense materials by developing the innovation capacities of defense manufacturers (the ability to draw from technological innovation, whatever its origins). On the other hand, in order to limit the defense innovation capacities in non-allied (or even allied) countries, defense tries to confine the defense innovation-related diffusion of competences to the national territory, thus preventing the diffusion, by means of dual technologies, of information on the technological content of the country's defense innovation. Duality is therefore considered in relation with strategic autonomy constraints.

While often present at national level, the challenge is however manifest in international cooperation, particularly at the European Union level (cooperation in manufacturing certain equipment and establishment of European defense groups such as Nexter and recently KMW, or in the control of exports of dual technologies within the Joint Research Center (JRC) of the European Commission), but also in transatlantic cooperation (F35 development partnership). The innovation environment is quite often international. Indeed, the challenge of duality is to capture and/or emit technology beyond the defense industries. Therefore, it makes no sense to consider national borders as boundaries. On the contrary, seizing opportunities beyond the national territory is the proper approach. The dual potential of a technology may in fact be related to the specificity of the innovation produced on another territory (because of its specific production factors, its uses or other institutional elements characteristic to this territory). In this case, while meeting the above-mentioned strategic constraint, which strongly depends on the respective technology, this potential must be taken into consideration.

Technology is therefore central to the DIS and, even if the governance of duality is highly constrained by strategy challenges of defense, the object itself may appear beyond national borders. There are two ways to perceive this. The first one is related to the strategic challenge of defense and it often corresponds to national, political and institutional borders. The second one corresponds more specifically to the identification of the technological perimeter within which the dual object can develop. There is no reason to confine this perimeter to the national borders. The most relevant approach appears to be that of TIS under the constraint of national strategic challenges of defense.

Summarizing all these elements, a DIS is studied within a defense strategic unified territory, typically the national territory, with the exception of international cooperation, notably in the European Union. For a specific technology, DIS is a set of institutions in the defense and civilian industries that contribute to an innovation process within an institutional space constrained by the strategic challenges of defense innovation. It is characterized by the set of formal and informal mechanisms for transfer and cooperation, which are involved throughout the innovation process. It determines the diffusion potential of a technology between these two fields in various sectors. Based on this potential, governments implement policies aimed at facilitating or constraining the dual development of a technology.

Drawing from the representation applied to localized production systems proposed by Le Goff and Carluer (2002), Figure 3.1 shows a DIS diagram. The advantage of this analysis is that it points out the phenomena of action and feedback characteristic to an IS and it proposes a grid for the analysis of duality depending on the stage of technological development at which it emerges and on the institutions involved. Thus described, the study of duality can be similar to that of a TIS. This approach enables a novel implementation in practice of the principles of duality.

The diagram (Meunier 2019) in Figure 3.1 shows the various objects through which duality can be observed (knowledge, technologies, products or services and finally uses). Some of the key actors present at each stage are also represented. Moreover, this diagram, a simplified reality in which the defense and civilian industries are clearly distinct, has the advantage of showing the complexity of the system of interactions between these two industrial environments. The feedback loops within each industry, and also among industrial sectors are taken into consideration in the analysis. These loops are involved in the development of the Internet, and they are also instrumental in understanding how the Internet technology has developed. As pointed out by Serfati (2008), in the United States, the development of the

Internet rapidly led to division into two separate networks (Milinet and Arpanet) after the failed attempts at direct collaboration. The two developments cannot be considered fully compartmentalized, but it is through indirect mechanisms inherent to the American IS as a whole that these interactions were established (Serfati 2005), one of them having to wait for the other's output to emerge in order to be able to finally appropriate it and integrate it in its concept.

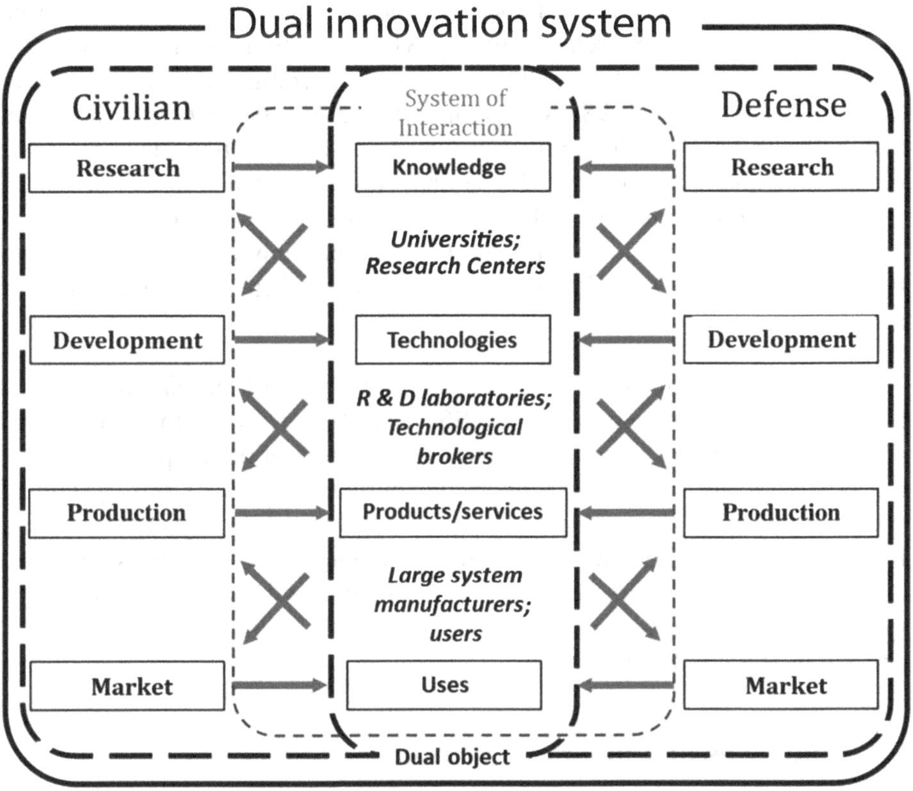

Figure 3.1. *Dual innovation system*

This approach shows the whole complexity of duality, which involves the existence of many distinct but complementary approaches within this systemic framework of analysis assuming multiple interdependences. There are two large categories of approaches on this subject.

IS-based approaches apprehend the whole, trying to clarify its systemic organization and understand its governance mechanisms. They have the advantage of highlighting the role of various actors, the manner in which they interact within the system and observing the manner in which the system evolves. These analyses are however rarely able to quantitatively measure duality, as they try to approach it in all its complexity.

On the other hand, other approaches do not deny the systemic character of duality, but they focus on a specific element of the system. This can be illustrated by analyses related to knowledge within an IS on transfer mechanisms (Guillou *et al.* 2009), an essential component of the system (Molas-Gallart 1997, 1998; Molas-Gallart and Sinclair 1999; Bellais and Guichard 2006), on technological proximity as construction element of the system (Guichard 2004b), etc. These analyses make it possible to focus on one DIS component; they have the advantage of a more in-depth specification of its characteristics and they can possibly conduct quantitative studies that, in a DIS-related context, enable a better understanding of duality.

The next part of this book presents this type of empirical analysis, highlighting the knowledge within DIS. The objective is to measure a dual potential by means of knowledge. Then it is the role of public policies and of the private sector to jointly support the implementation of this system in order to better use this potential: policies "deal with the organizational and informational requirements (e.g. mixed laboratories, networks, internal organization of the firm, information disclosure and learning), allowing a system (a firm, a sector, a country) to realize its duality potential" (Cowan and Foray 1995, p. 859).

3.3. Objectives and functions of a DIS

3.3.1. *In economic and technological terms*

The approaches presented in the first sections of this book show that technological duality pursues both economic objectives (economies of scope, economies of scale, market diversification, optimization of defense budgets, etc.) and technological objectives (higher technical performances, shorter development delays, diversification of innovation potentials, etc.). To meet these objectives, DIS articulates three main functions (Meunier 2019).

3.3.1.1. *Function 1: identify the actors*

This function is logically at the core of a DIS, as it delimits the perimeter. The objective is to identify the set of actors contributing to the innovation process of a given technology in order to follow their evolution. On the one hand, public authorities are able to support the dual development of a system by supporting the emergence and development of actors in both industrial segments and, on the other hand, similarly to a field of strategic activity for a market, DIS delimits the space within which companies must deploy their dual innovation strategy. Similar to a TIS, according to constraints related to the regulatory system and to the technology geostrategic context, these actors can only be located on a national or international territory, and inside or at the intersection of several sectoral systems. From this perspective, DIS mobilizes all the complementary resources required for the dual development of a technology, in the form of nonfinancial or financial assets and human capital.

3.3.1.2. *Function 2: organize dual cooperation*

In order to set up and then maintain a DIS, a set of mechanisms must be implemented in order to encourage and/or constrain the organizations to get involved. Within DIS, this cooperation is dual, meaning that it involves actors oriented toward the civilian industries and actors oriented toward the defense industries (knowing that some of them may have a dual civilian–defense orientation). As noted by Bergek *et al.* (2008b), not all the mechanisms are exclusively market- or government-related; they also originate in the opportunities identified by the entrepreneurial actors during a cumulative process of actor–system interactions. Therefore, public authorities play a central role in DIS organization, but a variety of other actors also influence this organization for a more or less dual purpose, depending on their interests. Knowledge is however the fundamental resource of such a system, while learning that enables knowledge dissemination is the most important process (Lundvall 1992). The objective of public authorities is therefore to support incentives favoring the dual learning process. Hence, the learning process within DIS enables a dual dissemination of knowledge between the actors in the civilian industries and those in the defense industries. This ensures technology sustainability by maintaining the knowledge base needed within a variety of actors whose civilian and defense orientation leads to a weakening of the innovation cycle, often very significant in the defense field.

3.3.1.3. *Function 3: create synergies*

As for the last function, it is related to the dual performance of DIS. Being both economic and technological, this performance depends on synergies developed between actors. The system effect depends on these synergies. They lead to economies of scope, scale and variety (Guichard and Heisbourg 2004), which determine the economic performance of companies and speed up timetable and event planning (Cowan and Foray 1995) – for example, faster or better performance within the same time – which are crucial for technological performance. These synergies generate positive externalities, which are essential for cluster formation. In the form of spillovers, they influence knowledge production in particular, and thus directly reinforce the system's dual performance. Moreover, by reducing also the uncertainty related to the innovation process and reinforcing technological legitimacy, they support cluster dynamics and its economic and technological performance.

These three functions show that DIS is a useful tool in the management of defense innovation policy and industrial policy, beyond the traditional boundaries of DITB. Indeed, according to Bergek *et al.*, the manner in which a technology is perceived influences the institutional perimeter within which its study is relevant (Bergek *et al.* 2008a). If studied within the framework of a specific application – as is the case for the defense application according to the DITB concept – the considered perimeter is confined to the actors concerned by this precise application. On the other hand, it is possible to study a technology beyond this perimeter by considering all its possible applications and, from this perspective, the institutional perimeter taken into account is wider. Innovation policy and industrial policy are thus rooted in a wider context, offering more diversified cooperation perspectives, in terms of both technological input and output. While such an opening cannot be considered at the scale of the whole DITB, as the perimeter may become too wide, it proves to be relevant at the scale of a specific technology with dual potential.

3.3.2. *Duality measure within a DIS*

As shown in Chapter 1, duality is a multidimensional concept, whose definition is subject to interpretation. Consequently, it is difficult to clearly distinguish between what is dual and what is not. This difficulty is partly reduced when focusing on knowledge, since only one dimension of DIS is studied. It is nevertheless necessary to accurately define knowledge duality.

According to the definition of DIS, duality is related to a joint production process. In the case of technological duality, and more precisely of dual knowledge, this joint production may relate to the same knowledge or to different but related knowledge. These two situations may be referred to by the terms “similarity” and “complementarity”.

The notion of similarity-related duality means that the dual potential concerns the production of one piece of knowledge, one group of knowledge units or even a TKS as a whole, in the civilian and defense industries simultaneously; on the other hand, the notion of complementary duality means that the dual potential concerns the complementarity of the innovation activities in the two segments of industries. This means that the production of one piece of knowledge, one group of knowledge units or one TKS as a whole, in the civilian industries or in the defense industries, requires the production of complementary knowledge originating in the other sector. Two remarks are worth being added to the definition of these terms.

First, these two dimensions are not inseparable. This means that the notion of similarity-related duality does not imply the exclusion of the notion of complementarity, and conversely. Beyond the presence or absence of both phenomena, their intensity in each TKS studied is important.

As will be presented in more detail in the next part of the book, the structure of the knowledge graphs resulting from patent analysis shows that knowledge is very widely distributed among organizations. Seldom does knowledge exclusively originate in a precise environment (at least as far as component knowledge is concerned). Moreover, the production of one piece of knowledge usually requires knowledge from another technological class. This means that each piece of knowledge or technological class strongly depends on its technological environment. This means that both phenomena are almost systematically observable. Consequently, the proportion in which they are represented is worth being studied.

The analysis of knowledge flows reveals a dual potential that can be divided into two categories. But this potential can be used to a higher or lower degree. This means that the companies can be more or less aware of these knowledge proximities and use them in their innovation actions. To analyze this aspect, it is possible to measure the proportion in which the flows between civilian and defense sectors correspond to the potential that would have been measured. In this case, the potential is referred to as revealed or underlying.

This so-called "revealed" potential is opposed to the "underlying" potential and does not necessarily involve the use of dual potential. Indeed, it is a matter of observing the actual flows of knowledge between the defense and the civilian sectors. In the case of revealed similarity potential, besides working on the same knowledge, direct links between knowledge produced in the defense and civilian sectors are established (one actor for each environment). The same logic is applicable to the notion of revealed complementarity. Knowledge produced in one industrial segment is directly used in another industrial segment.

This does not necessarily imply that the actors are involved in a process of joint production of knowledge. Knowledge exchange is possible without cooperation between actors; moreover, due to limits related to the nature of data used in the empirical part, knowledge can unawarely be exchanged, which consequently yields no dual innovation strategy. But duality cannot be used unless there is joint production. Therefore, the notions of revealed and underlying potential enable a more precise characterization of the nature of dual potential, but cannot be used to predict the strategies developed by the two parties.

3.3.3. *DIS for the autonomous vehicle*

The study of the autonomous vehicle offers an illustration of how DIS can be used. This section does not aim to define and specifically study a DIS. It is an illustration of how this framework of analysis can be used to study an emerging technology (or more likely a technological system), which presents an interest for the military and civilian sectors (Meunier 2019).

Considering the example of France, a very quick overview shows that there is a diversity of actors (university, laboratories, companies, etc.), depending on several sectors (automotive, electronics, telecommunication, etc.), mobilizing various technologies (photonics, optronics, optic, etc.) and whose activities are divided between defense sectors and civilian sectors. This broad range of actors can be integrated using a DIS-based approach. Public authorities are thus in a position to support their emergence/development in order to ensure the dual nature of the ecosystem, while the

DIS actors organize their strategies by implementing long-term industrial cooperation. This is the perspective adopted by DGA when financing within the Scorpion program, the development of autonomous vehicles carried out by Safran, surrounded by a "France team" with both civilian and military members, composed of universities and research laboratories (Mines Paristech, INRIA, Institut Pascal, CREC of Saint-Cyr Coëtquidan, Paris Dauphine, LAAS and IRSTEA) and industrial partners (Effidence, Technical Studio, Squadrone, Kompaï robotics, Sominex and 4D virtualiz).

The DIS-based approach can be used to reflect on the interaction between various defense-oriented programs, such as the above-mentioned DGA one, and also civilian programs, such as Safran, Valeo and the Ulis project, centered on one of the DIS technological components – the all-weather camera – financed by the former General Directorate for industrial competitiveness (Direction générale de la compétitivité, de l'industrie (DGCIS)), in partnership with the Single Interministry Fund (Fond unique interministériel (FUI)), whose action is rooted in the policy of poles of competitiveness and aims to encourage cooperation in R&D projects, budgeted by the Ministry of Industry and by the Ministry of Defense (currently Ministry of Armed Forces). Here, the Mov'eo and ViaMéca poles are led by the Ministry of Industry, Astech is led by the Ministry of Armed Forces and all integrate defense and civilian manufacturers. This incentive policy supports a dual process of knowledge dissemination, which is highlighted by the DIS-based analysis.

Finally, it appears that building synergies is necessary for the emergence of this technology and also for structuring a high-performance industrial sector. Indeed, the autonomous vehicle mobilizes many technologies spanning a diversity of complementary actors. They belong to the automotive (system integrators for the civilian sectors) and aeronautics sectors, particularly in the field of defense (for sensors such as Lidar), but also the digital sector (for artificial intelligence technologies), etc. The synergies between these actors draw upon the competitive edges of each of them. If they monopolize all the technological components in the digital field, the presence of giant American digital companies in this technological race is nevertheless a threat for the strategic autonomy of a country like France. The synergies between defense programs and civilian programs are a means for the long-term preservation of these competences on the territory. Hence, identifying a French DIS would enable an arbitrage between economic and technological performances, on both the short and long terms, on its own or in partnership with other European countries that are relatively independent from the United States.

Considering innovation at the scale of the technical system and from a dual perspective would enable a better adequacy between innovation policy and industrial policy. In France, the objective of the Agency for Defense Innovation is, according to Florence Parly (Minister of the Armed Forces, on August 28 during MEDEF summer university), to open defense innovation to the outside world and build its international presence. From this perspective, innovation management at the scale of the technical system makes it possible to rethink the institutional perimeter, beyond that of DITB. This requires the implementation of specific empirical methods enabling the analysis of the innovation process at the level of knowledge production. Consequently, it is possible to identify within DITB all the actors involved in this process and analyze their contributions and the way in which they interact, not only among them, but also with the rest of the industrial sectors for a given technical system.

3.4. Conclusion

The literature review, spanning from the introduction of duality as a concept until recent developments, shows the complexity of its expressions. While technological aspects are essential, they are not the only axis to be considered in this analysis. As a first step, a synthesis evidenced the diversity of objects that could be qualified as dual, and then pointed out the governance questions this raises. The definition of the DIS takes into consideration these two axes. When considered as a whole, it offers the advantage of taking into account the complexity of the interactions implied by duality; furthermore, a step by step analysis of duality provides an in-depth view on the various matters related to each stage in the lifecycle of the technology.

The next developments unfold within this framework of analysis; they focus essentially on the first layer. If the analysis is inserted within the global framework offered by DIS, the study will have a general coverage and facilitates the extension of the proposed argument. The main contribution of this approach is to show, first, that the perimeter of the DIS must be built in relation to the technical characteristics of a specific technological system, and, second, that this will depend on the institutional constraints related to the strategic challenges of defense innovation.

Conclusion to Part 2

This second part presented the reader with a full unfolding of an analysis that was used first to identify technological knowledge systems, then to evaluate their dual nature, both from the perspective of their internal coherences and their influences. The articulation of the theoretical context of economic dominance with that of technological coherence offered the possibility of thoroughly using patent data in an analysis of duality.

The first point of added value of this part is that it enabled the interconnection of several tools resulting from two distinct theoretical sets. Showing the interest of two approaches to methodological foundations that are different but fully compatible in theoretical terms opens the way for new methodological work on the analysis of knowledge production in general, and on technological duality in particular. Indeed, these indicators bring complementary perspectives on knowledge production, allowing the analysis to include complex characteristics of technological innovation.

The second prominent element of this part is to have shown the interest of patent data for addressing matters of technological duality. Indeed, while military innovation has a particular relation with patents – which is also the case in many other domains – this should not be an impediment for defense economists using this source of information. There are methodological solutions that enable their use and, if researchers take the required interpretation precautions, they prove to be particularly relevant for the study of duality which, by definition, concerns innovations with an influence beyond the military domain.

Finally, this part made it possible to propose an analysis of duality that reveals the diversity of situations. Indeed, using this approach in the analysis of 26 TKS involved in different industrial domains, composed of various technologies, this work shows that, beyond a binary perspective on duality that would be to simply tell whether such or such technological system is dual or not, it is interesting to show the characteristics concerned by this duality, in order to better understand how it can be used by the companies and how it points out a continuum of technological duality with multiple characteristics.

PART 2

Methodological Tools and Empirical Study of the Duality of Technological Systems

Introduction to Part 2

The first part of the book highlighted the multifactorial nature of dual technological innovation. Among these factors, technology, and more precisely the mobilization of knowledge within technologies, plays an upstream role in the structuring of the dual innovation system. Consequently, in order to evaluate the dual potential of these technologies, the second part proposes a set of tools for studying the organization and interactions of knowledge for various technological knowledge systems (TKS).

The first step in order to observe the organization of knowledge and thus evaluate the dual potential of TKS is to define the technological perimeter to be evaluated. The theoretical framework is provided by economic dominance theory (Perroux 1948) and the tools used are those of the influence graph theory (IGT) resulting from it (Lantner 1974; Defourny and Thorbecke 1984; Lequeux 2002; Gallo 2006; Lebert *et al.* 2016). The objective is to measure the synergies in knowledge production within a defense environment in order to define the relevant TKS to be studied.

The dual potential is then evaluated from two complementary perspectives. The dual potential of TKS is first evaluated by studying the structuring of knowledge within them. This involves the industrial coherence theory in its technological application (Teece *et al.* 1994; Cohen 1997; Piscitello 2000; Krafft *et al.* 2011; Nasiriyar *et al.* 2013). This enables a comparison between knowledge structure within a defense environment and knowledge structure within the global environment.

Finally, drawing on a dominance-based approach, a more detailed presentation of the dual potential of TKS will be provided, which will serve particularly to provide a better understanding of how each side establishes its relations with the rest of the knowledge environment. This last contribution indicates the role that companies play in structuring these relations.

Choosing to develop a complete set of methodological tools, focused on an essential aspect of duality, this work aims to offer the means that future works can use to go beyond the numerous case studies already proposed in the literature and to provide economists and practitioners with a set of metrics that will help them compare the diversity of situations in which technological duality can be observed.

This assumes an understanding of how knowledge analysis tools can be used to understand technological production and how they can be used to measure cognitive proximities between several environments.

This part is organized into three chapters: the first identifies the TKS to be studied, while the following two chapters evaluate their dual potentials in terms of technological coherence and then of influence.

Preliminary data presentation

For the sake of a smoother and more accessible presentation, data are presented in this section. The reader thus has an overview of the data to be used in the entire empirical part and which can serve as a reference.

Company database

The source of basic information is provided by the top corporate R&D investors (IPTS, European Commission). It includes information on 2,000 groups and their 500,000 subsidiaries, which in 2013 accounted for 90% of the worldwide expenses in private research and development (R&D). Companies are distributed in 30 industrial sectors based on their main activity.

This data case covering the period 2010–2012 comprises the references of patent filings for Scoreboard companies (IPTS 2013). This COR&DIP database is the result of a collaboration between EC-JRC and OECD and it was built according to the procedure described by Dernis *et al.* (2015).

Turnover	16,854,415.9 million euros
Mean turnover	8,427.2 million euros
Turnover standard deviation	735.4 million euros
Total R&D expense	538 763.8 million euros
Mean R&D expense	264.8 million euros
Standard deviation of R&D expense	735.4 million euros

Table I.1. *Statistics of the studied companies*

Patent data

The data related to the patents in this database are obtained from the European Patent Office's Worldwide Patent Statistical Database (PATSTAT). This database is composed of several tables interrelated by a unique patent identifier (appln_id). It offers in particular information on the inventors, the International Patent Classification (IPC), dates, offices and citations in these patents (EPO 2014, by Rassenfosse *et al.* 2014).

This work uses mainly information related to IPC and citations. They serve to build the technological flow and technological co-occurrence matrices. The principle is that, when a patent is filed, it is both referenced in the technological classes (according to IPC, in particular) and it references a certain number of sources, notably patents, which it cites. It is by the intermediary of these two pieces of information that it is possible to build the technological co-occurrence matrices (technological classes referenced together in a patent) and technological flow matrices (technological classes interrelated by a citation link). Since the validity period of the data is 2010–2012, backward citations are used here. This means that, based on a list of patents, the cited patents are retrieved. The opposite approach would be to use forward citations, meaning citations of a patent after its publication, which is less relevant on such a short term. It is worth noting here that there are two reasons for which a patent may cite another patent. The first reason is that the author of the patent cited this patent as a reference; they are then aware of the relationship in terms of knowledge. The second reason is that the examiner working for the intellectual property office added a reference they deemed relevant. In the latter case, the author may not be aware of this relationship.

Data extraction procedure

The patents in the Scoreboard base are related to PATSAT by a unique identification number (appln_id). The process unfolds as follows:

1) extraction of basic information: for the Scoreboard companies, within the table (TLS211_PAT_PUBLN) and using the unique identification number of patents (appln_id), information on filing authority, type of publication (only patents are retained here), filing date (appln_filing_date) and publication number (pat_publn_id) are retrieved;

2) extraction of citation information: for Scoreboard companies, in the table (TLS212_CITATION) and using the publication number (pat_publn_id), the references on the cited patents are retrieved: the number of cited patents (cited_pat_publn_id et cited_appln_id);

3) extraction of information concerning technological classes: for the cited and citing patents, within table (TLS209_APPLN_IPC), the numbers of technological classes of IPC are retrieved (ipc_class_symbol);

4) extraction of information concerning patent families: for the cited and citing patents, within table (TLS219_INPADOC_FAM), the numbers of the patent families are retrieved (innpadoc_family_id). A patent family is a set of patents related to the same innovation.

The final dataset is built based on patent families (the interest of these families will be presented further on) and includes the following information:

– unique identification number of the patents (appln_id);

– references of the patent filing offices (publn_auth);

– filing date (appln_filing_date);

– technological classes (ipc_class_symbol);

– family numbers (innpadoc_family_id).

Citation data scope

After duplicate data removal, autocitation elimination and missing data cleanup, the dataset comprises the information contained in Table I.2.

Number of companies that filed patent families with the studied offices	1,655
Number of citing patent families	2,341,491
Number of unique citing patent families	2,341,491
Number of citing defense patent families	367,185
Number of unique citing defense patent families	254,154
Average number of citing patent families per company	221.86
Average number of unique citing patent family per company	153.56
Number of unique technological classes for citing patent families	621
Average number of unique technological classes per citing patent family	2.72
Number of cited patent families	1,974,306
Number of unique cited patent families	1,087,362
Average number of cited patent families per company	1,192.93
Average number of cited unique patent families per company	657.01
Number of unique technological classes for the cited patent families	638
Average number of unique technological classes per cited patent family	3.11

Table I.2. *Statistics of patent data*

4

Identification of Technological Knowledge Systems in Defense

4.1. Introduction

This chapter aims to identify technological knowledge systems (TKS), whose dual nature will then be studied. It is the foundation on which the rest of the empirical work relies.

In order to identify a relevant set of TKS, this chapter delimits a specific knowledge environment that is adapted to the dual study object. This involves delimiting two perimeters: on the one hand, a set of knowledge dedicated to the defense field and, on the other hand, the set of knowledge used in all innovation activities, or in other terms, the global knowledge environment. These two perimeters identified from company data are referred to as the "defense knowledge environment" and "global knowledge environment", respectively.

This chapter offers the opportunity to introduce economic dominance theory (EDT). It is used here to identify TKS within the defense knowledge environment and to subsequently analyze the dual potential of these TKS by studying their relations with the global knowledge environment. EDT originated in the work of Perroux (1994), which relies on a structural analysis of the economy founded on an asymmetrical representation of so-called "dominance" relations between the elements of a structure. The analysis of these relations highlights the phenomena of dependence, interdependence and autarky, which shape the structure. In this chapter, the use of EDT-derived tools offers a solution for the localization and measurement of synergies between pieces of knowledge, and consequently for delimiting TKS based on patent data.

This chapter reviews the foundations of EDT, and then describes the methodological tools that can be applied to patent data for knowledge production study. Then it clarifies the method for identifying synergies within a structure, and finally identifies TKS, which are in the end briefly presented.

4.2. EDT and analysis of knowledge flows

4.2.1. *Economic dominance theory*

EDT is presented here mainly according to the works of Lantner and Lebert (2015). As recalled by Lebert and Younsi (2015), the foundation of EDT is twofold: theoretical and methodological. From a theoretical perspective, EDT derives from the works conducted by Perroux on power (dominance) relations in economy. According to these works, the economic world is perceived as a set of domination relations, which can be obvious or concealed (Perroux 1994). It is methodologically related to the mathematical theory of graphs, which, since its introduction at the end of the 1940s (Bavelas 1948; Luce and Perry 1949; Leavitt 1951) followed by the more formal analyses conducted at the University of Michigan (Harary and Norman 1953; Cartwright *et al.* 1965), is a privileged tool of sociometric studies, also referred to as "social network analysis" (SNA). Freeman (2004) points out that the "Sorbonne school", particularly through Flament *et al.* (1963) and Berge (1958), established the first interpretation of these writings, "which explicitly shows that a broad range of social problems could be understood as particular cases of a general structural model" (p. 114).

The works of Ponsard (1967, 1968) and those of Lantner follow the development of the theoretical framework proposed by Perroux and deploy structural analysis tools relying on the mathematical theory of graphs for the formal representation of dominance relations. These researches lead to EDT. Until present, it was mainly applied to the analysis of interindustrial relations. It is first mobilized within a national framework, in order to study the relations of dependence and interdependence between productive sectors, as represented by national accounting (Lantner 1974) and then, from an international perspective, in order to study the relations of domination in international exchanges (Lebert and Younsi 2015). It is nevertheless worth noting that the EDT was not exclusively applied to industrial flows. It was particularly employed for the analysis of capitalistic flows in the media industry (Lequeux 2002) and for the analysis of information flows in order to study the power relations in organizations (Gallo 2006).

It is only recently that it was for the first time applied to knowledge flows. Lebert (2016) studied interterritorial knowledge flows by the intermediary of the analysis of patent citations in order to measure the resilience of territories and, second, to explain this resilience by studying the domination relations between the technologies within the territories themselves. The approach is different here. The objective is the *a priori* study of intertechnological knowledge flows in order to explain a dual innovation dynamics.

Knowledge flows are one structure of exchange among others. For a good understanding of the interest that EDT presents for such works, it is worth presenting the formal application of this theory to the analysis of an arbitrary structure of exchanges, before applying it to knowledge flows.

For this purpose, a structure of exchanges between n poles is considered. This structure corresponds to a square matrix of n rows denoted by i and of n columns denoted by j, whose elements denoted by x_{ij} correspond to the flows between the various emitting and receiving poles. Let us denote by X_i the production of ith pole, by $X_i - \sum_{j=1}^{n} x_{ij} = Y_i$ the "request" from outside the structure and by $X_j - \sum_{i=1}^{n} x_{ij} = W_j$ "the added value" of pole j. The matrix with "technical coefficients" in the format $n \times n$ and composed of elements $a_{ij} = x_{ij}/X_j$ is thus calculated. The input output (IO) system $AX = Y$ is obtained with $A = [I - a]$, known as "Leontief matrix". Similarly, the matrix t of "production coefficients" of the form $n \times n$ composed of elements $t_{ij} = x_{ij}/X_i$ is calculated. In matrix format, the system IO $X^R T = W^R$ is obtained, where $T = [I - t]$, X^R is the row vector of X_j and W^R is the row vector of W_j. The diagonals of matrices A and T are composed of the same coefficients; they represent the loops associated with each pole, meaning the flows going directly from the ith pole to the ith pole.

There are many bridges between IO analysis and SNA, particularly due to the works of Salancik (1986), Bonacich and Lloyd (2001) and Friedkin

(1991), who use instruments and methods issued from IO analysis in SNA, and more recently Gallo (2006), who introduced in the IO analysis quantitative measures from the works of Lantner. Indeed, the structure of the IO analysis represents a set of relations between various poles that can be perceived, according to Perroux, as relations of domination directly or indirectly exerted between these poles. Then the IO method, as mentioned by Gallo (2006), enables the measurement of the mutual influence of these poles.

The objective of EDT is to measure and analyze these influences within a network. The instrument it uses for this purpose is influence graph theory (IGT), which uses the work conducted on fluence or transfer graph theory (Ponsard 1968) and extends it while enabling the distinction between structural dependence and interdependence within a network (Lantner and Lebert 2015). As pointed out by Lantner, the advantage of IGT compared to fluence graph theory (FGT) is that it enables, on the one hand, a better study of signal diffusion within a structure and, on the other hand, the analysis of the effects of multiple perturbations on the structure, while FGT does not seem adequate for this type of analysis. The interest of IGT is therefore that it is able to perceive, within an arbitrary linear system, the "global" influence exerted by one pole on the other. But studying this global influence requires taking into consideration what happens in the rest of the structure, therefore independently of the link between the two poles. It is particularly these structural phenomena that IGT can analyze in order to evidence the amplification effects in these relations. IGT therefore enables "the reflection on the arrangement and articulations of this structure; this leads to global indicators" (Lantner and Lebert 2015).

In 2013, Lebert and Lantner (2013a) recall the rules for building an influence graph:

1) each pole of the graph represents an entity i of the structure;

2) the arcs interconnecting poles correspond to the flows (x_{ij}) between poles i and j; their orientation depends on the "dominant influence", which can be either the offer (for example, in the direction of the flow of goods) or the demand (for example, in the direction of the monetary compensation). Then a first weighting of these arcs corresponds to either the technical coefficients a_{ij}, or to production coefficients t_{ij}, from which the value of "loops" $l_i \equiv 1 - a_{ii} = 1 - t_{ii}$ is deduced;

3) the dominant influence defines the orientation of the connections with the outside of the structure. It is centrifugal when the offer is dominant and centripetal otherwise. A second weighting of these flows corresponds to what does not circulate in the structure: $w_i \equiv W_i/X_i = 1 - \sum_{i=1}^{n} a_{ij} \geq 0$, when the offer is dominant, and $y_i \equiv Y_i/X_i = 1 - \sum_{j=1}^{n} t_{ij} \geq 0$, when the demand is dominant.

According to IGT, this structure is studied by calculating the determinant of the matrix, associated with various configurations of the graph. The value of the determinant D can be calculated from two opposite topological expressions, namely that of tree structures and that of circularities. They are characterized as follows:

– *tree structures*: the determinant is the sum of the values of tree structures. A "tree structure" being a partial graph that includes the relations with the outside and in which the indegrees for each pole (number of ingoing connections) are strictly equal to 1, then the outdegrees can be arbitrary (a tree structure integrating a root, if an additional pole is introduced, where all the external flows weighted by y_i or w_j end up) (Lebert and Younsi 2015);

– *circularities*: the determinant is the sum of the values of circularities. A circuit is a series of arcs ("paths") whose poles at the ends are identical. A Hamiltonian partial graph (HPG) is a partial graph whose poles have indegrees (number of receptions) and outdegrees (number of emissions) strictly equal to 1 (Lebert and Younsi 2015).

Then we have:

$$D \equiv \sum_{1}^{K} A_k = \sum_{1}^{L} G_l$$

where:

– k: number of tree structures, and A_k, the value of a tree structure:

$$A_k = \prod_{ij \in k} t_{ij}$$

– l: the number of HPG, G_l, the value of a HPG and c, the number of circuits in the HPG:

$$G_l = (-1)^c \prod_{ij \in l} t_{ij}$$

Based on the value of the structure determinant, it is possible to measure the importance of dominance (associated with tree structures) and circularities. These circularities unfold, on the one hand, into relations of interdependence and, on the other hand, into autarky. This involves the calculation of several theoretical values of the determinant. The positioning of these various values in Figures 4.1–4.4 makes it easier to follow the methodological explanations.

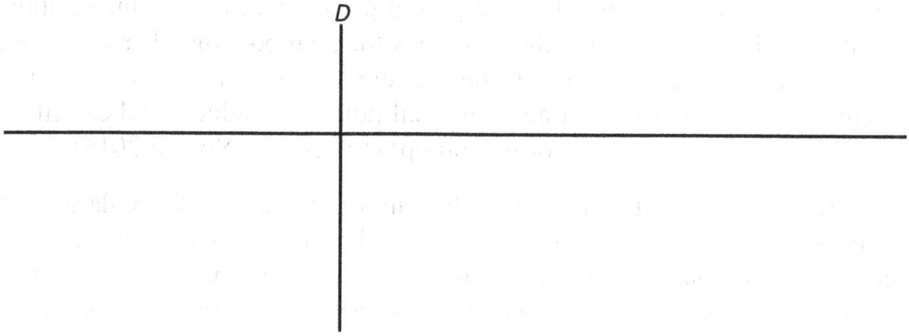

Figure 4.1. *Structural indicators (1)*

4.2.1.1. *Minimal and maximal values of the determinant*

Minimal and maximal values of the determinant depend on the connections between the structure and its outside environment.

Considering a graph whose orientation is given by the dominant offer, the minimal value of the determinant is equal to the product of y_i (or else to the product of w_i):

$$D \geq \prod_{i=1}^{n} y_i$$

Indeed, according to the theorem of the flowers (Lantner and Lebert 2013a), for a structure with n poles, if each of them is in autarky except for the connections with the outside, there is only one HPG composed of n loops, whose determinant is equal to the values of these loops. Or, in such a configuration, the value of these loops l_i is minimal and corresponds to coefficients y_i of connection with the outside. The emergence of an additional arc between two poles of the structure leads by necessity to an increase in the value of the determinant; therefore, the value of D is minimal:

$$mD = \prod_{i=1}^{n} y_i$$

This is why the gap between the minimal value of the determinant mD and the real value of the determinant is a good indicator of the importance of dependence (dominance) relations in the structure.

Similarly, considering a graph oriented according to the dominant offer, the maximal value of the determinant is a function of y_i (or else of w_i):

$$D \leq 1 - \prod_{i=1}^{n} (1 - y_i)$$

Indeed, according to the theorem of upper bounds (Lantner and Lebert 2013a), in an exchange structure in which there is no auto-consumption, the value of loops is equal to 1 (see above); the product of the values of the loops is also equal to 1. The maximal value of the determinant (defined as the sum of values of HPG of the structure) is therefore obtained when the structure is entirely organized according to dependence relations:

$$MD = \prod_{i=1}^{n} l_i - \prod_{i=1}^{n} (1 - y_i) = 1 - \prod_{i=1}^{n} (1 - y_i)$$

This is why the gap between the maximal value of the determinant MD and the real value of the determinant is a good indicator of the importance of circularities (interdependences) in the structure.

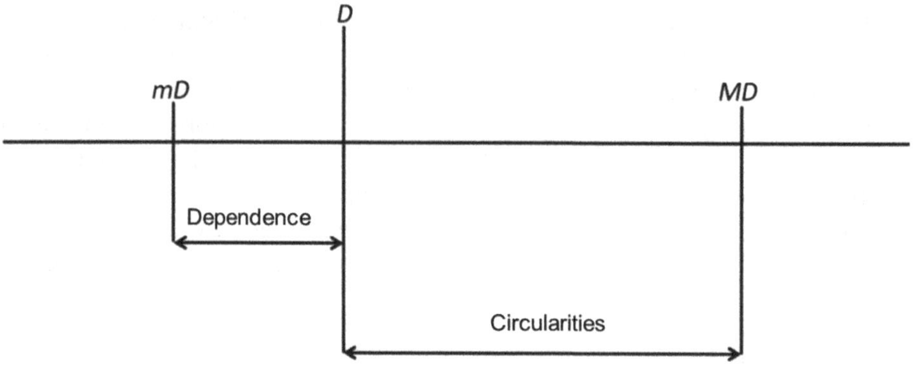

Figure 4.2. *Structural indicators (2)*

4.2.1.2. *Absolute bounds of the determinant*

It is known that:

$$\prod_{i=1}^{n} y_i \leq D \leq 1 - \prod_{i=1}^{n} (1 - y_i)$$

As previously defined, $y_i \geq 0$. Therefore, the product of y_i is necessarily greater or equal to 0. Moreover, $y_i \leq 1$, therefore the minimal value of $\prod_{i=1}^{n}(1 - y_i)$ is 0, by extension $1 - \prod_{i=1}^{n}(1 - y_i) \leq 1$. Then:

$$0 \leq D \leq 1$$

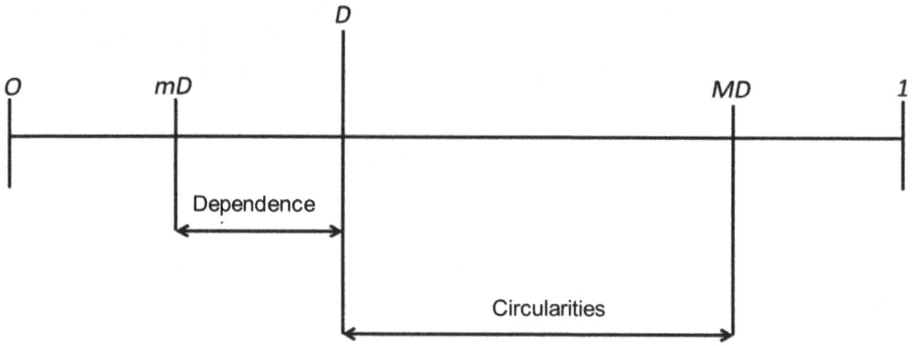

Figure 4.3. *Structural indicators (3)*

4.2.1.3. *The upper bound of the determinant in case of autarky*

In case of autarky, the maximal value of the determinant has the same form, except that the value of one of the loops is not 1. Considering once again a graph whose orientation is given by the dominant offer, the maximal value of the determinant is then:

$$D \leq \prod_{i=1}^{n} l_i - \prod_{i=1}^{n} (l_i - y_i) < 1 - \prod_{i=1}^{n} (1 - y_i)$$

Indeed, in case of autarky, for at least one pole i, auto-consumption is not zero. Then for this pole, one value of the loop is below 1 (see above). This is why the product of the loops is also below 1. Moreover, for each pole i, the value of the loop below 1 reduces the value of the arcs to $1 - t_{ii} - y_i = l_i - y_i$. The maximal value of the determinant of a structure involving auto-consumption (autarky) is therefore:

$$MaD = \prod_{i=1}^{n} l_i - \prod_{i=1}^{n} (l_i - y_i)$$

This is why the gap between the maximal value of the determinant MD and the value of the determinant considering the autarky is a good indicator of the importance of autarky within the structure.

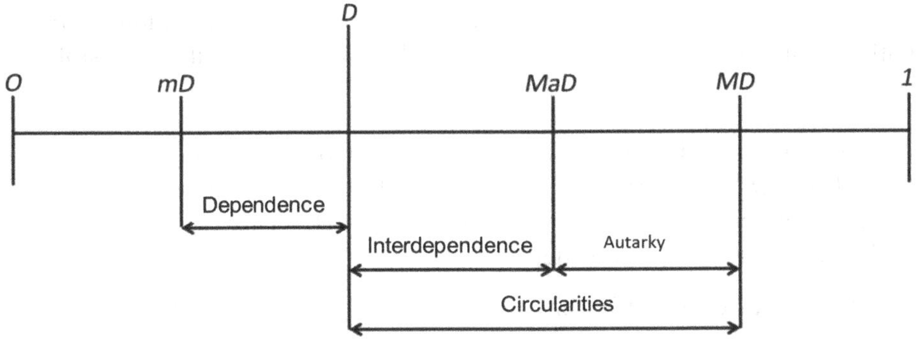

Figure 4.4. *Structural indicators (4)*

Besides the value of the determinant, the notion of partition (Lebert and Younsi 2015) is needed in order to analyze the structure of relations and identify TKS. It corresponds to the analysis of dependence and interdependence relations between subsets of the structure. This involves a separate consideration of the connections between certain poles of the graph. In other terms, it is the consideration within a complete matrix of subsets defining submatrices.

It is also possible to take one part separately from the rest and to calculate the determinant of each submatrix in order to measure its dependence, interdependence and autarky such as they were defined above. It is especially interesting to consider the relations between two parts of the matrix. This makes it possible to measure the importance of the same phenomena between the subsets. Indeed, the theorem of partial interdependences states that the measure of a connection between the subsets of a matrix is given by the difference between the product of the determinants of submatrices and the determinant of the complete matrix (Lantner and Lebert 2013a):

$$I = \prod p\, D_p - D$$

with:

– D: determinant of the complete matrix;

– D_p: determinants of submatrices.

It is thus possible to analyze the interactions between various subsets within a structure. In order to simplify the calculations, it is possible to consider one structure without autarky.

If the structure is divided into three parts and, as shown in Figure 4.5, $D_1 = 1$ and $D_2 = 1$, parts 1 and 2 composed of only one pole, the partition theorem indicates that $D_S = D_1 \times D_2 \times D_3 \geq D$. This means that the difference between D_S and D depends on:

– the values of a and b, for example on the circularities between parts 1 and 2;

– the values of c and d, for example on the circularities between parts 2 and 3;

– the values of e and f, for example on the circularities between parts 1 and 3.

The partition theorem therefore enables the measurement of the global interdependence between all the parts of the structure, by calculating here the difference between D_S and D, and the measurement of the interdependence by pairs of parts depending on the circularities through them.

The sum of these circularities taken two by two does not amount to the value of $D_S - D$. Certain circuits cannot be apprehended unless three or more parts are considered. The difference $D_S - D$ and the sum of interdependences between the parts taken two by two correspond to the weight of long circularities (for example, those that pass through at least three parts) in the structure.

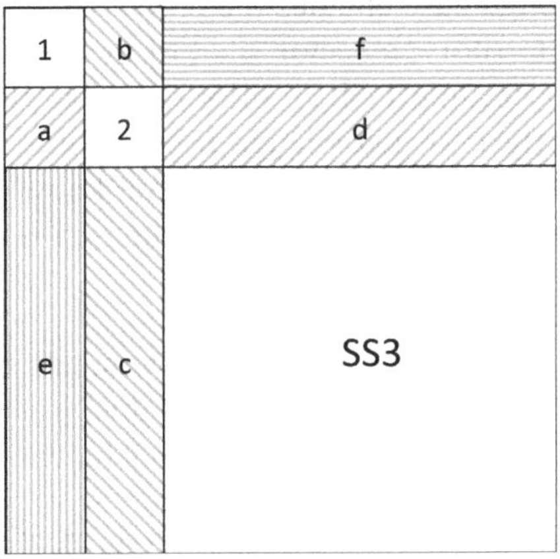

Figure 4.5. *The determinant of submatrices*

COMMENT ON FIGURE 4.5.–

– D_1: *determinant of substructure 1*;

– D_2: *determinant of substructure 2*;

– D_3: *determinant of substructure SS3*;

– a: *coefficient of the flow going out of 1 and into 2*;

– b: *coefficient of the flow going into 1 and out of 2*;

– c: *set of coefficients of flows going out of 2 and into SS3*;

– d: *set of coefficients of flow going into 2 and out of SS3.*

Therefore, the interdependence of substructures can be written as:

$$I_2 = D_1 \times D_2 \times D_3 - D$$

4.2.2. *Application to knowledge analysis through patents*

As already noted, there are several methods for apprehending a knowledge environment. The tools offered by IGT are one of these methods. This theory can be applied if patent data are understood similarly to a knowledge base.

The first part provided a presentation of the knowledge base concept. As explained, the knowledge base enables the representation for one unit, which can be a company, a territory, a sector, etc., of the knowledge it handles. As already mentioned, according to IGT information must be structured as an IO system. In the analysis of knowledge production using IGT, knowledge bases must enable the identification of input knowledge leading to the production of output knowledge. This representation is obtained by building technological flow matrices.

It is possible to build technological flow matrices using information related to patent intercitations. To understand this, it is first of all important to correctly figure the information contained in a patent.

Upon its filing with an intellectual property protection office, a patent is classified into one or several technological classes (TCs), depending on the nature of the innovation that it protects. There are several such classifications. The classification considered here is the International Patent Classification (IPC), used by all the offices providing data for this study (USPTO, EPO and all the offices of the Europe of Fifteen).

Moreover, similar to a research article, a patent must cite its sources. It must mention the patents on which it relies. Each patent lists a set of TCs, which can be divided into two categories. First, those in which the patent is directly referenced, known as “citing” classes; then, those in which the cited patents are referenced, known as “cited”.

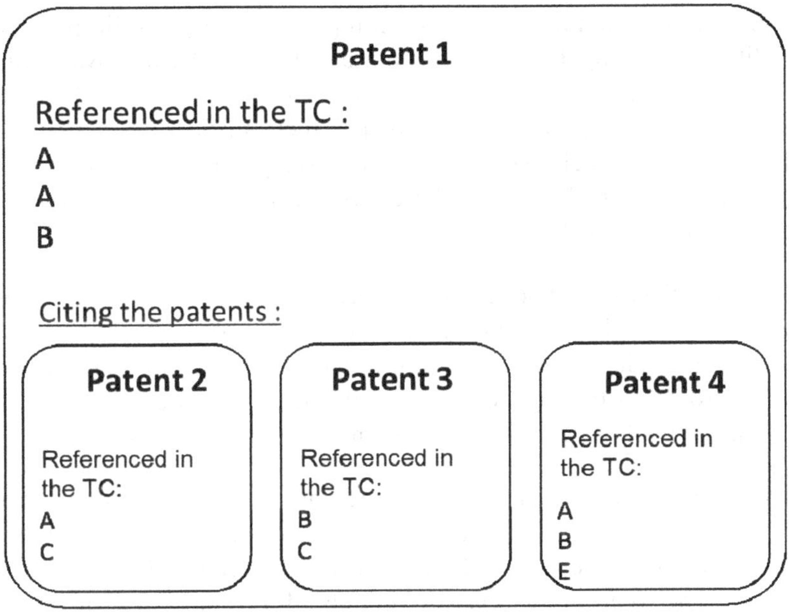

Figure 4.6. *Representation of a patent structure*

As illustrated in Figure 4.6, patent 1 helps identify two "citing" classes: A and B. Class A is counted twice. This happens because, for reasons related to ranking credibility at the finest level, the use in the economic literature and the power of the required calculation, IPC was not used at its finest level. Consequently, certain TCs that can be distinguished at the finest level appear as identical here. Similarly, there are four "cited" classes: A (twice), B (twice), C (twice) and E.

For the above-mentioned reasons, this work relies on a backward approach. This means that the technological flows are established by studying the citations of previous patents as they appear in a selected patent. This method is the opposite of the analysis of forward citations, which involves the study of later citations of a previously selected patent (which is impossible at the time this study is conducted, given the lack of hindsight). The analysis relies on the capacities of absorption and on technological combinations, rather than on technology diffusion capacities.

A similar approach at the scale of company patent portfolio provides the possibility of drawing for each of them a list of all the backward citations and thus considering each of them as a component – layer – of the matrix of global flows. Overlapping these "layers" then suffices to obtain a large matrix of all the technological flows corresponding to the sample of company patent portfolio studied here (see Verspagen 2004 for more details on the construction of flow matrices).

Following the example of the patent presented in Figure 4.6, it is possible to provide a detailed explanation on the quantification of technological flows in the matrix. Technological flows are in fact weighted in several successive ways, according to the principle that each family of patents (whose setting up is described below) accounts for "1" in the aggregate matrix.

First, there is the weighting inside the patent. In this example, there are three "citing" TCs (A + A + B) and seven "cited" ICs (A + A + B + B + C + C + E). Therefore, there are 21 possible combinations (3 × 7). Then, each connection between two classes counts for one part of these 21 combinations, for example, the connection A→A counts for 4/21^{e}, the connection B→E for 1/21^{e}, etc.

Second, there is the weighting related to companies that own the patent. If the respective patent is owned by only one company, then it is not subject to this weighting. On the other hand, if several companies are co-owners of a patent, then the value of the technological flows associated with it is equally divided between the various companies (fractional counting). Concretely, if companies X and Y are co-owners of patent 1, then the technological flows are divided into 42 parts, instead of 21. For the company X, the connection A→B now accounts for 4/42^{e}, and the connection B for 1/42^{e}, etc. The same is true for company Y.

Third, there is the weighting related to families of patents. Since this work relates to several offices for intellectual property protection, the focus is on families of patents, rather than on patents. Based on these families, several patents filed in various offices and dealing with the same invention[1] (Dernis and Khan 2004) can be grouped. Indeed, the same invention can be

1 To consolidate these families, we used the numbers "d'inpadoc_family_id" proposed in the PATSTAT base, which enables the grouping of all the patents that refer directly or by the intermediary of a third patent to the patent of origin.

the object of a patent in the United States, another one in Europe, a specific one for the French office, etc. Each patent includes a list of "citing" TCs and "cited" TCs. Each office is more or less independent and uses its own methods to identify the "citing" TC as well as the cited patents, and thus the "cited" TC for each patent (Mérindol and Fortune 2009); in a series of patents this leads to gaps in the list of TCs, even when they belong to the same family. It is therefore important, when aggregating these patents, to avoid overestimating or underestimating the value of technological connections. For this purpose, it is commonly the case that only single connections are taken into consideration in each patent (for example, an American patent citing a German patent and a French patent belonging to the same family as the American patent, having the same "citing" TC and which cites the same German patent, group identical citations that must be counted only once). In fact, double data are considered to refer to the same technological connections. In order to clarify this point, it is sufficient to consider that patent 1 belongs to a family containing only one other patent, namely patent 5. This is referenced in three "citing" TCs, namely A (twice) and B. On the other hand, it cites, besides patents 2, 3 and 4, patent 6 referenced in classes B and C. The TCs cited by patent 5 are as follows: A (twice), B (three times), C (three times) and E. Hence, this patent lists all the technological links already identified in patent 1 and adds a set of links associated with the emergence of additional TCs. Consequently, instead of (3 × 7 × 2) 42, there are (3 × 9 × 2) 54 possible technological combinations. Then, for company X the link A→B accounts for $6/54^{e}$ and the link B→E for $1/54^{e}$, etc. The same is valid for company Y.

Based on the previous example, identical layers of the following form can be identified for companies X and Y.

The sum of the set of layers is an input output system of technological flows of these companies. The study of this input output system makes it possible to analyze the relation of influence in the knowledge production process.

The first benefit of the analysis of the matrices of technological flows in support of EDT is the identification of synergies between pieces of knowledge and, consequently, the identification of TKS within a knowledge environment.

(a) Cited (rows) / Citing (columns)

	A	B	C	D	E
A	4/54	2/54	0	0	0
B	6/54	3/54	0	0	0
C	6/54	3/54	0	0	0
D	0	0	0	0	0
E	2/54	1/54	0	0	0

(b) Cited (rows) / Citing (columns)

	A	B	C	D	E
A	4/54	2/54	0	0	0
B	6/54	3/54	0	0	0
C	6/54	3/54	0	0	0
D	0	0	0	0	0
E	2/54	1/54	0	0	0

Figure 4.7. *Representation of the layers of the matrix of technological flows. (a) Company x; (b) Company y*

4.3. Graph theory applied to technological knowledge systems

As already mentioned, obtaining the list of pieces of knowledge contained in a defense technological system raises several problems. The concept of TKS was introduced in order to address them. The objective of this section is to find in the knowledge bases of companies a set of TKS whose dual nature is worth studying.

4.3.1. *TKS identification method*

Here, TKS are identified based on the patent data of defense companies. There are two arguments for this choice. First, though duality is approached in this work as a mutual relation in the production of knowledge, considering the information used here, there is a significant imbalance between the two parts. Indeed, only 65 out of 2,000 companies surveyed have an activity in the field of defense[2]. These companies are identified using data from SIPRI (SIPRI Arms Industry Database 2002–2014), which provides each year a list of the 100 companies having the highest turnover in this field, as well as their overall turnover. These companies account for 368,254 filed patents, compared to 5,251,233 for the whole sample. Second, the defense sector is characterized by a certain unity in the use of knowledge. Effectively, in

2 The weight of the defense activity varies between 1% and 100% of the turnover of these companies.

the defense knowledge environment, knowledge is specifically intended for applications in the field of defense. By contrast, the civilian sector is not characterized by a specific use of knowledge and it counts a wide variety of applications. This is why the application in the defense field is a particularity, which justifies the fact that companies focusing on this application are the first ones to be analyzed.

This approach does not affect the mutual nature of duality such as previously defined; the connection from civilian to defense and from defense to civilian will be explored. On the other hand, this guarantees the utility of the TKS to be studied to the defense field. In order to achieve the identification of TKS, the first stage involves the definition of the environment of defense knowledge.

The environment of defense knowledge is built from knowledge bases of defense companies. The proposal made here is to consider at different scales the technological flows within a company whose defense activity is minimal, and those observed in a company that is fully or significantly dedicated to defense activities.

Similar to the analyses conducted by Piscitello (2000, 2005) on company diversification, this amounts to weighting the results of the analysis of company knowledge bases by the part represented by defense activity in the company turnover. This makes it possible to assign a higher value to the technological connections achieved in a company whose defense activity is significant. This approach highlights the technological connections specific to the defense activity within the knowledge bases of defense companies.

To follow this principle, the value of each layer representing the knowledge base of a defense company is weighted by the percentage of the turnover of each company related to defense activity. For this purpose, the data published by SIPRI (SIPRI Arms Industry Database) give access to this part of the turnover of the top 100 defense manufacturers and to the weighted results.

The matrix obtained is then a section of the global input output system proportional to the defense part. This matrix of defense technological flows consequently represents the environment of defense knowledge within which the TKS are identified. The matrix comprising all the technological flows of all the companies without weighting the turnover in whatever field is the global matrix of technological flows and it corresponds to the global knowledge environment. The resulting structure resumes a set of poles representing the TCs interconnected by oriented and weighted links representing the citations.

In order to measure the interdependences between the poles of such a structure (where there is no autarky) by means of IGT, the method involves the comparison of the interdependence scores of all possible partitions P to a main part constituted of two poles and a complementary part constituted of all the other poles. Then, for each of the possible partitions P, it is possible to prove that the sum of intra- and interpart interdependences is greater or equal to the general interdependence of the structure.

A synergy $S_P > 0$ corresponds to a simultaneous existence, for a partition P, of interdependences inside both parts. With D_{p1} interdependences in the part with two poles and D_{p2} interdependences in the complementary part, finding the strongest synergies S_P amounts to finding $1 - D_{p1}$ weighted by the strongest $1 - D_{p2}$, for example, the interdependences in the main part weighted by the strongest interdependences in the complementary part. It is thus possible to measure for all the poles the combinations of the two most synergetic poles that do not harm the synergies in the rest of the structure, and thus rank the connections between these poles depending on these synergies (see Meunier 2018 for further details on the method).

4.3.2. *Application to knowledge flows*

In order to consider only the technologies that are part of the core of the structure and thus avoid a wider consideration of synergies associated with the General Purpose Technologies for example (Bresnahan 2010), a cutting threshold is positioned.

For this purpose, the interdependence scores obtained are normed between "0" and "1"; the "0" score represents the strongest interdependence between two poles in the structure and the "1" score represents the absence of interdependence. Then the scores of relative synergy between two poles are obtained.

These relative synergy scores are classified within a symmetric matrix. It is interpreted as a distance matrix whose diagonal elements are equal to 0.

The graphical representation of this matrix is a dendrogram, a fraction of which is presented in Figure 4.8. The study of this dendrogram, which represents the synergies between the TCs of the defense environment, enables the identification of TKS.

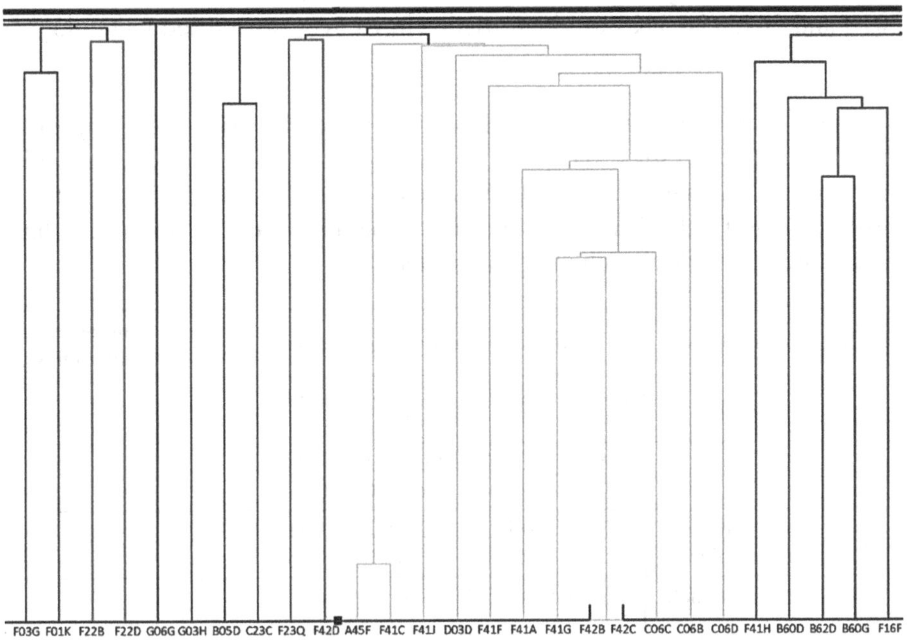

Figure 4.8. *Section of dendrogram. For a color version of this figure, see www.iste.co.uk/meunier/innovation.zip*

In order to obtain the most relevant possible results, a successive iteration method was chosen. Each iteration corresponds to a cutting level. The lower the cutting level, the larger the number of technologies included in the analysis. It gets increasingly lower as more TCs are included in the analysis. The finest cutting level chosen is 35% of the maximum score, and decreases by 5% steps until reaching at the finest level a 1% score. This makes it possible to focus on the strongest synergies in the environment of defense technological knowledge (12 technologies at the threshold of 35%) and to display the interdependences that are added as the number of studied technologies increases. *In fine*, these two elements make it possible to choose the most relevant cutting level for each TKS. According to this approach, TKS whose synergies are the highest at the cutting threshold are the most synergetic in the defense environment and therefore the most characteristic.

Based on the synergies observed in the defense environment between 2010 and 2012, 26 TKS are identified. They cover diversified technological fields.

These 26 TKS are listed in Table 4.1; they are classified according to the force of their synergies, therefore depending on the cutting level at which they appear. The name of each TKS is given as an illustration; it refers to the most obvious field of application, but all the TKS can, by definition, have applications in various technological systems.

TKS	Technologies	Number of technological classes	Number of technologies
1	Missiles	F41F F41A F41G F42B F42C C06B C06C C06D	8
2	Armament*	A45F F41C F41J D03D F41F F41A F41G F42B F42C C06B C06C C06D	12
3	Engines and turbines	F03B F16J F23C F02K F04D F01D F02C F23R F23D F23N F24H F02G	12
4	Defense vehicle	F41H B60D B62D B60G F16F	5
5	Communication	G06Q G06F H04L H04B H04W H04J	6
6	Guiding	H01P H01Q G01S G01C G08G G05D	6
7	Aircraft	B64C B64D	2
8	Remote guidance*	G06Q G06F H04L H04B H04W H04J H03H H01P H01Q G01S G01C G08G G05D	13
9	Drone*	H03G H03F H04M H03D H04K G05B G06N G06Q G06F H04L H04B H04W H04J H03H H01P H01Q G01S G01C G08G G05D B64C B64D	25
10	Defense drone *	F41H B60D B62D B60G F16F H03G H03F H04M H03D H04K G05B G06N G06Q G06F H04L H04B H04W H04J H03H H01P H01Q G01S G01C G08G G05D B64C B64D	30
11	Petrochemistry	B01D B01J C07C C10G C10L C07B C01B	8
12	Tires	B29B B32B B29C B29D B60C C08K C08L C08F D02G	10

TKS	Technologies	Number of technological classes	Number of technologies
13	Running gear of the vehicle*	B29K B28B B29B B32B B29C B29D B60C C08K C08L C08F D02G D07B C08C B29L C08J C08G	16
14	Electric systems	H02J H02M G05F H02P	4
15	Electric motors*	H01M H02J H02M G05F H02P H02K F03D H02H B60L	9
16	Vehicle in general	B60W B60K F16H F16D B60T	5
17	Electric vehicle	H01M H02J H02M G05F H02P H02K F03D H02H B60L B60W B60K F16H F16D B60T	14
18	Optics, image data processing	G01N G01J H01S G02B G02F H04N G06K G06T	8
19	Electronics	H01L H05K H01R H02G	4
20	Sensors*	G01N G01J H01S G02B G02F H04N G06K G06T G03B H01L H05K H01R H02G	12
21	Biochemistry	C12M C12P C12N C12Q C07H C40B	6
22	Light signals	B60Q F21S F21V F21L F21Y	5
23	Vehicle fitting	A47C B60N B60R E06C	4
24	Metal works	B21B C21D C22C C22F B22F	5
25	Combustion engine	F16N F01M F01L F02D F02B F02M F16K F01N	8
26	Metal works	B23C B24D B24B B23F	4

Table 4.1. *Technological Knowledge Systems (TKS). The TKS marked by * are complex TKS. This means they are composed of technologies of another TKS. For example, the Armament TKS comprises technologies of the Missiles TKS*

There are two categories of TKS: The first one is constituted of simple TKS, therefore independent of any other TKS; the second one groups complex TKS, meaning that they are composed of a group of TKS (depending on the force of synergies). These two levels of TKS make it possible to understand the synergies of knowledge at various levels, which enriches the analysis in the study of duality. Complex TKS are marked by an asterisk in Table 4.1.

TKS are on average composed of 9.2 technologies, a little over 6.1 technologies for simple TKS and 16.3 technologies for complex TKS. As expected, the TKS identified at the highest level of synergy are those whose military specificity seems strongest (missiles and armament in general). It is however not surprising to find a significant number of TKS in the more generic fields of knowledge, such as electronics, jet power systems or vehicles. The technologies strongly attached to aeronautics are particularly represented by SCT_3, SCT_7, SCT_9 and SCT_{10}. This is because a large number of defense companies associate civilian and defense aeronautics, which explains the current denomination of the defense aeronautics sector. Nevertheless, going beyond the companies in this sector makes it possible to point out a wider technological diversity within defense companies.

4.4. Conclusion

The application of IGT to the analysis of knowledge flows points out relations of dependence, interdependence and dominance in the process of knowledge production.

This first application of these tools to the environment of defense knowledge revealed synergies associated with defense technological innovation. The 26 TKS identified will be the material for the analysis of dual potential in the following chapters using both a coherence analysis and once again the tools of IGT.

5

Evaluation of the Dual Potential of Technological Knowledge Systems: Analysis in Terms of Coherence

5.1. Introduction

In this chapter, the analysis of duality relates to the structuring of knowledge inside technological knowledge systems. It involves a historical study, followed by a study of technological knowledge systems (TKS) in two knowledge environments that are differentiated based on company data covering the period between 2010 and 2012. The objective is to study how TKS are structured in order to understand how this organization of knowledge, internal to TKS, can influence their dual potential.

This chapter proposes an analysis of duality depending on the relevance of knowledge associations. The theoretical concept referred to as "coherence" emerged in the 1990s through the works of Teece *et al.* (1994), who tried to understand the relevance of company diversification strategies by analyzing the resulting coherence of competence associations. These coherence analyses, which originally related to the study of competences within companies, were then adapted and enriched in the context of knowledge analysis in order to assess the technological coherence of diversified companies (Piscitello 2000), industrial sectors (Krafft *et al.* 2011) and technological programs (Cohen 1997). They contribute to a better understanding of knowledge structuring and, in this work on duality, they allow a comparison between knowledge structuring in the field of defense and in the global environment.

This chapter first revisits the origins of coherence theory and the methodological foundations for various measurements of technological coherence. The following section presents and explains the duality indicators developed on the basis of this theory. They are then applied to the TKS of this sample in order to propose various scales of duality concerning their internal structures. An analysis of the results obtained is then conducted.

5.2. Technological coherence

5.2.1. *Theory of relatedness and coherence*

In economics, the origins of the analysis of coherence can be found in the literature on company diversification. For a better understanding of diversification strategies, the concept of relatedness (Ansoff 1957, 1965) was developed. It provides the possibility of analyzing the coherence of company portfolios of activities, especially technological ones. The study of these relations combines two additional dimensions:

– first, the study of relations between activities through the functional relations between them. In this case, the flows between activities are taken into account and they enable the measurement of the link (Fan and Lang 2000; Rondi and Vannoni 2005);

– second, the relation between the activities based on a portfolio of shared resources. In this case, the combinations of resources determine the relation; the considered resources can be "human" resources (Farjoun 1994), "technologies" (Robins and Wiersema 1995), etc. These analyses have particularly given rise to the development of measurements of coherence (Teece *et al.* 1994). These measurements are applied here to a specific type of resource: technological knowledge.

According to Foss and Christensen (2001), the technological coherence of a company involves the efficient management of an exploration/exploitation dilemma (March 1991). This dilemma results from the various uses of existing knowledge, which amounts to either using known technological combinations or exploring new opportunities: "the essence of exploitation is the refinement and extension of existing competencies, technologies, and paradigms [...]. The essence of exploration is experimentation with new alternatives" (March 1991, p. 85). It appears that this dilemma is solved in time, as companies first explore opportunities and then exploit the most profitable ones (Fauchart and Keilbach 2009) and is therefore structuring in the lifecycle of a technology.

These analyses of diversification originate in the works of Penrose (1959), who points out that company performance does not solely depend on the number of available resources, but also on their interrelations. An activity is then associated with an articulation of resources. But various activities can rely on similar articulations of resources and thus give rise to synergies between activities. The exploitation of synergies between various interrelated activities is the foundation of diversification strategies (Ansoff 1965; Chandler 1962). Therefore, the structure of the company resources determines the diversification diagram that is best able to increase its performances. There are a certain number of companies with similar diversifications around the same profiles of interrelated resources.

Moreover, Penrose points out that this diversification is not necessarily done by means of already existing products (exploitation of synergies between two already known activities); it also involves the search for new opportunities in relation to already existing resources (Penrose 1959). Indeed, the information referring to the synergetic potential between various resources is not always *a priori* available to companies. It often happens that only after having tested combinations of resources are companies able to precisely know the synergetic potential. Therefore, company diversification involves the reconciliation of two alternatives. This is why this situation is referred to as the dilemma between exploration and exploitation (March 1991).

On the one hand, the exploitation of already known synergies between company resources increases their "relatedness" (Montgomery 1994; Rumelt 1974). On the other hand, the exploration of new relations between the company resources whose synergetic potential is not yet known can potentially lead to the addition of new activities (Nesta and Saviotti 2005) or to discarding those that generate prohibitive organizational costs (Reed 2001). It appears that there is an optimum of diversification related to the nature of competences that the company mobilizes and associates.

The concept of slack proposed by Penrose (1959) facilitates the understanding of this reconciliation between the exploitation of existing relations and the exploration of relations whose potential is uncertain. This slack corresponds to a set of possible relations between the resources of each company, not necessarily exploited by the company. Each of them can tap into this pool of resources either to exploit combinations that are commonly used by companies, or to explore new combinations.

Dibiaggio and Meschi (2010) employ Penrose's terminology in order to study, instead of diversification, technological innovation in companies. Their hypothesis is that innovation potential, similar to diversification potential, is related to the capacity of companies to use "slack", which is technological in this case. The "technological slack" exclusively concerns resources in terms of knowledge and is observed in the knowledge base of companies. It corresponds to all the possible relations between technological pieces of knowledge in a company. The potential architectural knowledge whose development they enable is, as expressed by Penrose, a "structure of opportunity" for the company (Cohendet and Gaffard 2010, p. 73). This structure of opportunity determines the potential of innovation of companies and it can be studied through the exploration–exploitation dilemma.

The measurement of company coherence derives from the concept of relatedness, as described above. A company is all the more coherent as it increasingly articulates already interrelated competences (Teece *et al.* 1994). This signifies that diversification is the result of exploiting synergies between complementary resources that the company has available. The implementation of relatedness is influenced by the dynamic process of the exploration–exploitation dilemma. Therefore, the level of company coherence is in turn influenced by this experimentation during the process of company diversification (Piscitello 2000). The same is true for the technological coherence during the innovation process.

This influences the manner in which the knowledge base of a company is represented, because of two major properties of the process of knowledge production presented in the first part: cumulative and correlational aspects (Krafft *et al.* 2011).

Similar to the theoretical model for knowledge dissemination presented in Chapter 2, these aspects are apprehended by means of the typology proposed by Henderson and Clark (1990), between *component knowledge* and *architectural knowledge*. Then, if the knowledge base of a company is considered as a network, according to this typology, the dynamic of its motions can be studied at two levels:

– nodes: these represent the "component knowledge". Their appearance or disappearance indicates the company decision to develop or, on the contrary, to cease developing certain pieces of component knowledge;

– links: these represent the "architectural knowledge". Technological recombinations represent modifications in the architectural technological knowledge of a company.

In this case, it is possible to study, in terms of both "component knowledge" and "architectural knowledge", the technological exploitation or exploration of companies. This amounts to considering, according to Foss and Christensen (2001), that the technological coherence of a company is related to a dynamic management of the exploration–exploitation dilemma, whose efficiency can be measured. It is then possible to reinterpret the analyses introduced by Teece *et al.* (1994) on coherence. Relying in particular on the works developed since then (Piscitello 2000, 2005; Nesta and Saviotti 2006; Krafft *et al.* 2011; Nasiriyar *et al.* 2013), it is thus possible to measure a technological coherence.

The dynamics between exploration and exploitation is apprehended by combining two complementary perspectives: a theoretical configuration and a concrete configuration of knowledge bases. The theoretical configuration corresponds to the first works conducted on the measurements of coherence by Teece *et al.* (1994). In the case of technological coherence, it means allowing component knowledge to freely interrelate inside a company. Nevertheless, the global coherence scores of companies are closely related to the structural representation of their knowledge bases (Nesta and Saviotti 2006). But this theoretical structural representation, all possible relations being considered, does not allow the representation of the concrete articulation of knowledge in a company. Indeed, two companies managing the same technologies and in the same proportion, but with a different association, would obtain identical scores of theoretical coherence. Architectural knowledge is therefore not taken into account here.

On the other hand, the concrete configuration takes this architecture into account and retains the concretely observable articulation of the company knowledge base (Nasiriyar *et al.* 2013).

5.2.2. *Duality scale in relation to TKS internal structure*

This section presents the original indicators relying on the analysis of the exploration–exploitation dilemma based on patent data. These original indicators will be employed to provide an evaluation of the dual potential of TKS. Therefore, they are at the core of this work.

The preliminary processing of patent data is similar to that made by El Younsi *et al.* (2015); the reader can therefore refer to it for further details.

Coherence indices are built in two stages from co-occurrence matrices. First, the technological relatedness is measured. For this, an "expected" number of co-occurrences between technologies are calculated using a hypergeometric law. The relatedness (τ_{ij}) between technologies i and j depends on the difference between the actual and expected number of cooccurrences. If (τ_{ij}) is high, for example if the number of observed links J_{ij} between the technological classes i and j is higher than the number of expected links (μ_{ij}), the two technologies are linked. The greater and more positive the difference, the stronger their relatedness (Teece *et al.* 1994).

We have:

$$\mu_{ij} = E(X_{ij} = x) = \frac{O_i O_j}{B}$$

where:

– B: set of filed patent families;

– $p_{bi} = 1$: if the patent family references technology i, 0 otherwise;

– $O_i = \sum_b p_{bi}$: total number of times when technology i is referenced among all the patent families;

– J_{ij}: number of occurrences of the association of technologies i and j, and therefore $J_{ij} = \sum_b p_{bi} p_{bj}$;

– X_{ij}: random hypergeometric variable of the number of patent families associated with technologies i and j (with a population B, a number of embodiments O_i and a sample of size O_j) whose variance is equal to σ_{ij}^2 :

$$\sigma_{ij}^2 = \mu_{ij}\left(\frac{B - O_i}{B}\right)\left(\frac{B - O_j}{B - 1}\right)$$

Therefore, the technological link is written as:

$$\tau_{ij} = \frac{J_{ij} - \mu_{ij}}{\sigma_{ij}}$$

The set of links between technologies is listed in a matrix of technological relations.

Then, considering the knowledge base of company k represented by a set of patent families, $p_{ki} = 1$ if the patent family filed by company k references technology i, 0 otherwise. P_k is the number of technological classes in which company k is active. A set of indicators is built with the same formula, in which the adjacency matrix M_{ij}^{kIndic} is used in order to specify the technological relations retained for each of them:

$$Indic_k = \frac{1}{P_k}\sum_i C_{ki}\left(\frac{\sum_{j\neq i}\tau_{ij}M_{ij}^{Indic_k}P_{kj}}{\sum_{j\neq i}M_{ij}^{k}P_{kj}}\right)$$

Then $Indic_k \in 0, +\infty$ designates the indicators related to company k, where:

– i: technological class compared to all the other technologies produced by this company ;

– τ_{ij}: index of technological relatedness between i and j ;

– C_{ki}: vector of technological classes in which the company is active;

– $P_{kj} = \sum_j p_{kj}$: the number of patent families referencing the technological class of company k.

Then four indicators are built:

– for total coherence CT_k: adjacency matrix $M_{ij}^{CT_k}$, whose format is $T \times T$, is a matrix of 1 whose diagonal elements are 0; it takes into account all the possible relations between the technologies used in the knowledge base of company k;

– for core coherence CC_k: the adjacency matrix $M_{ij}^{CC_k}$ integrates the strength of technological links in the space of production of company innovations. While CC_k associates the company technologies in $t_k(t_k - 1)/2$ links, the objective is to associate them all in only $t_k - 1$ links (for example in a tree) and retain only the association – given the values τ_{ij} – that produces the highest total tree weighting. In other words, the definition of $M_{ij}^{CC_k}$ relies on a *weighted maximum spanning tree* process and $M_{ij}^{CC_k} = 1$ if ij belongs to the maximum spanning tree, 0 otherwise;

– for the observed coherence CO_k: the adjacency matrix $M_{ij}^{CO_k}$ accounts for the actually observed links between technologies in the knowledge base, with $M_{ij}^{CO_k} = 1$ if relation ij is actually observed in one of the patent families in the knowledge base of company k, 0 otherwise;

– for the extended coherence CE_k: the adjacency matrix $M_{ij}^{CE_k}$ accounts for the actually identified links between technologies in the knowledge base and of all the links of the core; $M_{ij}^{CE_k} = 1$ if relation ij is actually observed in one of the patent families in the knowledge base of company k or belongs to the maximum spanning tree, 0 otherwise.

All these indicators make it possible to measure the importance of the phenomena of exploitation and exploration in the knowledge bases, as listed below:

– "exploit the obvious technological links": these are technological combinations that the actors in a knowledge environment commonly achieve;

– "explore strange technological associations": these are not the most frequently found in the whole sample of patents. From this perspective, these relations are a differentiating factor;

– "do not exploit obvious technological associations": these are often found in the sample of patents and can be expected to "quite readily" contribute to creating innovation locally. From this perspective, not exploiting them is a distinction factor. Distinction and differentiation represent the exploration.

In concrete terms, this is measured by means of gaps between the various indicators previously presented:

– measurement of exploitation: the gap between the value of total coherence and observed coherence:

$$Exploit_k = \frac{CO_k - CT_k}{CC_k - CT_k}$$

– measurement of differentiation: the gap between the value of core coherence and extended coherence:

$$Diff_k = \frac{CC_k - CE_k}{CC_k - CT_k}$$

– measurement of distinction: the gap between the value of observed coherence and extended coherence:

$$Dist_k = \frac{CE_k - CO_k}{CC_k - CT_k}$$

– measurement of exploration: the gap between the value of core coherence and observed coherence:

$$Explor_k = \frac{CC_k - CO_k}{CC_k - CT_k}$$

To apply the measurements of coherence to the study of duality, the above presented indicators must be transposed at the level of TKS. For this purpose, instead of studying the knowledge base of a company, coherence scores of TKS are calculated. It is sufficient to consider TKS as a set of technological classes. Then the formula for calculating the indicators is:

$$Indic_S = \frac{1}{P_S} \sum_i C_{si} \left(\frac{\sum_{j \neq i} \tau_{ij} M_{ij}^{Indic_S} P_{sj}}{\sum_{j \neq i} M_{ij}^{S} P_{sj}} \right)$$

with:

– $Indic_S \in 0, +\infty$: indicators related to TKS;

– i: technological class compared to all the other technologies of TKS;

– τ_{ij}: index of technological relation between i and j ;

– C_{si}: vector of technological classes composing TKS;

– $P_{sj} = \sum_j p_{sj}$: number of patent families referencing the technological class j.

The construction of matrices $M_{ij}^{Indic_s}$ is similar to that of company indices, except that it does not involve a company perimeter.

Therefore, all the measurements enabling the apprehension of the exploration–exploitation dilemma can be calculated at TKS level. It is thus possible to have a historic overview of the structuring of these TKS and draw the first conclusions in terms of duality.

In order to build the scale of duality, the defense knowledge environment should be compared to the global environment. First of all, the defense knowledge environment serves to perceive the specificities related to the defense activity in the structuring of technological relations within TKS. This requires formulating the hypothesis according to which the aggregation of all the patents, patent families filed by the defense companies, generates a group effect. In other words, the fact of having gathered the defense companies enables the group to concentrate technological relations that are linked to the innovation activity in this field. In other terms, technological relations concerning the defense activity are overrepresented in this knowledge environment. This enables the calculation of the scores of technological relation τ_{ij}^{d} capturing the specificity of the defense activity.

As for the global knowledge environment, it corresponds to indicators such as those presented in the beginning of this section. This environment is not strictly speaking a civilian environment, as it is built from all the technological co-occurrences between 2010 and 2012. Building a civilian perimeter would have been risky, as the R&D activities in these industries cover all the technological fields and the civilian nature of their innovation is not enough to create a group effect that is sufficiently strong compared to sectoral effects, for example. It does not give the value of the civilian link, but a value of the technological link beyond all sectoral or industrial specifications of the innovation activity. It is a generic value of the technological link.

It is by comparing the measurements in the defense knowledge environment and in the global knowledge environment that the indicators enable the evaluation of the dual potential of TKS. Indeed, the general idea is that the comparison between what is specifically coherent in a defense activity and what is globally coherent makes it possible to capture what is simultaneously coherent in both sets, thus revealing the proximities of knowledge presenting, consequently, a dual potential.

The construction of scales of "internal" duality relies on the analysis of TKS by means of coherence indicators. This analysis is completed by the analysis in terms of influence, which concerns the relations between TKS and the rest of the knowledge environment. The scales of duality are built on the basis of five indicators, which rely on the coherence indicators and especially on the measurements used for probing the exploration–exploitation dilemma.

The first internal indicator deals with the technological core of TKS. This indicator is expected to measure the extent to which the technological core of TKS is stable from one knowledge environment to another, or in other terms from one domain to another. A technological core that does not change from one knowledge environment to another means that the strongest (and most frequent) relations are the same in both environments, which, in the present case, means for both defense and non-defense companies that use TKS technologies. This indicator is referred to as "ID_1" for "duality of the technological core".

For a TKS, this stability can be measured by means of a ratio between the number of technological core relations shared by both knowledge environments and the total number of technological core relations.

Let A_s^i be the set of $n-1$ technological core relations $\{t_1 \ldots t_n\}$ presented in the architecture of TKS_s with respect to environment $i \equiv \{D, G\}$, where D is the knowledge environment of defense companies and G is the global knowledge environment.

Then, $\forall_s$:

$$ID_1 = \frac{(A_s^D \cap A_s^G)}{n-1}$$

The second indicator refers particularly to the architectural knowledge of TKS. This indicator is expected to reflect, beyond the technological core, the manner in which knowledge is actually articulated in both environments, and then to measure the coherence of this articulation. If, for a TKS, the coherence observed in the defense knowledge environment (which is a part of the global knowledge environment) represents a small part of the coherence observed in the global environment, this means that the architectural knowledge supporting this TKS is outside defense companies; in other terms, it is not specific to this activity and therefore it is dual. This indicator is referred to as "ID_2" that stands for "duality of architectural knowledge".

For a TKS, this dissemination of architectural knowledge can be measured by the ratio of the concrete coherences with respect to two environments.

Let CO_s^i be the observed coherence of TKS_s in environment $i \equiv \{D, G\}$, where D is the knowledge environment of defense companies and G is the global knowledge environment.

Then, $\forall_s$:

$$ID_2 = \frac{CO_s^D}{CO_s^G}$$

The third and the fourth indicators focus on the exploration part within a TKS. The third indicator measures the extent to which the architectural knowledge of a TKS does not rely on the technological core of the defense knowledge environment. If this architectural knowledge is not specific to the technological core of defense companies, this means it is not specific to them, and therefore it is dual. This indicator is denoted by "ID_3", which stands for "exploration duality".

For a TKS, non-specificity can be measured by the exploration ratio with respect to an environment.

Let CO_s^D be the observed coherence, CT_s^D the total coherence and CC_s^D the core coherence of TKS_s in the knowledge environment of defense companies.

Then, $\forall_s$:

$$ID_3 = \frac{CC_s^D - CO_s^D}{CC_s^D - CT_s^D}$$

The fourth indicator measures the extent to which architectural knowledge is fixed in the two knowledge environments, revealing a similar level of stability in the technological system, and thus measuring the proportion in which defense companies and other innovation actors can simultaneously explore new technological combinations within a TKS and therefore, using the expression of Cowan and Foray, save calendar and event time (Cowan and Foray 1995). This indicator is denoted by "ID_4", which stands for "combined exploration duality".

For a TKS, simultaneity in exploration efforts can be measured by the ratio of exploration ratios for the two environments.

Let CO_s^i be the observed coherence, CT_s^i the total coherence and CC_s^i the coherence of the core of TKS_s in environment $i = \{D, G\}$ enabling the calculation of the exploration ratio of TKS_s in the defense environment.

Then, $\forall_s$:

$$ID_4 = \frac{(CC_s^D - CO_s^D)/(CC_s^D - CT_s^D)}{(CC_s^G - CO_s^G)/(CC_s^G - CT_s^G)}$$

Finally, the fifth indicator concerns specifically the part of duality related to isolated component knowledge. This indicator measures the extent to which component knowledge is assimilated in the defense knowledge environment without developing a specific architectural knowledge. If a piece of component knowledge is isolated, and it is isolated both in a defense knowledge environment and in the global knowledge environment, this indicates that its integration did not require the development of architectural knowledge specific to defense companies. In other terms, the architectural knowledge of this TKS does not rely on the technological core of defense companies and it consequently plays a marginal role in the integration of component knowledge of this TKS in the defense industries. This indicator is denoted by "ID_5" for the "duality of isolated component knowledge".

For a TKS, the secondary nature of this architectural knowledge can be measured by the ratio of the distinction ratio in the defense knowledge environment to the distinction ratio in the global environment.

Let CE_S^D be the coherence of concrete technological relations to which the relations with unused core technologies are added. Using the previously defined elements, it is possible to calculate the distinction ratio with respect to the two environments within TKS_S.

Then, $\forall_S$:

$$ID_5 = \frac{(CE_S^D - CO_S^D)/(CC_S^D - CT_S^D)}{(CE_S^G - CO_S^G)/(CC_S^G - CT_S^G)}$$

In order to create a scale of duality that can be used for ranking TKS on each of these duality components, all these indicators are normalized between 0 and 1. This facilitates the comparison of TKS when all these dimensions have to be considered simultaneously:

$$D_i = \frac{(ID_i) - \min(ID_i)}{\max(ID_i) - \min(ID_i)}$$

These five indicators constitute the scales of duality related to the internal structure of TKS. They compose the tools that are used in this chapter for the study of the dual potential and, according to the theoretical model, they do not use a binary approach to address this question, but they define a continuum of the technological duality. They utilize the notions of architectural and component knowledge in order to point out the technological proximities between the defense technological environment and the rest of the knowledge environment, which constitutes the basis of the model presented in the first part. Duality is evaluated with respect to a form of balance between the defense and civilian industries; the unbalanced profiles that can give rise to technological spin-offs are not assimilated to duality.

5.3. Analysis of the duality of technological knowledge systems

The measurements of internal duality are now applied to 26 TKS and the results are analyzed.

	Global knowledge environment			Defense knowledge environment		
Indicators	Mean	Standard deviation	Median	Mean	Standard deviation	Median
Total coherence	27.39	23.15	24.42	5	3.48	3.94
Core coherence	135.67	43.29	116.31	25.21	6.04	22.43
Observed coherence	29.41	23.27	25.81	6.97	4.34	5.49
Extended coherence	29.42	23.27	25.82	7.01	4.37	5.52
Exploration ratio	0.98	0.02	0.99	0.9	0.05	0.92
Exploitation ratio	0.02	0.02	0.01	0.1	0.05	0.08
Distinction ratio	0.097780	0.052646	0.084170	0.000087	0.000178	0.000022
Differentiation ratio	0.98	0.02	0.99	0.9	0.05	0.91

Table 5.1. *Statistics of coherence*

A first note on the scores of coherence: as expected, they are lower in the defense knowledge environment than in the global knowledge environment, because defense is a small part of the global environment.

Then, referring to the exploration–exploitation dilemma, as expected, the scores of exploitation are on average higher in the defense knowledge environment. This can be explained by the fact that TKS were selected due to their influence in the defense companies, which means that this knowledge is currently used by these companies. They consequently have higher chances to be put in relation in patent families filed by defense companies and therefore to belong to the technological core of the defense knowledge environment, and hence increase its exploitation.

Over the period 1980–2013, as the exploration ratio, as defined, structurally dominates the distribution of innovation activities within companies, its predominant nature is reinforced here. This happens because TKS are constituted based on the analysis of a field of innovation (defense activity) that is relatively marginal in terms of patent filing.

Indicators	Mean	Standard deviation	Median
Total coherence	26.15	7.29	25.46
Core coherence	123.89	37.10	118.68
Observed coherence	28.54	7.13	27.96
Extended coherence	28.55	7.13	27.97
Exploitation ratio	0.03	0.01	0.03
Exploration ratio	0.97	0.01	0.97
Distinction ratio	0.00017	0.00012	0.00015
Differentiation ratio	0.97	0.01	0.97

Table 5.2. *Descriptive statistics of the measurements of coherence from 2010 to 2012*

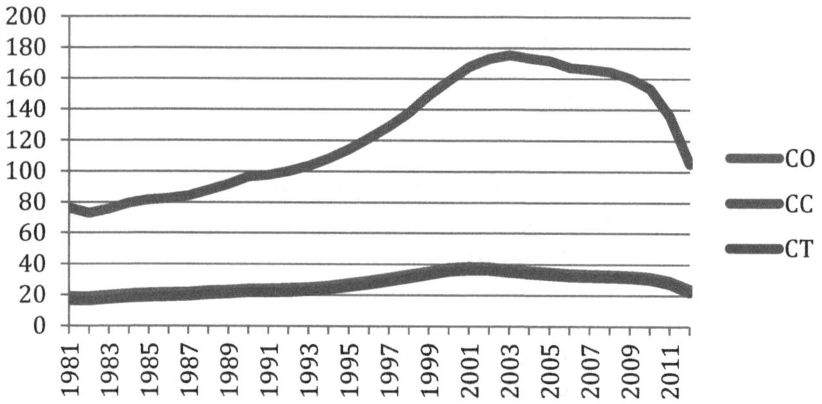

Figure 5.1. *Evolution of the mean coherence scores of TKS. For a color version of this figure, see www.iste.co.uk/meunier/innovation.zip*

Figure 5.1 shows a regular increase in the coherence scores of TKS in the global environment until early 2000, followed by a period of slight decline, which accelerates by the end of the period. This acceleration is due to the decrease in the amount of available data (not all the patents of the last period were available when this work was conducted).

It appears that overall this analysis shows an increase in the coherence of TKS. This means an increase in the number of times when the technological relations with respect to these TKS appear in the global environment, which leads to the assumption that the dual potential of these TKS would have a stronger impact nowadays than 30 years ago, due to the wider dissemination of their architectural knowledge in the global technological environment. This first result is nevertheless far from being conclusive.

Indeed, the increase in the value of the observed coherence is a general tendency. Its scope extends beyond the TKS studied here and is simply explained by the increase in the technological references in the patents, thus generating the increase in the observed technological combinations. Moreover, it seems logical that these TKS, having been identified by means of data related to the period 2010–2012, should correspond to the technological paradigm valid during that period, and consequently, their coherence should be relatively higher during that period than in the past. Finally, a more in-depth analysis of the data shows a wide disparity from one TKS to another, which enables the identification of several groups of TKS with a quite distinct evolution, a more interesting approach.

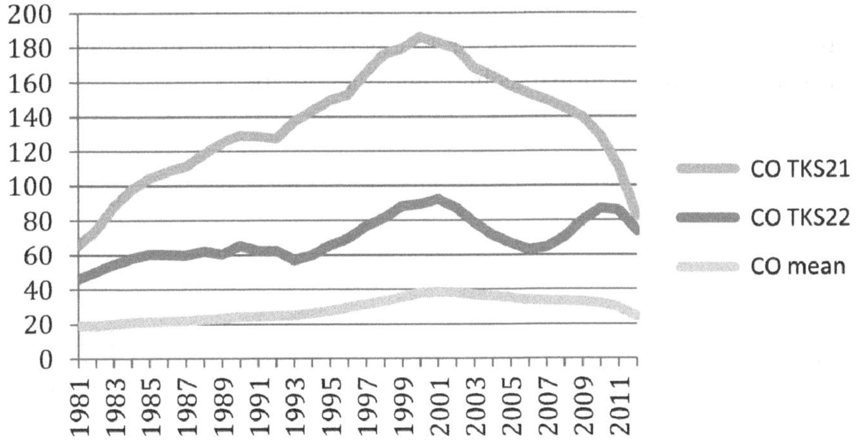

Figure 5.2. *Observed coherences (1). For a color version of this figure, see www.iste.co.uk/meunier/innovation.zip*

Figure 5.2 shows the evolution of the scores of observed coherence of TKS_{21} and TKS_{22} between 1981 and 2012. These two TKS (organic chemistry and light signals) are the only ones whose coherence scores are largely above the mean.

To explain this, it is worth noting that these TKS are relatively peripheral in the companies (see Chapter 4). Consequently, they are not clearly marked by the influence of this activity, which can explain the levels of coherence above those of TKS more marked by the specificities of defense innovation.

Moreover, these two TKS are focused on the technological classes that, in the three figure classification, are combined (C12 for the first and F21 for the second), while the other TKS are more diversified, even within a three-digit classification. The knowledge of TKS_{21} and TKS_{22} is therefore institutionally recognized for being interconnected, which explains why it makes sense to associate them. Finally, it seems that for the TKS_{21} associated with organic chemistry, there is a sectorial effect. Certainly, other studies conducted within UEA (Unité d'Economie Appliquée – ENSTA Paris) evidence a structurally high coherence level in the chemistry sector.

These two TKS are therefore constituted around highly coherent architectural knowledge. If they belong to defense companies, the latter can be carriers of strong dual potentials, which are all the wider as the technologies related to chemistry or to electrical equipment are among the most widespread in the global technological landscape.

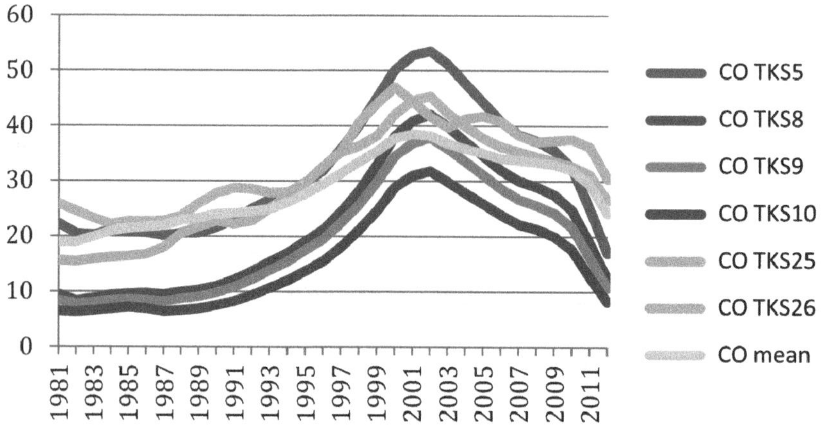

Figure 5.3. *Observed coherences (2). For a color version of this figure, see www.iste.co.uk/meunier/innovation.zip*

Figure 5.3 represents the second category of TKS characteristic of the sample. It is composed of three distinct situations. First, there is a group, TKS_8, TKS_9 and TKS_{10}, associated with aeronautics and whose scores of observed coherence are impacted by TKS_5, which associates the knowledge in information transmission and processing; then, TKS_{25}, which corresponds to knowledge related to combustion engines; and finally, TKS_{26}, which groups the technological knowledge on metal working.

While they refer to very different situations, the coherence scores of these three sets are all characterized by a trend reversal in early 2000. This trend reversal may correspond to a shift in the manner in which innovation corresponding to this knowledge is produced. This structuring seems particularly relevanting for TKS_8, TKS_9 and TKS_{10}, which are associated with drone technologies and are essential to defense companies.

This shift, which can be perceived as a change of technological paradigm, may have impacted the dual potential of these TKS. Indeed, it may have led to a gap between the defense and civilian technological domains, if this new paradigm did not develop in both domains; this would decrease the possibilities of interaction between the two domains.

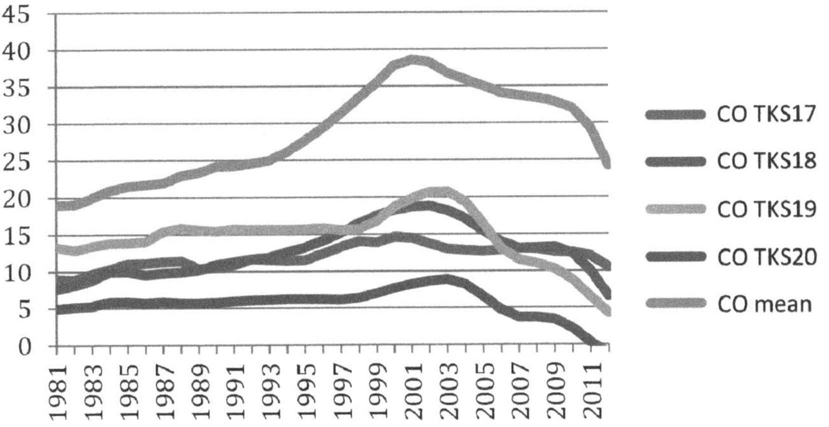

Figure 5.4. *Observed coherences (3). For a color version of this figure, see www.iste.co.uk/meunier/innovation.zip*

The third category is shown in Figure 5.4 and lists the TKS whose scores of observed coherence are steadily below the mean throughout the whole period. The concerned TKS are, on the one hand, TKS_{17}, which corresponds to an association of knowledge related to the electric vehicles, and TKS_{18}, TKS_{19}, and TKS_{20}, whose technological classes are useful when setting up sensors.

It can be easily understood that TKS_{17} corresponds to a relatively low level of coherence. Indeed, while there has been a breakthrough in recent years in the field of autonomous vehicles, this type of vehicle still has a minority share (0.59% of the sales in France, according to the Committee of French Car Manufacturers (Comité des constructeurs français d'automobiles (CCFA) in 2014).

Innovation in thermal vehicles facilitates other technological relations. The technologies related to vehicles in general, for example those presented in TKS_{16}, are often associated within patent families with technologies related to heat engines. Given how coherence scores are calculated, the presence of the technological classes of the vehicle without their association with an electric motor mechanically reduces the coherence of the technological relations of TKS.

The explanation is less obvious for TKS_{18}, TKS_{19} and TKS_{20}. Nevertheless, the low scores can be interpreted as a certain diversification in the use of sensors. Indeed, the latter are presently components of numerous technological artifacts, from drone to autonomous vehicle, including medical instruments, and concern many sectors. The coherence of the technological relations between these sensors is consequently strongly dependent on its use; it is affected by sectorial technological specificities. Hence, the sensors are manipulated through a certain architectural knowledge in the car industry, which is not the same in the medical industry, which reduces the global coherence of TKS_{18}, TKS_{19} and TKS_{20} generally dedicated to sensors.

Due to the low values of these scores, no conclusion can be drawn on the dual potential of these TKS. They nevertheless reveal that the underlying architectural knowledge is relatively less dominant than that of other TKS. Hence, for an equivalent score, the dual potential that will be measured in the following section has a less significant impact in terms of architectural knowledge than the dual potential in TKS_{21} or TKS_{22}, for example.

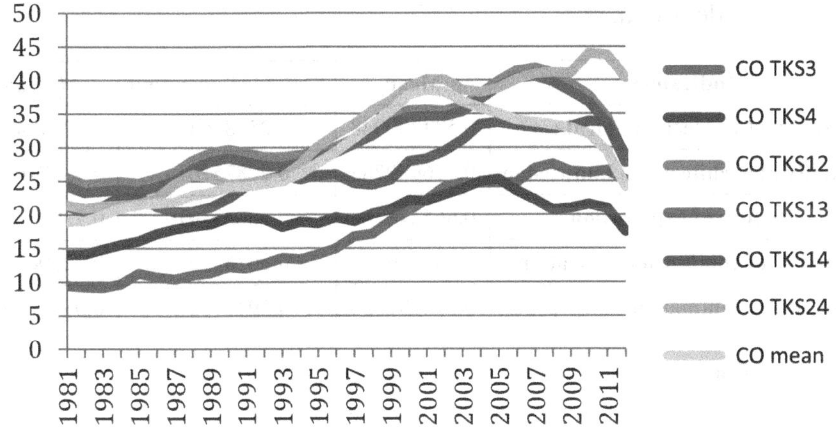

Figure 5.5. *Observed coherences (4). For a color version of this figure, see www.iste.co.uk/meunier/innovation.zip*

The last category of TKS is illustrated in Figure 5.5. It groups a set whose coherence scores had an ascending trend, without the reversal trend in 2000.

There are first TKS_3 and TKS_4, which are characteristic of the aeronautics defense industries, as they group knowledge that is especially found in missile design and in aircraft engine design. Their scores have increased over this period, without however reaching very high levels. This architectural knowledge was therefore reinforced, but its dissemination is limited by its specificity related to the aeronautics defense industry, which explains the relatively low scores that limit the global impact of the dual potential of these TKS.

The next scores are for TKS_{12}, TKS_{13}, TKS_{14} and TKS_{24}, which correspond to knowledge related to tires, vehicle running gears, electric systems, in general, and metal working. Their scores are high, above the mean of other TKS, which facilitates the dissemination of knowledge in their composition (due to dominant architectural knowledge) and thus the impact of their dual potentials.

For the period 2010–2012, during which, based on the available data, it is possible to distinguish between a defense knowledge environment and a global knowledge environment, all the indicators of duality are calculated for the 26 TKS identified.

Indicators	Mean	Standard deviation	Median
Duality of the technological core	0.524700948	0.254876466	0.527914947
Duality of architectural knowledge	0.476099783	0.228257014	0.432710157
Duality of exploration	0.665278565	0.286538019	0.739354998
Duality of combined exploration	0.686236981	0.262697637	0.725907504
Duality of component knowledge	0.080901836	0.191510277	0.038412929

Table 5.3. *Descriptive statistics of the indicators of internal duality*

To facilitate the understanding of the results, a main component analysis, which was conducted based on the duality scores of 26 TKS, made it possible to differentiate several profiles. These profiles correspond to a reality as, on the one hand, ACP explains approximately 90% of the scores and, on the other hand, the profiles appear logical with respect to the composition of TKS (the TKS that are close on the map are also similar in their compositions).

Component 1 appears strongly structured around the most synergetic TKS for the defense companies and duality indicators ID_1, ID_3 and ID_4, while component 2 explains ID_2 and ID_5. Component 1 reveals the role of the technological core, therefore the most central TKS are close to this axis, while component 2 takes the TKS as a whole and consequently aggregates the TKS that are secondary to defense.

Four TKS profiles were identified as follows:

- profile 1: mastered dual potential;
- profile 2: emerging dual potential;
- profile 3: dual potential of industrial production;
- profile 4: marginal dual potential.

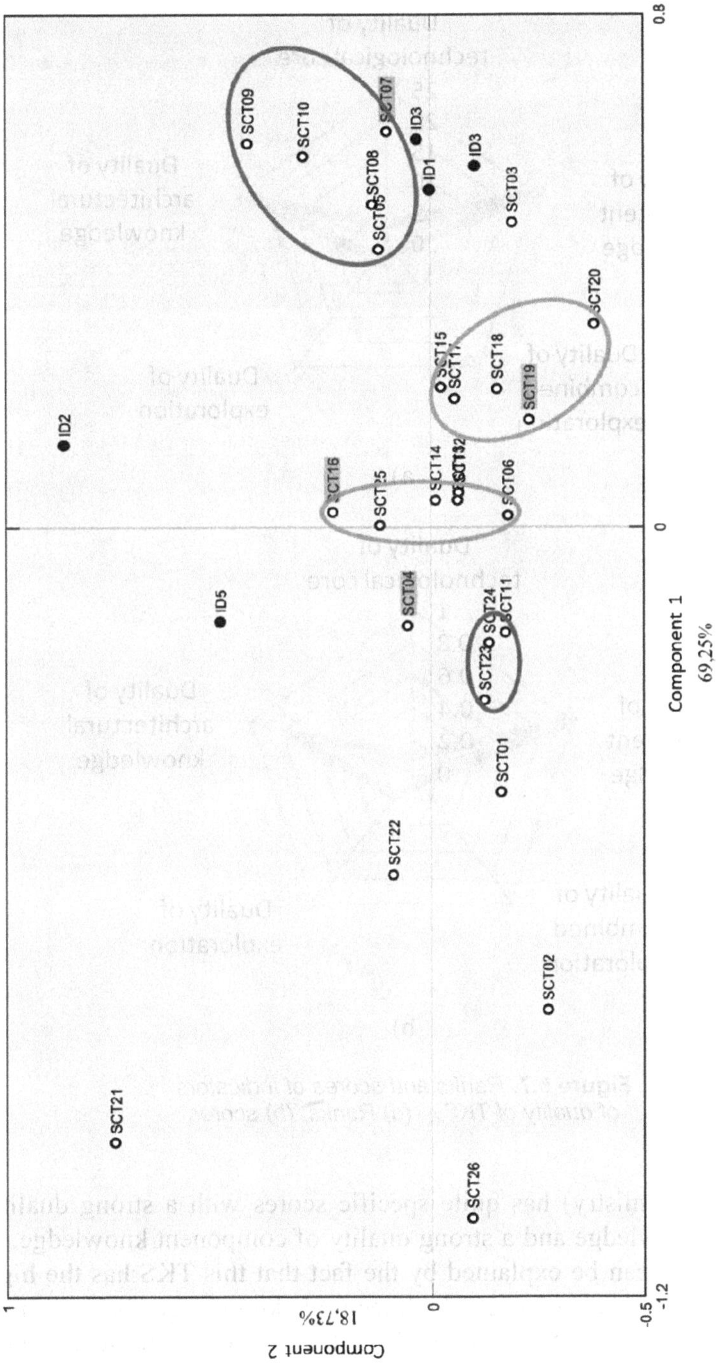

Figure 5.6. *ACP on duality scores. For a color version of this figure, see www.iste.co.uk/meunier/innovation.zip*

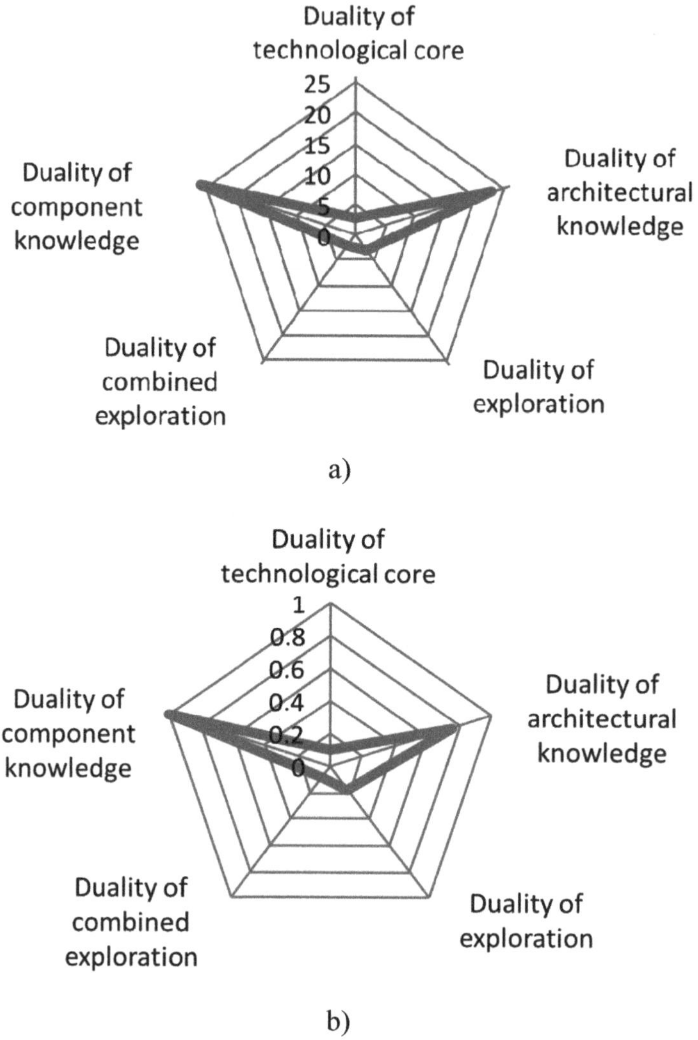

Figure 5.7. *Ranks and scores of indicators of duality of TKS_{21}. (a) Ranks; (b) scores*

TKS_{21} (biochemistry) has quite specific scores with a strong duality of architectural knowledge and a strong duality of component knowledge. This particular profile can be explained by the fact that this TKS has the highest score of observed coherence. Architectural knowledge being strongly associated with this TKS, it is involved both in the defense knowledge environment and in the global knowledge environment, though it is not part of the technological core of defense companies. This leads to high scores of duality of architectural knowledge and component knowledge. It appears that the particular position of this TKS is explained by the peripheral role played by defense in a TKS, otherwise a very structured one. Therefore, the dual potential of this TKS essentially concerns component knowledge integrated by means of an architectural knowledge widely shared beyond the defense industries. In association with the lack of centrality of this TKS, it appears that this dual potential can be qualified as peripheral.

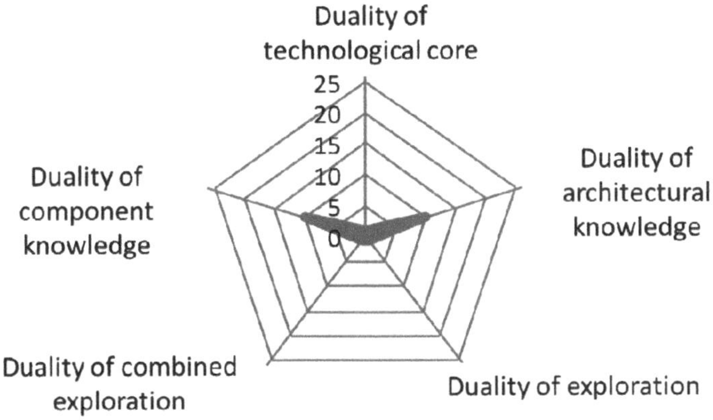

a)

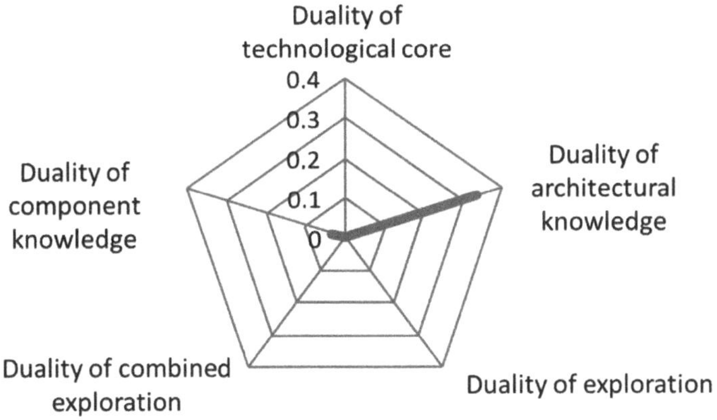

b)

Figure 5.8. *Ranks and scores of indicators of duality of TKS_{26}. (a) Ranks; (b) scores*

As for TKS_{26} (metals), it has low scores in all fields, and particularly for indicators ID_1, ID_2 and ID_3. This TKS is overall the least dual in the sample. This is related to the peripheral nature of this TKS in the defense environment (for the weaker synergies in the defense companies, see the Introduction to Part 2). This is why defense companies do not participate in the associated knowledge production. It is the typical case of a set of knowledge that is useful to the defense industry but for which defense companies use the knowledge production from other industrial sectors in order to integrate it to their own production. This situation is more similar to spin-ins than to duality. The notion of spin-in corresponds to the idea that instead of defense innovation being beneficial to civilian sectors, civilian innovations are beneficial to the military domain (Alic *et al.* 1992; Galbraith *et al.* 2004).

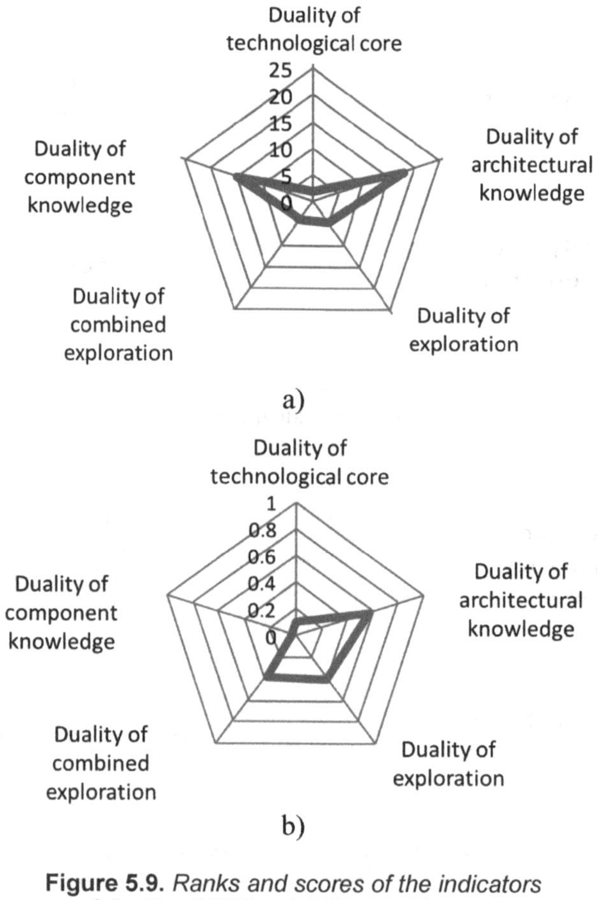

Figure 5.9. *Ranks and scores of the indicators of duality of TKS_{22}. (a) Ranks; (b) scores*

The situation of TKS_{22} (light signals) is intermediate with respect to the two previous ones. Like TKS_{26}, it has low scores, which are essentially drawn by the duality of component knowledge and architectural knowledge, similar to TKS_{21}. Therefore, its dual potential seems peripheral and even non-existing.

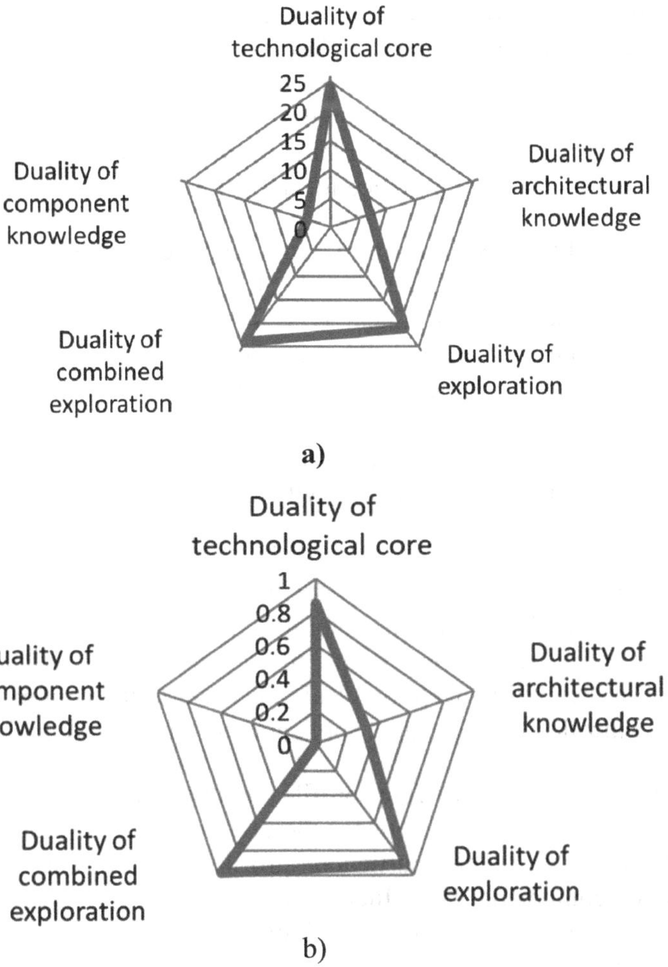

Figure 5.10. *Ranks and scores of indicators of duality of TKS_3. (a) Ranks; (b) scores*

Then, TKS_3 is at the opposite of the representation and has very high scores of duality for the technological core, exploration and combined exploration. This TKS, which gathers knowledge related to the development of aircraft engines, is indeed more central for companies in the defense aeronautics, which are an essential part in the defense companies of the studied sample. This explains the fact that these companies are the driving force in articulating this knowledge and that consequently, the attached architectural knowledge is part of their technological core. Moreover, the prevalence of defense companies explains the similarity of the technological core within the global environment and the defense environment. Furthermore, this TKS has a particular place within duality indicators related to exploration due to its importance for the defense industries.

The case of this TKS is therefore quite opposite to the two previous ones, as defense companies play an essential role in the technological core, while the rest of the global environment is a "follower". This explains why the duality of component knowledge is very low, as component knowledge is assembled depending on the technological core. On the other hand, the low score of the duality of architectural knowledge shows that beyond the technological core of defense companies, there is coherent architectural knowledge in which the defense activity does not seem to participate too strongly.

In the case of TKS_3, duality seems to correspond to a model of "integrated duality", in which defense companies feature technological expertise that is beyond the scope of defense. They are harmoniously embedded in the civilian technological landscape in the context of a precise and fully controlled technological application of the aircraft engine.

Finally, TKS_4 has a particular profile. Its dual potential seems low, with quite low scores all over, except for the architectural knowledge where the potential is higher. This particular profile can be explained by the technologies composing TKS. Indeed, while nearly all its technologies are generic technologies related to the vehicle, one of them is very marked by the defense activity, being in connection with armor, turret and camouflage technologies. It is therefore certainly the architectural knowledge related to generic technologies that drives the score high, while the defense aspect of one of the categories renders the TKS very specific.

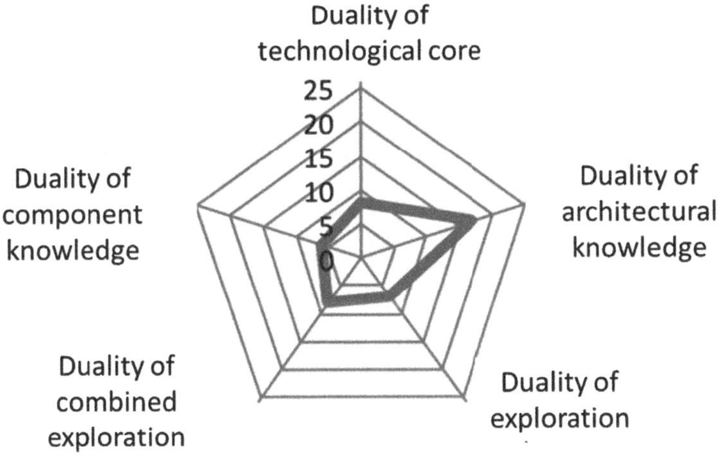

a)

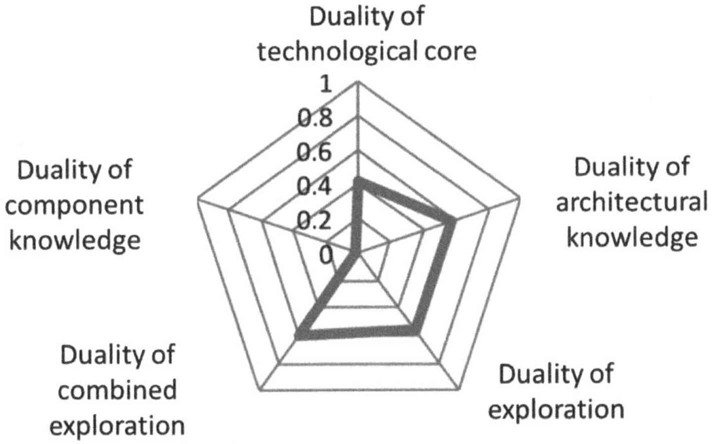

b)

Figure 5.11. *Ranks and scores of indicators of duality of TKS_4. (a) Ranks; (b) scores*

The four profiles are presented depending on their global level of duality, from the profile with the highest potential to the one whose potential is the lowest.

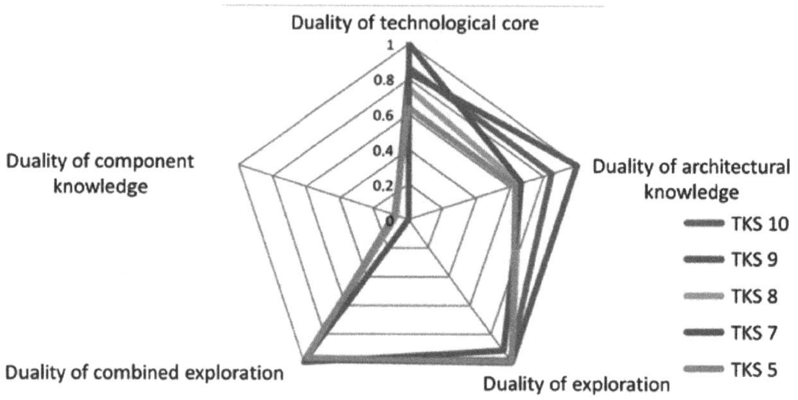

a)

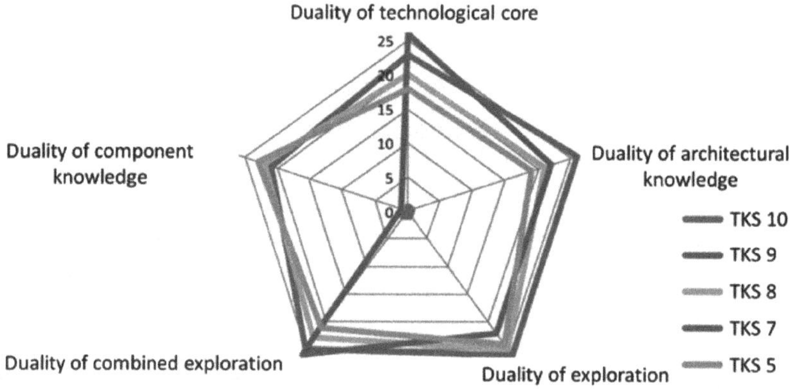

b)

Figure 5.12. *Profile 1 linked with aeronautics embedded systems. (a) TKS Scores; (b) TKS ranks. For a color version of this figure, see www.iste.co.uk/meunier/innovation.zip*

Profile 1 corresponds to a group of TKS linked with embedded systems and aeronautics (communication system, remote guidance and drones); they feature high scores on each duality indicator[1]. This profile is composed of TKS that are central in the innovation of defense companies but whose

1 Except for 7 whose component knowledge duality is 0, as it is composed of only two technological classes, which by definition brings its score to the lowest level for the duality of component knowledge and to the maximum level for the duality of technological core.

technologies are nowadays also necessary in the production of civilian goods. It seems trivial to show the dual nature of aeronautics, as it appears obvious (Moraillon 2001); nevertheless, beyond evidence, it is interesting to understand the characteristics of this duality.

This profile is different from the others due to the scores of duality of combined exploration that are above those of all other TKS, while displaying high scores of duality on the technological core and on the architectural knowledge. This means that for these TKS, the defense and civilian industries closely articulate this knowledge nowadays, and they have the opportunity to cooperate in technological exploration in order to extend these proximities between the two technological domains.

Indeed, it seems that the two technological domains nowadays use the same technological core, which means that the development of these TKS involves strong relations that are similar in the two knowledge environments. There is essentially no divergence in the combinations of knowledge between the defense and civilian industries. Cooperation for the technological development in the current technological paradigm can therefore be expected. More broadly, the same architectural knowledge is used in both environments, which facilitates the knowledge transfers between sectors. The proximity of architectural knowledge facilitates the insertion in one technological domain of component knowledge originating in another one.

This technological profile appears to be in line with the history and current structuring of aeronautics, a sector in which companies have already been dual for several decades (Depeyre 2013). The technologies that compose this profile are widely common to the civilian and defense fields. This very high technological similarity and the integration of these TKS in the eminently dual companies suggest a model of “controlled duality” both with respect to technology and to the strategy of companies.

Nevertheless, it appears that in the defense environment and in the civilian environment, companies explore new ways to articulate this knowledge. This duality of combined exploration offers, as described by Cowan and Foray, the possibility of saving calendar and event time in technological development. Moreover, collaborating in this exploration, the two technological domains have the opportunity to build together the norms and standards that constrain future developments; they can also take advantage of this opportunity in order to set up an institutional framework that may in the future facilitate this cooperation within a future duality. The already dual strategy of aeronautics companies is an indicator that the latter are able to play a role in the materialization of this potential.

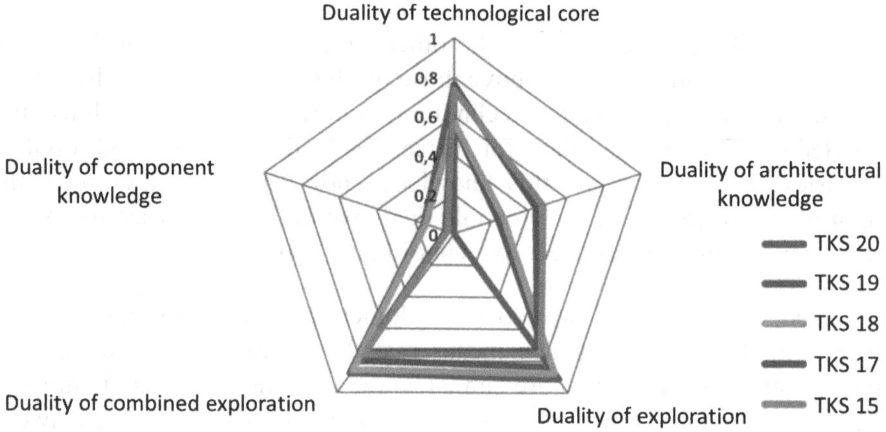

a)

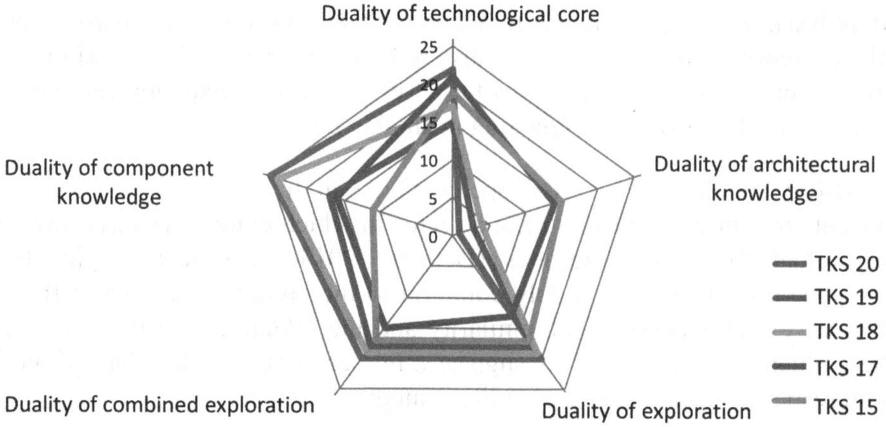

b)

Figure 5.13. *Profile 2 in relation to the autonomy of vehicles. (a) TKS scores; (b) TKS ranks. For a color version of this figure, see www.iste.co.uk/meunier/innovation.zip*

As for profile number two, it concerns TKS linked with the sensors, vehicles and electric motors. It is characterized by high duality scores for three components: duality of technological core, duality of exploration and duality of combined exploration. Here, the retained TKS are less central and have mean energy levels in the studied sample of TKS.

Similar to the previous case, here the high duality of the technological core can be interpreted as a convergence in the foundations of knowledge use in these TKS, which indicates they belong to the same technological paradigm. On the other hand, unlike profile 1, the low duality of architectural knowledge shows that defense companies use only a small part of the combinations of the coherent technological classes that could otherwise be used. This is certainly due to the specificity of uses in the defense field, but also, and especially, due to the application of these increasingly diversified technological systems in the rest of the technological landscape (development of autonomous vehicles, connected agricultural machineries, civilian drones or railway transportation).

Moreover, the high scores of duality of exploration and combined exploration show that defense companies participate in the exploration effort and can, within these "original" associations of knowledge, develop new opportunities of cooperation with the rest of the technological environment.

Globally, this profile presents an interesting dual potential, as it groups TKS whose level of coherence is rather low, which means that there is a certain diversity in the technological associations within which defense companies can certainly find opportunities to use their knowledge. Moreover, the respective knowledge serves the technological development of goods expected to thrive in the future, such as autonomous vehicles. These new applications require the development of new architectural knowledge. Car manufacturers or high technology experts who are currently involved in the development of the autonomous vehicle work on various architectures. Some focus on sensor quality, others on cartography or artificial intelligence (on this subject, see "The vehicle of the future", a report by the Academy of Technologies). Even though all these elements are required for the development of an autonomous vehicle, the balance of these various pieces of knowledge, which determines the dominant architectural knowledge, is not yet defined and there is yet no standard. Furthermore, since the articulation of these pieces of knowledge does not seem to disagree with the technological core of defense companies, and for some of them vehicle "intelligence" and autonomy are development axes (for example, Nexter, with Scorpion program), it appears that the latter could take part in the development of the civilian autonomous vehicle, and thus contribute to the elaboration of architectural knowledge; this will consequently enable them to more easily find new opportunities for their technologies, beyond the defense field. These TKS are hence associated rather with a duality of complementarity that is sustained by a high similarity at the level of the technological core. This seems to be a model "emerging duality", in which the role of defense companies needs to be clearly defined, unlike in the previous case.

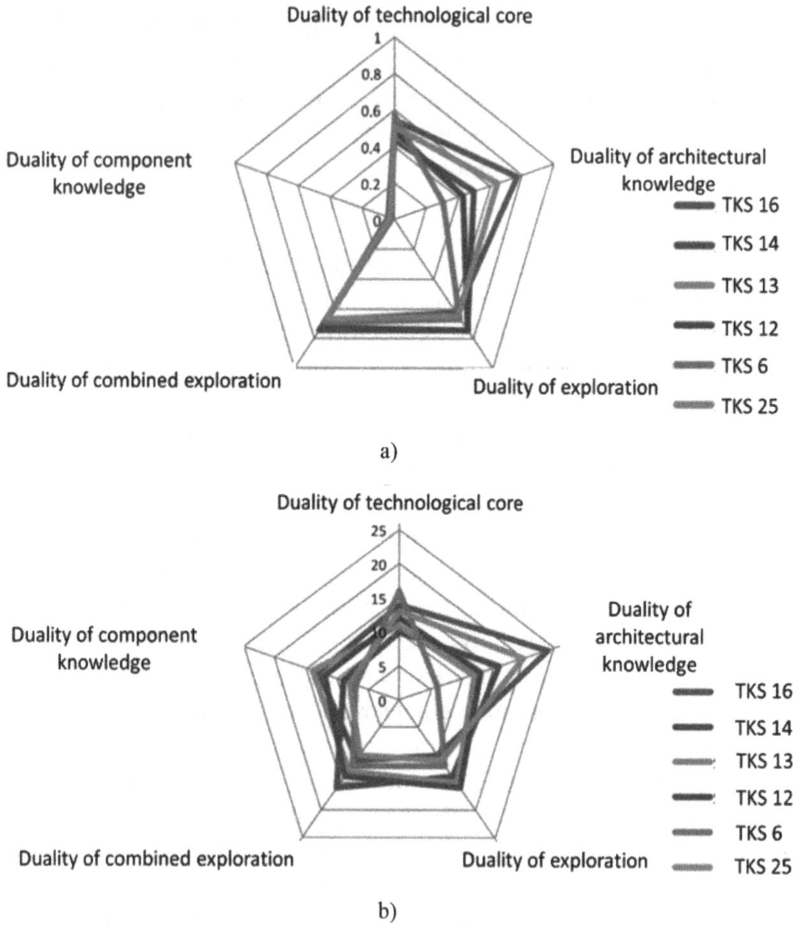

Figure 5.14. *Profile 3 in relation to generic technologies. (a) TKS scores; (b) TKS ranks. For a color version of this figure, see www.iste.co.uk/meunier/innovation.zip*

Profile number three is constituted of TKS with diverse domains of application (tires, guidance systems, technologies related to vehicles in general and electric systems), or generic technologies, which are present notably in the automobile sector. Their scores are lower overall than those of the previous profiles.

The first information that is worth noting here is that the concerned TKS are as central to defense companies as those of profile 2; nevertheless, their core duality scores are much lower. This means that the strong relations achieved in the defense knowledge environment are not similar to those in the global knowledge environment.

Hence, unlike the previous cases, there is not the same fundamental proximity of knowledge. Moreover, despite the lack of similarity between the strong relations, the duality of architectural knowledge is rather higher than that of the previous case. This can be explained by the fact that, for these TKS that are relatively peripheral for defense, the defense knowledge environment is upstream of the rest of technological production in this field. This is confirmed by the low scores in the duality of exploration and combined exploration.

Consequently, defense companies "use" knowledge produced elsewhere in a relatively close architectural knowledge. On the other hand, in order to adapt these architectures to the specificities of the military industries, defense companies add specific knowledge pertaining to their technological core, which explains the low scores of the duality of component knowledge.

The dual potential of this profile seems far lower than the previous ones, particularly in terms of duality of similarity. By contrast, the profile of these TKS suggests that in these TKS there is a distribution of roles among the companies in the two technological domains. The significant maturity of the concerned technologies suggests that industrial production is largely rationalized. Hence, each of these two technological domains is specialized in the field in which it has the greatest advantages. The model of duality is therefore a mature model of "duality of industrial production" strongly marked by a complementarity between the two technological domains.

In this last profile, TKS are associated with petrochemistry, equipping any type of vehicle, and metal working. They all have low scores of duality.

In this case, the scores are so low that any reference to duality or even to "marginal duality" would be excessive. The only noteworthy element is that, for two out of three TKS (TKS_{11} and TKS_{24}), the duality of component knowledge seems relatively high; this indicates that the associations achieved in these TKS do not pertain to the technological core of defense companies and that they separately integrate component knowledge generated elsewhere.

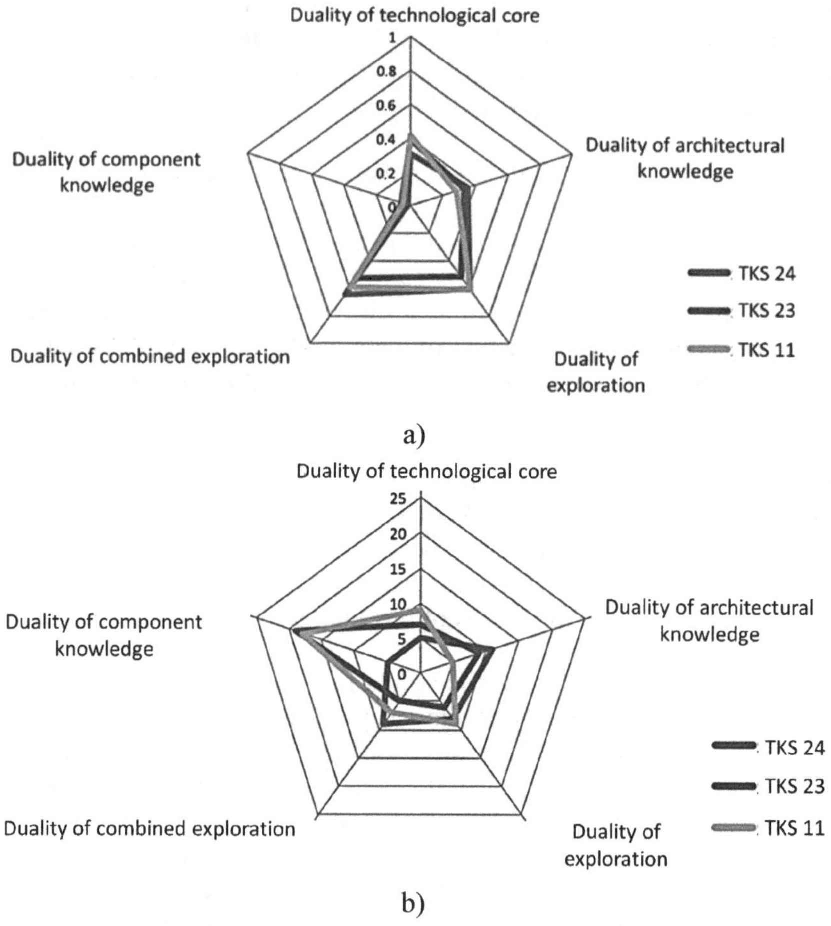

Figure 5.15. *Profile 4 in relation to generic technologies. (a) TKS scores; (b) TKS ranks. For a color version of this figure, see www.iste.co.uk/meunier/innovation.zip*

The last point that is worth explaining concerns TKS_1 and TKS_2 (Figure 5.16).

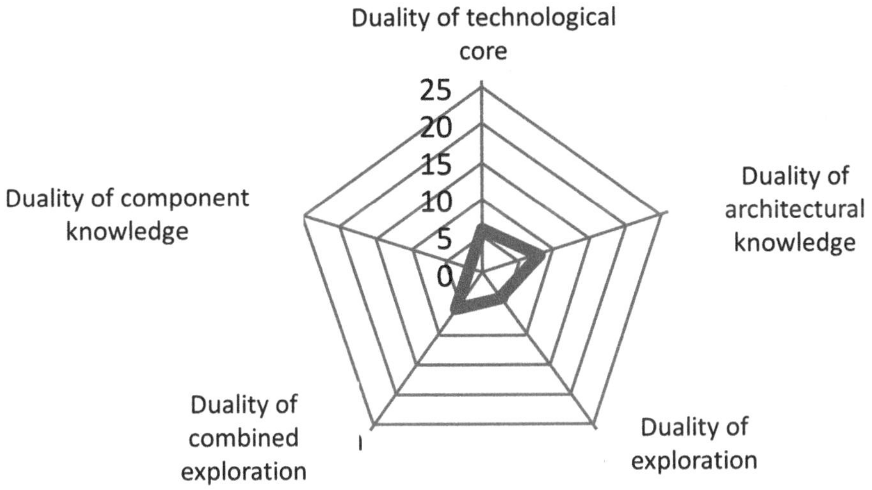

a)

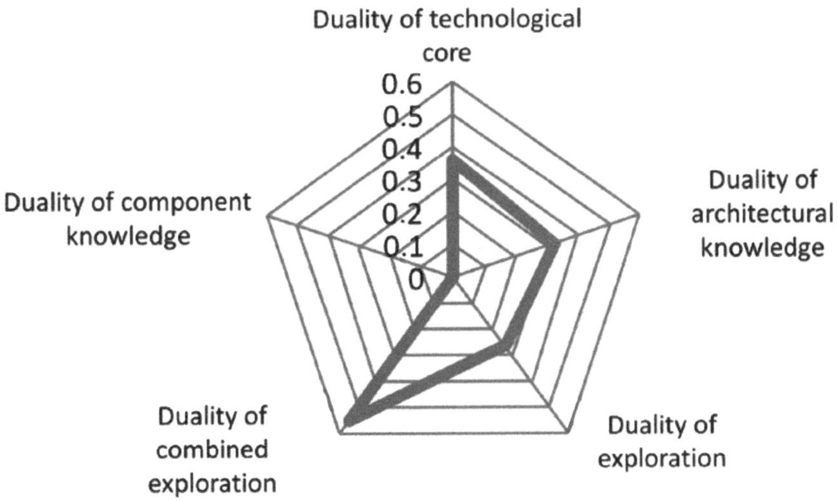

b)

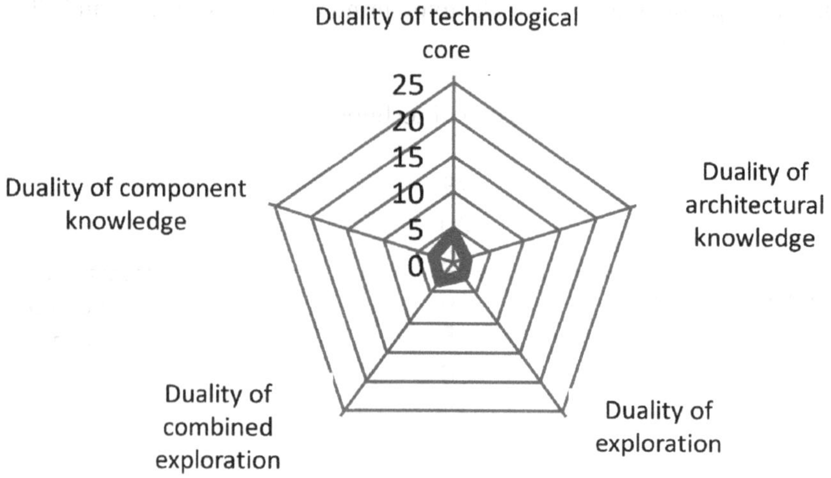

c)

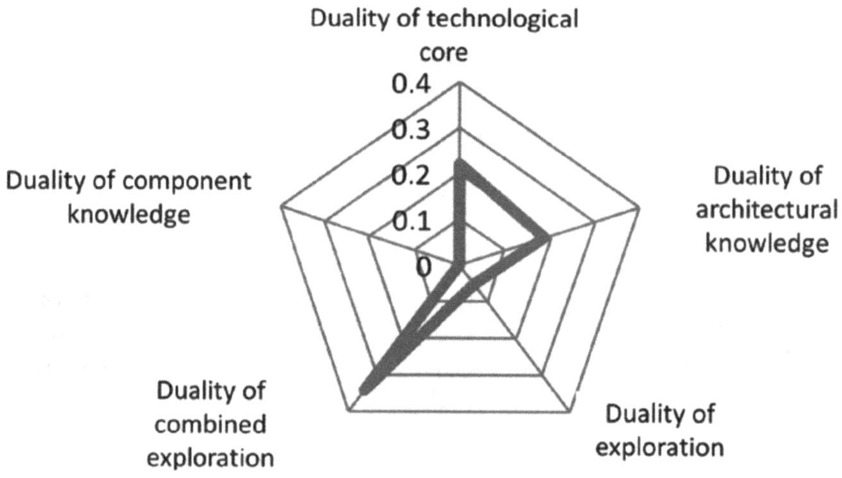

d)

Figure 5.16. *TKS that are central to defense industries. (a) TKS_1 ranks; (b) TKS_1 scores; (c) TKS_2 ranks; (d) TKS_2 scores (follow-up)*

The scores of duality of these TKS (missiles and armament) are the lowest. This is due to the obviously military nature of the technologies associated with these TKS. Therefore, in these fields defense seems to produce very specific technological associations and, if possible, interactions will more readily take the form of spin-offs, given the nearly complete absence of proximity in the production of knowledge between the civilian and the defense fields. Therefore, these TKS have a very limited dual potential.

5.4. Conclusion

This chapter is dedicated to highlighting the interest in using the theory of technological coherence for the study of the internal structure of TKS. This theoretical framework justified the proposal of several indicators of duality: duality of the technological core, duality of architectural knowledge, duality of exploration, duality of combined exploration and duality of component knowledge.

The analysis enables drawing a clear hierarchy of the dual potential of various TKS, taking into account the internal organization of knowledge between 2010 and 2012. This hierarchy points out the capacity of defense companies to participate in the technological development of guidance systems, civilian drones or autonomous cars. Repeating this type of analysis over several years would enable the definition of trends that may help not only the defense manufacturers in defining the strategy of dualization, but also public actors in the process of dual financing orientation.

It can consequently be completed by a domain and company-focused analysis in order to refine recommendations depending on more specific cases. The main objective was to show its relevance in the measurement of the dual potential. The definition of more precise recommendations requires complementary analyses that consider TKS and sectors individually over a longer period of time.

6

Analysis of the Dual Influence of Technological Knowledge Systems

6.1. Introduction

The objective of this chapter is to analyze the relations of a technological knowledge system (TKS) with its environment in order to understand the technological context in which duality is expressed. This makes it possible to distinguish, on the one hand, the influence exerted by a TKS through technologies structuring it and, on the other hand, the influence exerted by a TKS through technologies it is related to.

The previous chapter offered a way to understand the structuring of knowledge related to a TKS in particular. However, while a dual innovation system (DIS) is always defined in relation to a TKS, this does not mean that only the knowledge of the TKS is involved in its innovation dynamics. This is what happens at a large scale in the case of General Purpose Technologies (GPT) (Bresnahan 2010), which drives the dynamics of innovation of many TKS, without specifically characterizing them. A lot of knowledge, through its own progress, influences the progress of other knowledge. It is related to the correlational nature of knowledge production: the development of new pieces of knowledge offers the possibility of multiplying their possible combinations and recombinations (Fleming and Sorenson 2001; Sorenson and Fleming 2004), which opens the way to new developments. Hence, the richer the knowledge environment of a TKS, the higher its ability to be beneficial to the TKS and vice versa. Similarly, the fact that our TKS were constituted based on data from defense companies does not mean, and this reflects their entire dual nature, that only these companies participate in the dynamics of the TKS. Hence, what is valid for knowledge is also valid for companies, and identifying the weight of companies that contribute to a TKS depending on their relation to the defense domains offers information on the duality dynamics of a TKS.

This chapter relies on economic dominance theory, and more precisely on the tools of influence graph theory (IGT presented in Chapter 4). These tools are used for the study of both the internal dynamics of each TKS and the relations between the TKS and its environment.

For this purpose, the influence of the TKS is studied with, on the one hand, the influence related to relations inside a TKS and relations that the TKS builds with the rest of the structure (interdependency inside a part and between parts) and, on the other hand, the influence associated with the egocentric network (Lebert and Younsi 2015), which involves determining the knowledge directly related to the development of a TKS and measuring interdependences. Taken together, these elements enable an understanding of the TKS innovation dynamics. It is worth taking into account these internal and external elements in the analysis of duality of a TKS, not only for the evaluation of the dual potential, as in the previous chapter, but also for establishing the role of companies and technologies in the setup of a DIS.

For this purpose, this chapter first revisits the influence that pieces of knowledge exert on each other in the development of a TKS and explains in detail the measurements of the influence using two main concepts: centrality of cohesion and egocentricity. Methodological aspects are approached subsequently. Then, these methods are adapted to the study of TKS. Finally, these results are analyzed in relation to duality.

6.2. Influence and duality

The dual potential of TKS was defined in Part 1 depending on the cognitive proximities between the defense and civilian industries. But beyond this analysis that focuses on the internal structure of TKS, understanding the influence exerted by the production of one or several pieces of knowledge (TKS) on the production of other pieces of knowledge makes it possible to take into account other forms of proximity, which highlight technological inputs and outputs.

6.2.1. *Internal influence and external influence*

Duality can be summarized by establishing a relation between the civilian and defense industries in the development of a technology. While this relation is mutual, this does not mean it is symmetrical. Indeed, identifying TKS from the knowledge bases of defense companies necessarily puts defense companies at the core of the analysis. This means that the participation of defense companies should not be dealt with similarly to that of strictly civilian ones.

Indeed, the synergies of defense companies enabled the definition of the borders of TKS. The hypothesis formulated in this chapter is that the contribution of defense companies, in terms of the knowledge environment, to the total synergies of a TKS (for example, the synergies measured in the global environment) enables the measurement of the dual potential of a TKS. In other words, the force of synergies observed in the defense environment, compared to those observed in the global environment, provides information on the capacity of defense companies to integrate in the global environment for a given TKS. Calculating various contributions, various dimensions of this duality are distinguished.

Nevertheless, while this approach gives an indication on the dual potential of a TKS, it does not offer information on the perimeter of companies that participate in the dual innovation dynamics of the TKS. Once more, this participation cannot be apprehended as exactly the same for defense companies and civilian companies. The objective of this chapter is to show how influence measurements can play a role in the definition of the perimeter of a dual system of innovation by offering measurements of the involvement of companies in the technological development of a TKS, whether or not they have an acknowledged activity in defense. Two complementary pieces of information should be distinguished, as they do not have the same significance or importance for the two categories of companies.

On the one hand, it is possible to measure the participation of companies to TKS as such (technologies that define it, strictly speaking); this gives information on their involvement in TKS innovation dynamics and makes it possible to know the companies that participate in a DIS, strictly speaking. On the other hand, it is possible to identify among these companies those that contribute to the links between defense TKS and the rest of the technological environment. These companies contribute to the process of TKS knowledge dissemination, and therefore potentially to its duality. Indeed, this knowledge, which is not specific to this TKS, but is connected with it, participates in its evolution, either by supplying it with the external inputs it requires, or by offering opportunities to the technologies that compose it, beyond the strict framework of this defense TKS. This is the very essence of a dual process of knowledge dissemination. The following sections deal with the manner in which this relation is analyzed.

These analyses of the influence inside a TKS and in its direct technological environment make it possible to determine the dual potential of each TKS and also to evaluate the perimeter of civilian and defense companies that participate to the DIS related to each TKS.

The measurements of influence rely on the matrices of technological flows. Chapter 3 presented how these matrices are built from backwards citation data. These matrices point out the technological knowledge required for generating the supply for the production of other pieces of knowledge. In other terms, they enable the study of technological inputs.

At this stage, it is worth noting that these matrices can be used to find out, for a given technological class, not only the inputs that served to produce it, but also the knowledge generated using this technological class. Indeed, once the matrix is built, it is sufficient to consider the coefficients among the technologies, in either direction, in order to study the technological inputs and outputs. Hence, what is valid for one technological class is also valid for several technological classes, and therefore for a TKS. This is why the dependence and interdependence links that can be observed by IGT can prove interesting in the evaluation of the dual potential of TKS.

The interest that analyzing such relations has for the evaluation of a dual potential can be easily understood. Beyond the cognitive proximities related to the similarity of technological activities in the civilian and defense industries, this manner of apprehending the question makes it possible to evidence cognitive proximities related to spin-offs and/or to the spin-ins of knowledge produced by the civilian and/or defense domains.

The tools of IGT make it possible to use technological flow matrices. More specifically, IGT is used to analyze the relations in a TKS, between the TKS and its direct knowledge environment, and within its direct knowledge environment. Before going any further, it is important to revisit IGT in order to show how it can be used to analyze these relations in terms of influence.

As already presented in Chapter 4, Lantner (1974) shows that the calculation of a matrix determinant is an original and efficient way to measure the weight of trees and circuits in a weighted and oriented structure in order to measure the various forms of influence. The various values of the determinant make it possible to distribute the influence in a structure between dependence, interdependence and autarky. By construction, the value of these measurements takes into account both the number of poles propagating this influence and the force of the links between the poles. Hence, the influence of one pole on a large number of poles that are not interconnected can be similar to that exerted on a large number of weaker poles that are more strongly interconnected. Therefore, IGT can be used to apprehend the influence, on the one hand, depending on the number of poles involved and, on the other hand, depending on the links between these poles.

Compared to traditional IO analysis, taking into account the paths in the analysis is a significant contribution to the influence analysis. Indeed, distinguishing various categories of paths depending on their weightings, their orientations and their mutual or non-mutual nature makes it possible to divide the observation into several structural phenomena, which enable a wide enrichment of the analysis (Lantner and Lebert 2015).

In the analysis of TKS, what is measured is not the influence of one pole on the rest of the structure, but that of a set of poles, by definition interdependent. It is consequently a matter of studying one part (the TKS), its relation to an additional part, which is composed of knowledge that is external to the TKS, but is connected with it, and the manner in which pieces of knowledge of the additional part interact.

First, the calculation of the influence in the TKS is simpler. It is a matter of studying the interdependences within a part, independently of the links established with an additional part.

Then the partition theorem is used for the elaboration of indicators concerning the relation of a TKS with its environment: “the determinant of the structure of exchanges is smaller or equal to the product of determinants of the parts” (Lantner and Lebert 2013a, 2013b). Given that the TKS is a part of the complete graph, the interdependence between this part and the rest of the structure is measured by the difference between the product of the determinants of the two parts (TKS and non-TKS) and the determinant of the complete structure. This interdependence makes it possible to apprehend all the amplified effects generated by the circuits that interconnect the parts (Lebert 2016).

Finally, the influence of a TKS on the rest of the structure and the manner in which this additional part is structured is apprehended through various paths, which make it possible to distinguish various forms of influence. In order to isolate them, it is important to deal with a particular form of partition referred to as an "egocentric network" (Lebert and Younsi 2015).

The analysis of egocentric networks (or egocentricity) is a new approach, compared to the one presented in Chapter 4. It is used for the study of relations within a set of complementary poles directly linked to one or several poles defining a primary part (Lebert and Younsi 2015). Up to the present, the primary part was always presented as a single pole. Lebert and El Younsi used this tool in an analysis of international trade. Consequently, they use a specific partition that enables them to approach the position of a country (a pole) in relation to its trade partners. This structure is used here in order to present the method. It will be then extended to the case of a TKS, which corresponds to the case of a primary part composed of several poles. The analysis of the egocentric network is used to apprehend the influence of the direct knowledge environment on a TKS.

This involves as a first step considering the partition of a structure of three parts defined as follows:

– part 1: constituted by a pole, referred to as ego;

– part 2: directly connected to the ego, referred to as alter;

– part 3: the rest, which is not connected to the ego.

The objective of this partition is to analyze the circularities inside alter. The major interest of this tool is to be able to define alter in various modes, in the sense of distinguishing between various modes of connections between ego and alter so that the analysis of egocentricity can be decomposed into several structural phenomena. The alter network is centered on ego, therefore egocentricity is involved.

Several characteristics of egocentricity have already been presented by Lebert and Younsi (2015) as follows:

– D the determinant of the global structure and D_i the determinant of each part. But the parts P1 and P3 were defined in such a way that the interdependence between these parts is zero. Then, calling P4 and the part comprising P1 and P3: $D_4 = D_1 \times D_3$;

– according to the properties of the value of the determinant in an exchange structure in which the autarky of the poles is considered zero, the difference $1 - D$ enables the measurement of interdependence in a structure. Therefore, the value of $1 - D_2$ measures the value of the interdependence in the egocentric network;

– if C is the diagonal cofactor associated with the main pole P1, then the value of D_2 is always greater or equal to C. If $D_2 = C$, this means that the egocentric network internalizes all the circularities of the structure complementary to P1; in other words, there is no internalized circularity in part P3;

– finally, D_2 is always between C and 1.

The analysis of egocentricity does not take into account the long circularities that can be established in the complementary part, meaning the interdependence between parts 2 and 3.

Until present, these various perimeters have always served to analyze international trade data and were named according to the vocabulary associated with this type of analysis. These various modalities are summarized here, with different names, in order to be better applied to the analysis of knowledge flows:

– the egocentric network composed of all the poles to which the pole of the main part P1 directly sends flows (Lebert and Younsi 2015). This definition applied to the case of international trade defines the network of exportations of the main pole. In the case of a knowledge analysis, this makes it possible to delimit the borders of the network of direct spin-offs of a pole;

– the egocentric network of the set of poles from which the pole of the main part P1 directly receives flows. This definition applied to international trade defines the network of suppliers of the main pole. In the case of a knowledge analysis, this makes it possible to delimit the borders of the network of direct spin-ins of a pole;

– the egocentric network composed of the set of poles to which the pole of the main part P1 directly sends flows or from which it directly receives flows. This network makes it possible to synthesize the two previous approaches and defines, in the context of international trade, the limits of the network of trade partners of the main pole. In the context of knowledge analysis, it is the network of knowledge exchanges of a pole;

– the egocentric network composed of the set of poles that are simultaneously flow receivers and emitters; these are poles to which the pole of the main part P1 directly sends flows and from which it directly receives flows. Thus, it makes it possible to identify bilateral relations that the pole has with the rest of the structure, both from the perspective of international trade and from that of knowledge production: it is the network of bilateral exchanges;

– the analysis of egocentricity of a pole involves the study of interdependences in an *alter* network. The analysis of egocentric networks is one of the components enabling the evaluation of the influence that a TKS has on its environment.

The interest of the analysis of egocentricity of a TKS is to isolate the relations that the latter (ego) internalizes in order to focus on the relations between the alter poles. Indeed, TKS are by definition constituted around strong circularities that consequently influence the interdependences between TKS and the poles that are directly related to it. Considering only the determinant of the subpart constituted of poles in direct relation with the TKS (alter), it is possible to apprehend the structuring of these poles independently of the circularities or synergies internalized in the TKS, and thus assess the robustness of this complementary network.

Finally, the influence of a TKS is decomposed into several elements. On the one hand, the influence within and among the parts of a TKS: it is a matter of interdependences in the ego and between ego and alter. On the other hand, the influence related to the egocentric network is a matter of interdependences complementary to the TKS that appear in the rest of the knowledge environment in direct relation with the TKS (alter).

6.2.2. *Measures of influence*

For the sake of a smooth passage from the above-presented subject, the analysis of egocentricity of a TKS is first approached, before focusing on the measures related to intra- and interpart interdependence.

The measures presented here are inspired by those of Lebert and El Younsi (2015) and slightly adapted in order to be applied to an ego network defined as a set of poles.

Similar to Chapter 4, given the nature of data related to a structure of knowledge exchange, the determinant D of the complete structure is always between 0 and 1. In the analysis of the egocentricity of a pole, it is the value of the diagonal cofactor that sets a lower boundary on the value of the determinants of various egocentric networks; when this tool is applied to a TKS – that represents the main part whose value of determinant is denoted by D_{SCT} – it is the value of the determinant of the complementary part denoted by $D_{\overline{SCT}}$ that constitutes the lower boundary to the value of the determinants of various egocentric networks. The complementary part being a subpart of the complete matrix, $D_{\overline{SCT}}$ is necessarily greater or equal to 0; then the hierarchy below is established.

The four egocentric networks defined above help in distinguishing the various structural phenomena. The gaps between the various values of the determinants enable the measurement of these phenomena. Hence, it is important to clarify the hierarchy of these values. For this, it is worth recalling that the more the egocentric network represents a significant fraction of the circularities of the complementary part, the closer its determinant to de $D_{\overline{TKS}}$ and the closer it gets to 1 otherwise.

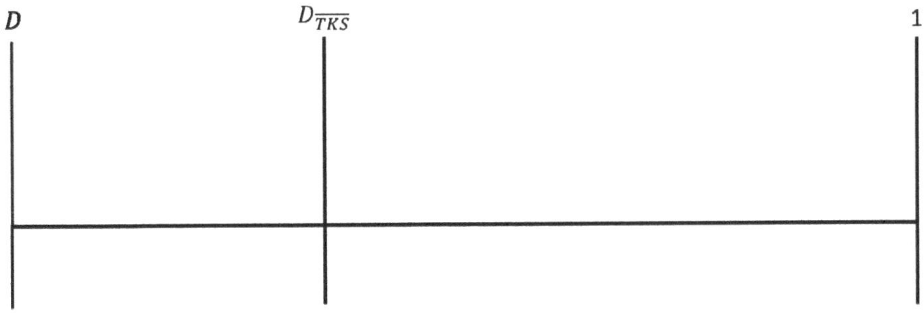

Figure 6.1. *Measures of influence (1)*

Hence, the largest egocentric network is, by definition, the network of knowledge exchanges, as it comprises all the direct ingoing and outgoing relations. On the other hand, the narrowest is the network of bilateral exchanges, as it contains only the poles emitting and receiving simultaneously to and from the main part. The networks of direct spin-offs and that of direct spin-ins are among the previous two. Nevertheless, for the latter two, an ambiguity persists, as it is impossible to *a priori* rank them. The various networks are denoted as follows: the network of direct spin-offs is denoted by D_X; the network of direct spin-ins is denoted by D_M; the network of knowledge exchanges is denoted by $D_{X \cup M}$ and the network of bilateral exchanges is denoted by $D_{X \cap M}$. The hierarchy shown in Figure 6.2 is then established.

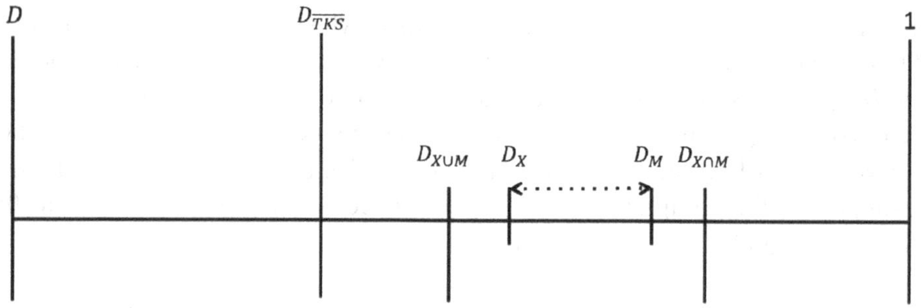

Figure 6.2. *Measures of influence (2)*

The four egocentric networks can be used to evidence seven structural phenomena listed in Lebert and El Younsi (2015). Some of them are simply renamed here, so that they better match the cases of knowledge flows (see Table 6.1).

The philosophy of these indicators is to valorize, for a TKS_i, various structural phenomena depending on the corresponding circularities. The stronger these circularities, the more they reflect a significant multiplying effect (Lantner 1974). Hence, the multiplying effects of a TKS can be discriminated depending on the various relations that a TKS has with its environment.

Indicators	Measures
Integration	$T_i = \frac{1 - D_{X_i \cap M_i}}{1 - D_{\overline{TKS_i}}}$
Inclusion	$I_i = \frac{1 - D_{X_i \cup M_i}}{1 - D_{\overline{TKS_i}}}$
Insertion through spin-offs	$R_i = \frac{1 - D_{X_i}}{1 - D_{\overline{TKS_i}}}$
Insertion through spin-ins	$A_i = \frac{1 - D_{M_i}}{1 - D_{\overline{TKS_i}}}$
Cognitive asymmetry	$S_i = \frac{D_{M_i} - D_{X_i}}{1 - D_{\overline{TKS_i}}}$
Knowledge transfers	$F_i = \frac{D_{X_i \cap M_i} - D_{X_i \cup M_i}}{1 - D_{\overline{TKS_i}}}$
Exclusion	$E_i = \frac{D_{M_i \cup X_i} - D_{\overline{TKS_i}}}{1 - D_{\overline{TKS_i}}}$

Table 6.1. *Indicators related to egocentric network*

These indicators can be used to apprehend the circularities between $D_{\overline{TKS}}$ and 1 (Figure 6.3); this is why they are measured with respect to this gap. All these indicators are represented on the axis of measures of egocentricity.

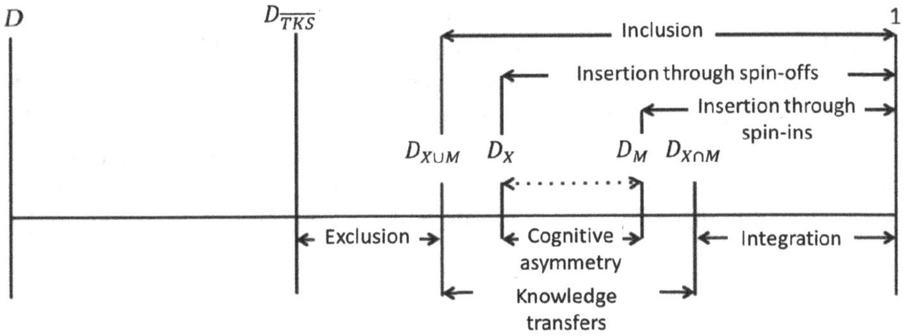

Figure 6.3. *Measures of influence (3)*

This first series of indicators enables the exploration of what happens in the egocentric network of the TKS. New indicators remain to be presented, as they enable the exploration of the relation between the TKS and its egocentric network. While the measures related to the egocentric network are calculated in the interval $\left[D_{\overline{TKS}}, 1\right]$, the measures related to the TKS and its relation with its egocentric network have values between D and $D_{\overline{TKS}}$.

In addition to this analysis of the egocentric network, the intrapart interdependence (inside the TKS) and interpart interdependence (between the TKS and the complementary part of the matrix) should be measured. Due to these interdependences, the centrality of cohesion of the TKS can be measured (Lebert *et al.* 2016; Lebert and Meunier 2017). Its denomination is explained by the fact that it measures the relations established by the TKS both within and with the rest of the structure.

It is the part situated on the left of $D_{\overline{SCT}}$ on the axis of measures of influence that is used to analyze these relations. It is in fact on this part of the axis that the interdependences between TKS and the rest of the structure can be measured. Up to the present, the analysis was limited to the valorization of the interdependence between ego and alter in order to measure the ego centrality (intermediary centrality). Here, the objective is to detail the components of this interdependence.

In their article in 2015, Lebert and El Younsi present the difference between D and the value of the diagonal cofactor (in this article, the ego network is assimilated to a pole) as a measure of the centrality of the pole intermediarity. In the case of a partition in which the main part is constituted of a single pole, this part measures both the interdependences between the main part and the complementary part, which are not included in the complementary part (theorem of partition), no interdependence being included in the main part. Indeed, as shown above, in this analysis of egocentricity of a pole, the circularities included in the complementary part are analyzed in the interval between the value of the diagonal cofactor and 1.

This centrality is denoted by $C_i = \frac{C_i - D}{1 - D}$. It can be readily understood that, in the case of a partition in which the main part is defined as a pole (without autarky), the circularities within this pole are zero. The entire interdependence is therefore strictly related to circularities between the main part and the complementary part, and to circularities in the complementary part. Nevertheless, in the general case, the interdependence between two parts depends on three elements: the circularities inside the main part, the circularities between the main part and the complementary part, and the circularities in the complementary part.

In the analysis of a TKS, the challenge is therefore to dissociate what concerns the interdependences internalized by the TKS from those concerning the relation between the TKS and its complementary network. This is equivalent to studying the part between D and $D_{\overline{SCT}_i}$ on the axis of measures of influence.

For this purpose, a new point of reference must be fixed on the axis of measures of influence. It is K, the product of the determinants of TKS, and of the complementary part $K = D_{TKS} \times D_{TKS}$. But according to the partition theorem, K, the product of the determinants of two subparts is smaller or equal to D, and since D_{TKS} is smaller or equal to 1, K is smaller or equal to $D_{\overline{TKS}}$. Therefore, K enables the distinction between two spaces on the left of $D_{\overline{TKS}}$ and evidencing two new indicators.

As previously, the philosophy of these indicators is to valorize, for a TKS, two structural phenomena depending on the values of their interdependences. These indicators make it possible to apprehend the circularities between D and D_{TKS}. This is why they are measured with respect to this gap. The centrality of cohesion as a whole is measured as a function of $1 - D$. When K tends to $D_{\overline{TKS}}$, this means that the TKS internalizes few circuits and vice versa. Two components of the centrality of cohesion can be distinguished: the one concerning the interpart interdependences referred to as "centrality of external cohesion", which measures the interactions between a TKS and its egocentric network (all these interactions are determined by the circuits defining the egocentric integration network, as by definition, there is no interdependence with one pole unless the latter is linked by a circuit, therefore by a bilateral relation) and the one concerning the intrapart interdependences referred to as "centrality of internal cohesion", which measures the self-sufficiency of a TKS.

For more clarity, the indicators of cohesion centrality will be named depending on what they designate in the case of a matrix of knowledge flow, therefore on the interaction between the knowledge of the TKS and the rest of the structure on the one hand, and on the self-sufficiency of the flows of knowledge internal to the TKS on the other hand.

Indicators	Measures
Centrality of external cohesion: interaction	$N_i = \dfrac{K_i - D}{D_{\overline{TKS_i}} - D}$
Centrality of internal cohesion: self-sufficiency	$O_i = \dfrac{D_{\overline{TKS_i}} - K_i}{D_{\ i} - D}$
Centrality of cohesion	$C_i = \dfrac{D_{\ i} - D}{1 - D}$

Table 6.2. *The indicators concerning intra- and interpart interdependences*

The measures of influence are therefore divided into two sets, which are distributed on the axis of measures of influence. On the one hand, there are the measures that enable the analysis of the egocentric network and, on the other hand, those that enable the analysis of the centrality of cohesion of TKS. Together they can be used to establish a complete overview of the interactions of a TKS in the matrix of technological flows.

When calculated globally, these measures are not strictly speaking indicators of the level of duality of TKS, but they make it possible to contextualize the analysis. In order to obtain information on the duality of TKS, it is important to measure the contribution of defense to various components of the influence of TKS. The next section is dedicated to this subject.

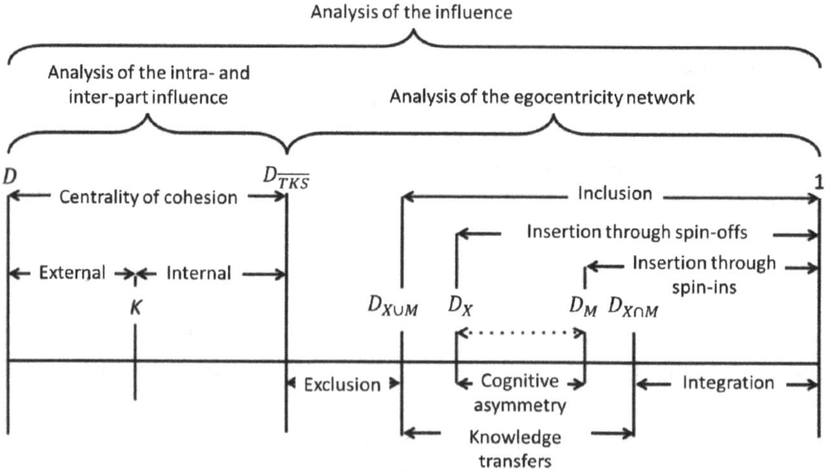

Figure 6.4. *Measures of influence (4)*

6.3. Dual analysis of influence

6.3.1. *The indicators*

The application of measures of influence to the study of duality of TKS does not rely on the creation of new indicators, but on the analysis of "contribution". This contribution enables the measurement of the role of various elements (for example, the companies) in the global structure. A cautious interpretation of the above presented indicators can be proposed depending on this contribution. The contribution is then not only a new indicator of the duality of TKS, but also a means to start drawing the perimeters of their corresponding DIS.

To approach the notion of contribution, the construction of the complete matrix should be represented as the sum of matrices of each company. In other terms, the structure of the exchanges of technological knowledge is a multigraph composed of as many graphs as there are companies in the database. Considering each graph of the company as a layer, the global matrix is therefore the sum of all the company layers (Figure 6.5).

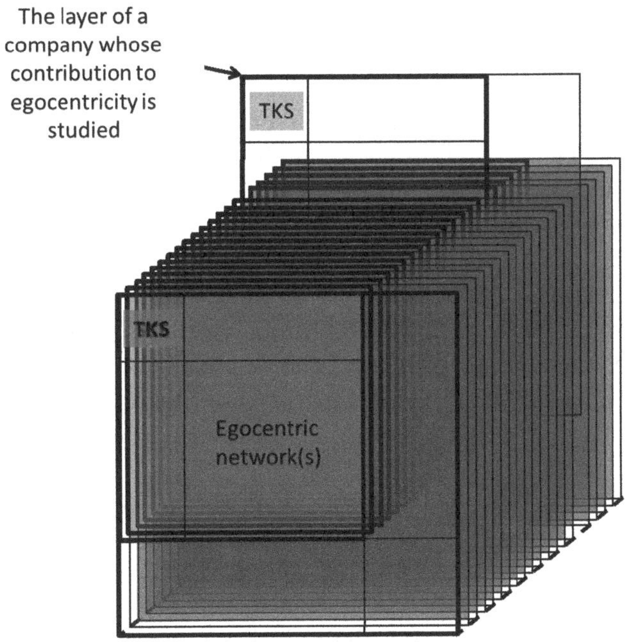

Figure 6.5. *The contribution of layers to influence*

The global structuring of knowledge flows is a function of the structuring of flows of each company, which makes it possible to evaluate to what extent the structuring of knowledge of a company contributes to the global structuring of knowledge. Finally, the contribution of a layer to the influence is apprehended through a partial (the coefficients of poles related to a company) subgraph (certain poles).

Similar to the layers of companies, it is possible to calculate the contribution of a whole knowledge environment. It is the purpose of this tool, which facilitates the specification, for each TKS, of which of the two knowledge environments (civilian or defense) contributes more to the scores of influence of a TKS.

In order to build the defense knowledge environment, the weightings of layers used in Chapter 4 must be summarized. They enable the consideration of technological relations of a company depending on the part of the turnover this company achieves in the defense industries (see Chapter 4 for further details on the method). Hence, all else being equal, the technological relations of a company that is very specialized in the field of defense are more strongly valorized within this environment than those achieved in a company oriented toward civilian applications.

In this manner, the layers of defense companies are divided into two groups, out of which the first one constitutes the defense knowledge environment. The second group is simply considered as a component of the global knowledge environment which, for lack of a better term, is referred to as "civilian knowledge environment". Each group can be considered as a layer whose value of coefficients is equal to the sum of the coefficients of layers composing it. Hence, the layer of defense knowledge environment enables the calculation, by TKS, of defense contribution to the various structural phenomena listed above. The defense knowledge environment and the civilian knowledge environment are therefore the two strictly complementary parts of the global knowledge environment.

To calculate the contribution of a company or of a knowledge environment composed of a set of companies, the technological coefficients of each layer must be calculated based on the gross knowledge flow corresponding to each company. Hence, the matrix of a company layer enables the study of the contribution of a company to various structural phenomena observed and measured at the aggregated level.

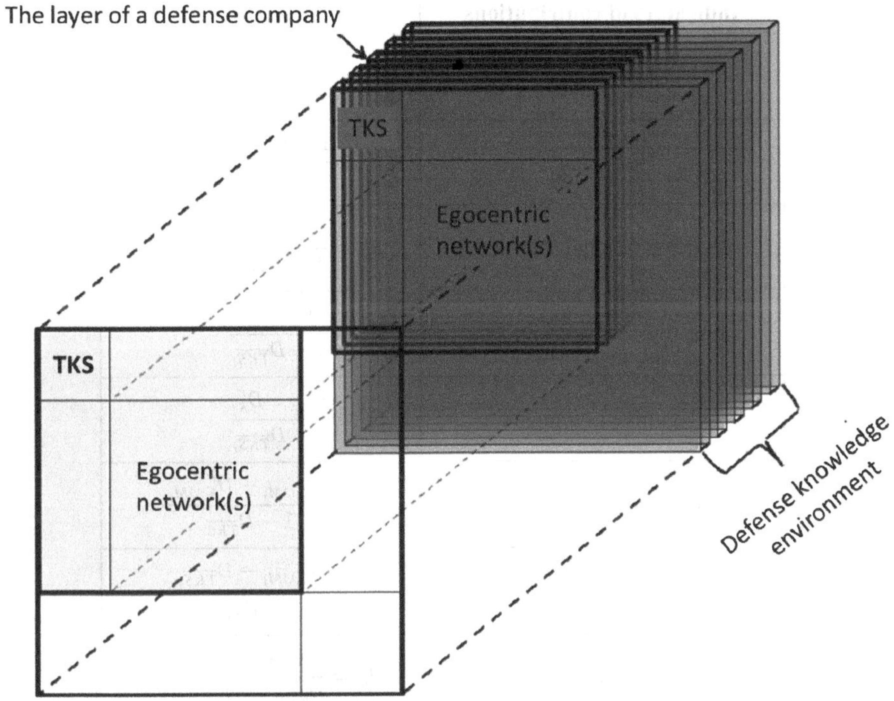

Figure 6.6. *The contribution to influence*

Each layer has corresponding technological coefficients that reflect the structural properties of layers and make it possible to understand the extent to which companies contribute to the properties of the global structure of exchanges. For example, in the context of influence, the formula of the contribution of c to the integration of TKS_i is calculated as follows:

$$T_i^c = \frac{1 - D^c_{X_i \cap M_i}}{1 - D_{\overline{TKS_i}}}$$

This corresponds to the value of integration for the TKS_i in the global matrix for the layer of knowledge environment c. It is calculated as a function of $1 - D_{\overline{SCT_i}}$, so that this contribution is a part of what is produced in the global structure.

Indicators of contributions	Measures
Integration	$T_i^c = \frac{1 - D^c_{X_i \cap M_i}}{1 - D_{\overline{TKS_i}}}$
Inclusion	$I_i^c = \frac{1 - D^c_{X_i \cup M_i}}{1 - D_{\overline{TKS_i}}}$
Insertion through spin-offs	$R_i^c = \frac{1 - D^c_{X_i}}{1 - D_{\overline{TKS_i}}}$
Insertion through spin-ins	$A_i^c = \frac{1 - D^c_{M_i}}{1 - D_{\overline{TKS_i}}}$
Cognitive asymmetry	$S_i^c = \frac{D^c_{M_i} - D^c_{X_i}}{1 - D_{\overline{TKS_i}}}$
Knowledge transfers	$F_i^c = \frac{D^c_{X_i \cap M_i} - D^c_{X_i \cup M_i}}{1 - D_{\overline{TKS_i}}}$
Exclusion	$E_i^c = \frac{D^c_{X_i \cup M_i} - D_{\overline{TKS_i}}}{1 - D_{\overline{TKS_i}}}$
Interaction	$N_i^c = \frac{K_i^c - D}{D_{\overline{TKS_i}} - D}$
Self-sufficiency	$O_i^c = \frac{D_{\overline{TKS_i}} - K_i^c}{D_{\overline{TKS_i}} - D}$
Centrality of cohesion	$C_i^c = \frac{D_{\overline{TKS_i}} - D}{1 - D}$

Table 6.3. *The measures of contribution*

On the one hand, the scores of influence calculated at the level of the global structure, which are technological characteristics of the TKS, are pointed out. These indicators inform on the influence of TKS on their knowledge environment. Strictly speaking, they do not provide information on the duality of TKS, but offer information on the technological relations that each TKS has with its knowledge environment, which is important information for the contextualization of the analysis of duality. On the other hand, there is the contribution of knowledge environments to various scores of influence of TKS, which offers information on the duality of TKS. As previously mentioned, as the TKS studied here are *a priori* considered in the defense industries, the more their technological trajectories depend on the defense knowledge environment, the less they are dual (and vice versa). These indicators of contribution therefore measure the dual potential of TKS and enable their comparison in quantitative terms. On this subject, not all the indicators of influence are relevant and only some of them are retained in the continuation of the analysis.

6.3.2. *Analysis of the duality of a TKS*

This involves applying the measures of the influence to the 26 TKS and calculating the contribution of the defense knowledge environment in order to better qualify the dual potential.

It is first a matter of the results of all the companies considered as a whole and by TKS, and then they are calculated at the scale of the knowledge environments. These results calculated in the global knowledge environment and the results of the contribution of the defense knowledge environment offer an overview of the influence of TKS and can be used to study their duality.

	Global knowledge environment		
	Mean	**Standard deviation**	**Median**
Centrality of cohesion	0.000178927	0.000133356	0.00012316
Self-sufficiency	0.365967598	0.132997969	0.362595759
Interaction	0.634032402	0.132997969	0.637404241
Inclusion	0.999867596	0.000143054	0.999962201
Insertion through spin-ins	0.999600991	0.000481901	0.999918591
Insertion through spin-offs	0.99957349	0.000321269	0.999672686
Asymmetry	-2.74792×10^{-05}	0.000279087	-8.3999×10^{-05}
Integration	0.999185396	0.000782634	0.999596134
Knowledge transfer	0.0006822	0.000644554	0.000352412

Table 6.4. *Statistics of influence in the global knowledge environment*

	Defense knowledge environment		
	Mean	**Standard deviation**	**Median**
Centrality of cohesion	0.000178971	0.000133393	0.00012316
Self-sufficiency	0.019609857	0.033089656	0.362595759
Interaction	0.038591981	0.013838245	0.999596134
Inclusion	0.046815432	0.009375126	0.999962201
Insertion through spin-ins	0.041540685	0.013915662	0.999918591
Insertion through spin-offs	0.043686234	0.009275805	0.999672686
Asymmetry	0.002145547	0.006152588	0.000106503
Integration	0.9803723397	0.033057292	0.637404241
Knowledge transfer	0.00822345	0.00695133	0.000352412

Table 6.5. *Statistics of defense contributions to influence*

The graphics in Figure 6.7 represent the scores of influence of the 26 TKS in the global knowledge environment. The eight graphics summarize the results of the indicators calculated in the global knowledge environment. For better readability, interaction and self-sufficiency are presented as percentages of the centrality of cohesion, while exclusion, being strictly equal to the part that is complementary to an inclusion of 1, is not represented.

First, this representation of data shows a high homogeneity in the structuring of the influence of TKS in the global knowledge environment. Overall, it seems that it is due to the distribution between interaction and self-sufficiency, as well as to the score of the centrality of cohesion as such that the first differences can be noted. As for the scores of egocentricity, they are very homogeneous and in a first instance they suggest only several exceptions.

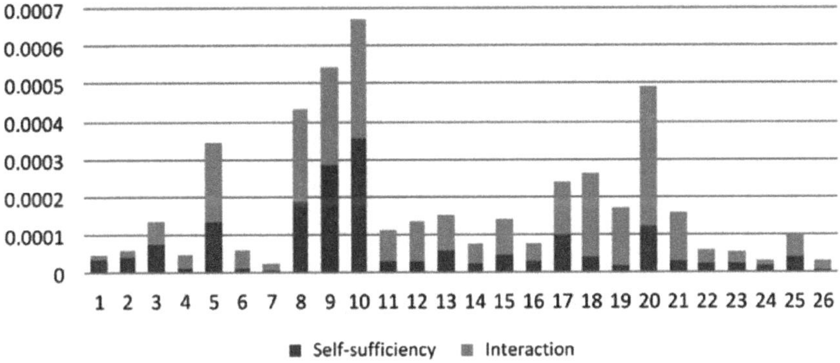
0.0007
0.0006
0.0005
0.0004
0.0003
0.0002
0.0001
0
1 2 3 4 5 6 7 8 9 10 11 12 13 14 15 16 17 18 19 20 21 22 23 24 25 26
Self-sufficiency
Interaction

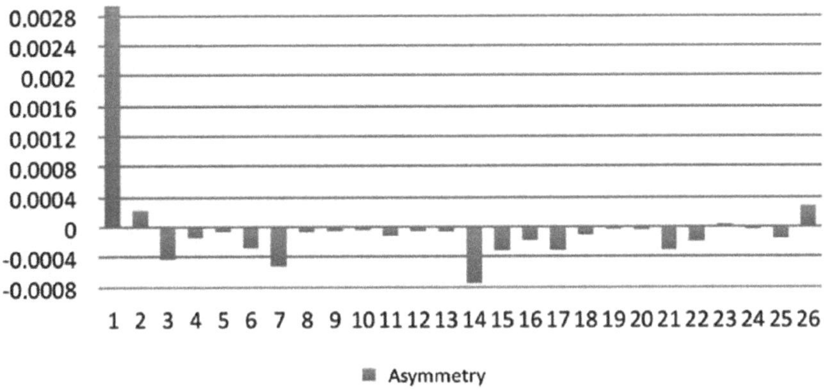
0.0028
0.0024
0.002
0.0016
0.0012
0.0008
0.0004
0
-0.0004
-0.0008
1 2 3 4 5 6 7 8 9 10 11 12 13 14 15 16 17 18 19 20 21 22 23 24 25 26
Asymmetry

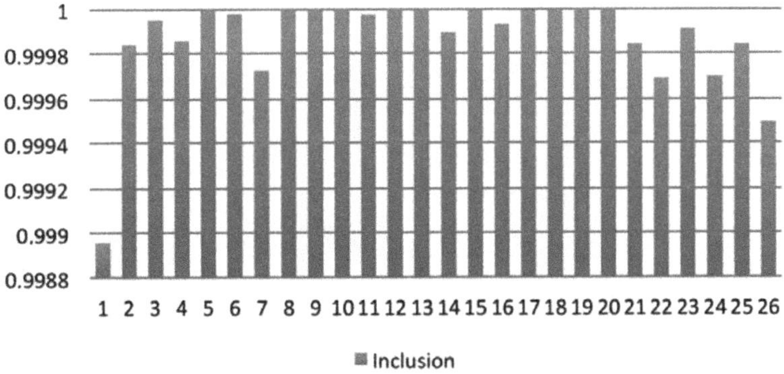
1
0.9998
0.9996
0.9994
0.9992
0.999
0.9988
1 2 3 4 5 6 7 8 9 10 11 12 13 14 15 16 17 18 19 20 21 22 23 24 25 26
Inclusion

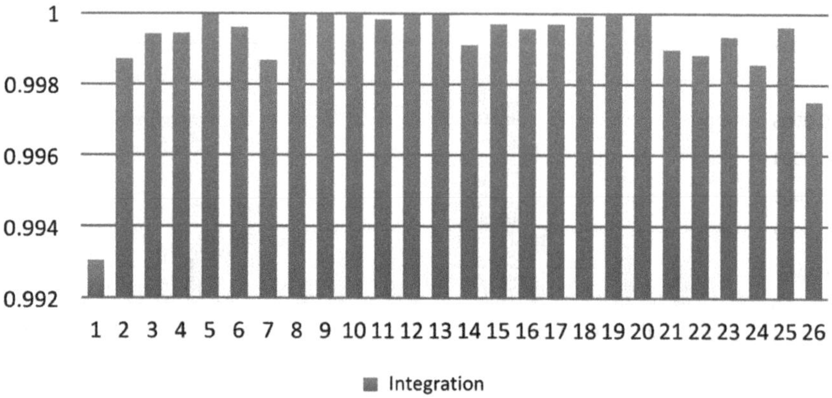
1
0.998
0.996
0.994
0.992
1 2 3 4 5 6 7 8 9 10 11 12 13 14 15 16 17 18 19 20 21 22 23 24 25 26
Integration

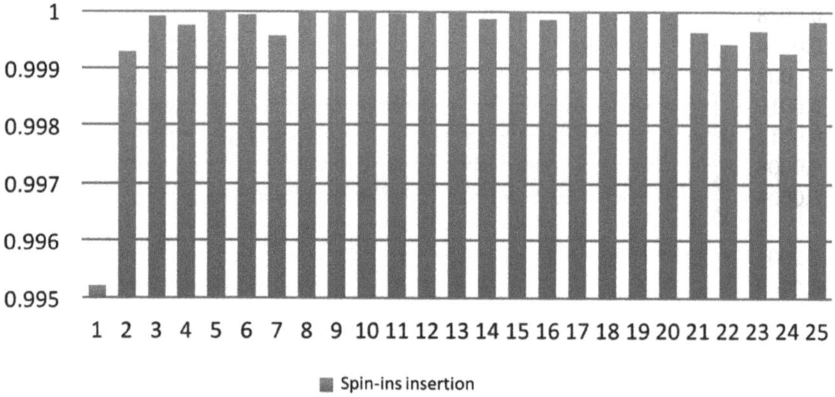
1
0.999
0.998
0.997
0.996
0.995
1 2 3 4 5 6 7 8 9 10 11 12 13 14 15 16 17 18 19 20 21 22 23 24 25
Spin-ins insertion

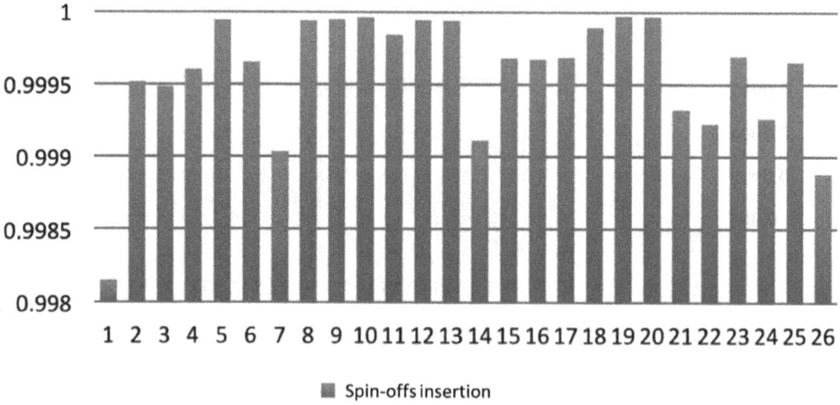
1
0.9995
0.999
0.9985
0.998
1 2 3 4 5 6 7 8 9 10 11 12 13 14 15 16 17 18 19 20 21 22 23 24 25 26
Spin-offs insertion

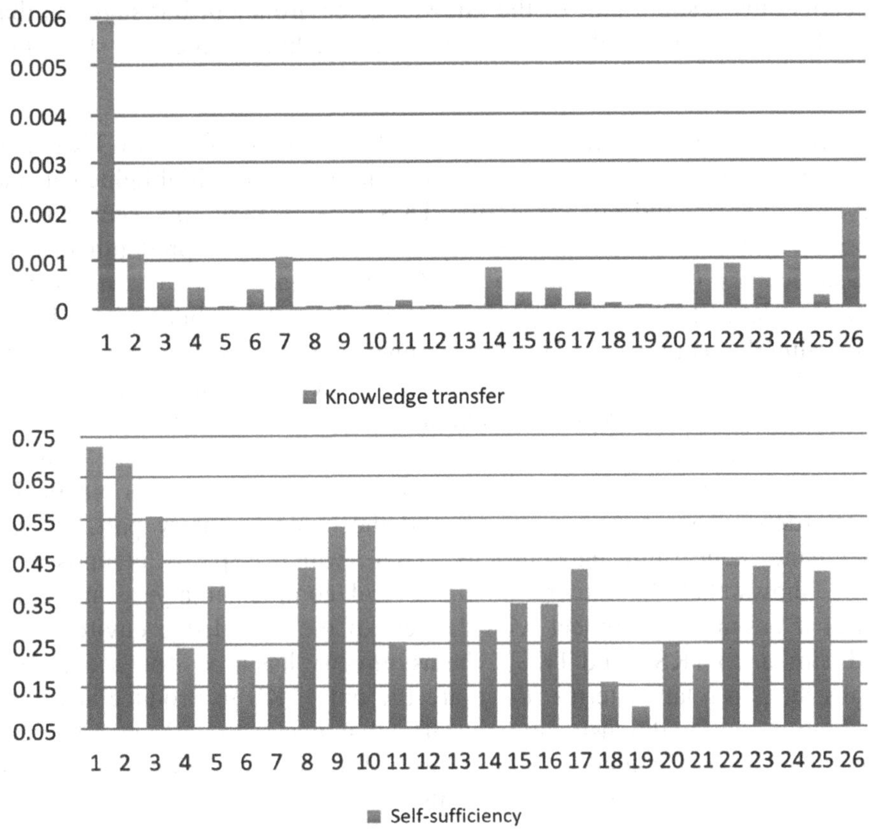

Figure 6.7. *Influence of the 26 TKS in the global knowledge environment. For a color version of this figure, see www.iste.co.uk/meunier/innovation.zip*

Nevertheless, only TKS_1 is distinguished in all respects, and particularly by its scores of egocentricity whose interaction (0.27621) reflects a very weak relation with the rest of the knowledge environment and whose scores of insertion through spin-ins or spin-offs (0.99521 and 0.99815), as well as the scores of integration and inclusion (0.99304 and 0.99895), show that the technologies to which this TKS is linked are not very interdependent. This means that this TKS is linked to few synergies in the rest of the structure. Hence, the very strong positive asymmetry that is beneficial only to this TKS (0.00293) concerns only the smallest share of the global structure. Finally,

TKS_1 has a very strong level of knowledge transfer (0.00591); this also concerns only a small part of the knowledge environment but suggests that this TKS is the intermediary of the two sets of knowledge that share few synergies.

Second, this presentation seems to confirm the specificity of TKS_1 and TKS_2 at the level of their internal organization, already highlighted in the previous chapter. Indeed, these two TKS have a very low centrality of cohesion (0.00005 and 0.00013), which is marked by a predominance of self-sufficiency (0.68422 and 0.558608). This means that their innovation dynamics depends most of all on innovations from the technological classes composing them at present. This predominance of internal circularities is one of the characteristics of the "aerospace and defense" domains that, for the 2010–2012 period, rank second among the sectors integrating the most circularities (calculations made in other studies conducted in the unit for applied economics with ENSTA Paris). This means that there is practically no interdependence between a TKS and the complementary part. On the other hand, concerning egocentricity, TKS_2, which is partly composed of TKS_1, shows that the integration of several complementary technologies makes it possible to connect with the rest of the knowledge environment. And, similar to TKS_{24} and TKS_{26}, the asymmetry has a positive score. This means that, in relative terms, these are the only TKS to produce at global level more synergy downstream (spin-offs) than upstream (spin-ins). In other terms, they have a tendency to be beneficial to the innovation dynamics of other technologies rather than tap into them.

Third, TKS_8, TKS_9 and TKS_{10} constitute another set. Their profile seems quite opposite to the above description. Indeed, if in this group, similar to the previous one, self-sufficiency scores are high (0.43373, 0.53015 and 0.53202), they are paired with very high scores of centrality of cohesion (0.00043, 0.00054 and 0.00067); this means that, in contrast to the previous case, the interaction between these TKS and the complementary part of the knowledge environment is important and, finally, that these TKS have a strong effect on the rest of the structure, controlling a large quantity of flow.

The other TKS are marked by lower self-sufficiency scores and also by low levels of centrality of intermediarity, with the exception of TKS_5 and TKS_{20}, which benefit from a relatively high centrality of intermediarity (0.00034 and 0.00049). However, in contrast to the previous case, these scores are associated with a low part of self-sufficiency (0.38864 and

0.24889). This means that the capacity of these TKS to influence their environment is high, but it rather goes through their capacity to interact with the rest of the knowledge environment rather than through the synergies they integrate. This is reinforced through their high scores of insertion, integration and inclusion, and means that these TKS interact with sets of knowledge that are at their turn interdependent.

Finally, the last element of context that is worth being evidenced is the highly negative asymmetry for three TKS_3, TKS_7 and TKS_{14} (–0.00042, –0.00051 and –0.00074). This means that, in the process of knowledge production, these TKS take particular advantage of synergies existing in the rest of the knowledge structure, while they bring only a small contribution to external synergies.

At the global scale, the challenges associated with the influence of TKS are related to:

– centrality of cohesion, meaning the capacity of a TKS to impact the production of knowledge in the rest of the structure. However, they are also related to the equilibrium between self-sufficiency and interaction within this centrality of cohesion, in other words, to the manner in which this impact is distributed between the internal structure of the TKS and the interdependence with the rest of the knowledge environment;

– inclusion and integration, meaning the value of synergies to which each TKS is connected. This information is completed by the knowledge transfer score that makes it possible to measure the gap between the value of synergies that are either upstream or downstream of the TKS and those located at both ends;

– asymmetry, meaning the difference between the value of these synergies downstream and those of synergies upstream of a TKS.

In order to represent the contribution of the defense industries to the above presented scores and thus address, strictly speaking, the matter of duality, only certain indicators were selected consistently with the above-presented challenges (Table 6.5). The retained variables are as follows:

– for the first challenge: self-sufficiency. The contribution to the interaction being the strict complement to a contribution to self-sufficiency of 1 for a given layer, it brings no additional information;

– for the second challenge: exclusion (complement to an inclusion of 1), integration and knowledge transfer. Exclusion was preferred to inclusion, as this way the three retained variables make it possible to cover the entire axis of egocentricity;

– for the third challenge: asymmetry.

Table 6.6 seems to show that the most central TKS in the defense knowledge environment, meaning the TKS classified among the first ones (see Chapter 4), have negative scores of contribution to asymmetry. The reverse applies for the less central. Even though asymmetry is globally negative, whether it is a matter of the global environment or of the contribution to the defense knowledge environment, this means that the defense environment participates more in the upstream synergies required for the constitution of TKS when the latter is central than when this TKS is not central (with respect to downstream synergies to which it participates). This could be interpreted as a strategy for securing technological supplies for the technologies that are the most important for defense. This seems to correspond to the uses in this field of activity. This hypothesis should be tested but this is beyond the scope of this study.

TKS	Self-sufficiency	Exclusion	Integration	Knowledge transfer	Asymmetry
1	0.243147	0.990498	0.008059	0.001443	–0.001055
2	0.226238	0.990751	0.008380	0.000868	–0.000513
3	0.005628	0.948035	0.051035	0.000930	–0.000914
4	0.000598	0.946730	0.050462	0.002808	–0.002284
5	0.000033	0.944788	0.053831	0.001381	–0.001216
6	0.003577	0.946394	0.045256	0.008350	–0.006574
7	0.015859	0.947928	0.044654	0.007417	–0.007387
8	0.001177	0.946069	0.053323	0.000608	–0.000457
9	0.003227	0.948915	0.050636	0.000448	–0.000305
10	0.003266	0.950623	0.049246	0.000130	–0.000130
11	0.000321	0.947468	0.043983	0.008549	–0.005573
12	0.002192	0.948133	0.051769	0.000098	–0.000083

TKS	Self-sufficiency	Exclusion	Integration	Knowledge transfer	Asymmetry
13	0.002740	0.948143	0.051760	0.000097	–0.000082
14	0.000092	0.953174	0.040026	0.006799	–0.006562
15	0.000162	0.944793	0.046136	0.009071	0.003774
16	0.000078	0.947262	0.038365	0.014373	–0.000012
17	0.000167	0.944851	0.046126	0.009023	0.003796
18	0.000104	0.945009	0.045737	0.009253	–0.008587
19	0.000021	0.946328	0.051807	0.001865	0.000207
20	0.000105	0.944854	0.054876	0.000270	0.000164
21	0.000013	0.985890	0.004222	0.009888	0.009150
22	0.000027	0.961647	0.010186	0.028167	0.014994
23	0.000171	0.948292	0.043886	0.007822	0.007236
24	0.000700	0.948271	0.037432	0.014297	0.004040
25	0.000163	0.948938	0.017543	0.033519	0.018783
26	0.243147	0.990498	0.008059	0.001443	–0.001055

Table 6.6. *Defense contributions to influence*

In order to process these data for the study of duality, a principal component analysis (PCA) is conducted here based on the data in Table 6.6; similar to the previous chapter, it will lead to various profiles.

This PCA (Figure 6.8) is widely determined by the first component related to the autarky scores of TKS. Component 1 makes it possible to identify a first group constituted of TKS_1 and TKS_2 (red circle). It is largely drawn by the defense contribution to self-sufficiency. As expected, this means that the synergies internal to these two TKS, whose technologies are very marked by their military uses, are highly dependent on the defense activity of companies. Therefore, this analysis confirms the eminently defense nature of these two TKS, whose internal synergies are significantly more related to defense innovation than for the other TKS.

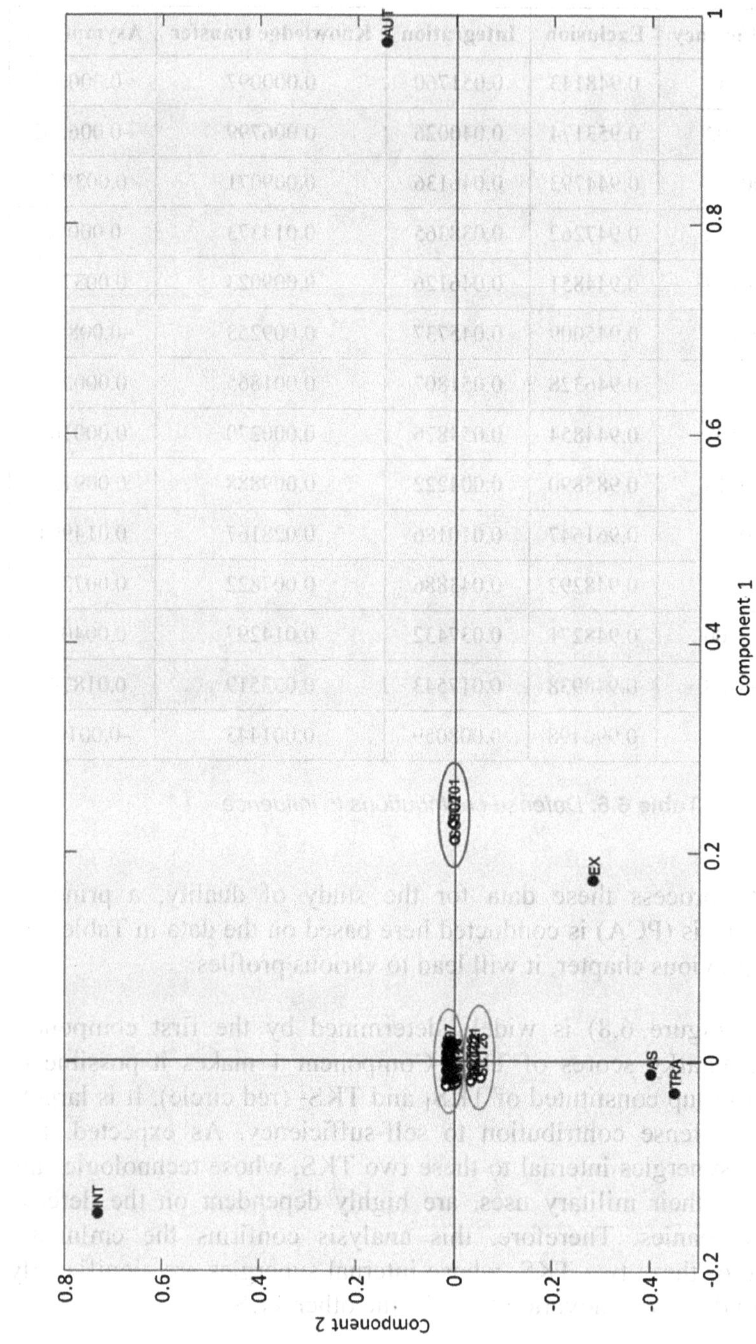

Figure 6.8. *PCA on the scores of influence of 26 TKS. For a color version of this figure, see www.iste.co.uk/meunier/innovation.zip*

Moreover, defense makes only a small contribution to the relation that TKS can have with the rest of the technological landscape. This analysis is consistent with the results presented in the previous chapter, revealing a lack of dual influence. Indeed, as anticipated, there are few interactions between the defense and civilian industries on these technologies.

Moreover, beyond PCA, it is worth noting that TKS_1 and TKS_2 are among the few TKS that produce more synergies downstream than they consume upstream. This seems to mean that, while there is no dual relation, there are knowledge transfers going on, and the latter are more favorable to downstream synergies than to upstream synergies.

Once more, as anticipated in the previous chapter, despite the low potential of coproduction in this field, there appears to be a potential for these technologies in terms of spin-offs. Nevertheless, it is worth noting that the contribution of defense companies is small, the latter being, in the context of this activity, dependent on upstream synergies.

By contrast, the contribution to self-sufficiency does not make it possible to clearly discriminate the other TKS. It is component 2, related to four other variables, which seems to be able to distinguish at least two groups of TKS among the remaining TKS. Indeed, these TKS are grouped at the center of a triangle delimited by the variables knowledge transfer and asymmetry on one vertex, exclusion on another vertex and integration for the last vertex.

For a more specific study of these TKS, a second PCA is conducted. For better clarity of representation, it does not take into account TKS_1 and TKS_2, and it focuses on the four variables that, given the first analysis, can define the profiles of distinct TKS.

This second PCA leads to the identification of four groups of TKS, which are very widely distributed along the axis of component 1.

First, referring to particular cases, it is worth citing TKS_{21} (biochemistry), whose position is strongly related to exclusion (and consequently to inclusion). Indeed, defense activity has an extremely low contribution to the inclusion of this TKS. This means that defense companies participate only to a little extent in circularities related to this TKS, either upstream or downstream. It should be recalled that, while it has relatively high scores of duality of architectural knowledge and component knowledge (see Chapter 5), the other characteristics of internal duality of this TKS are quite weak.

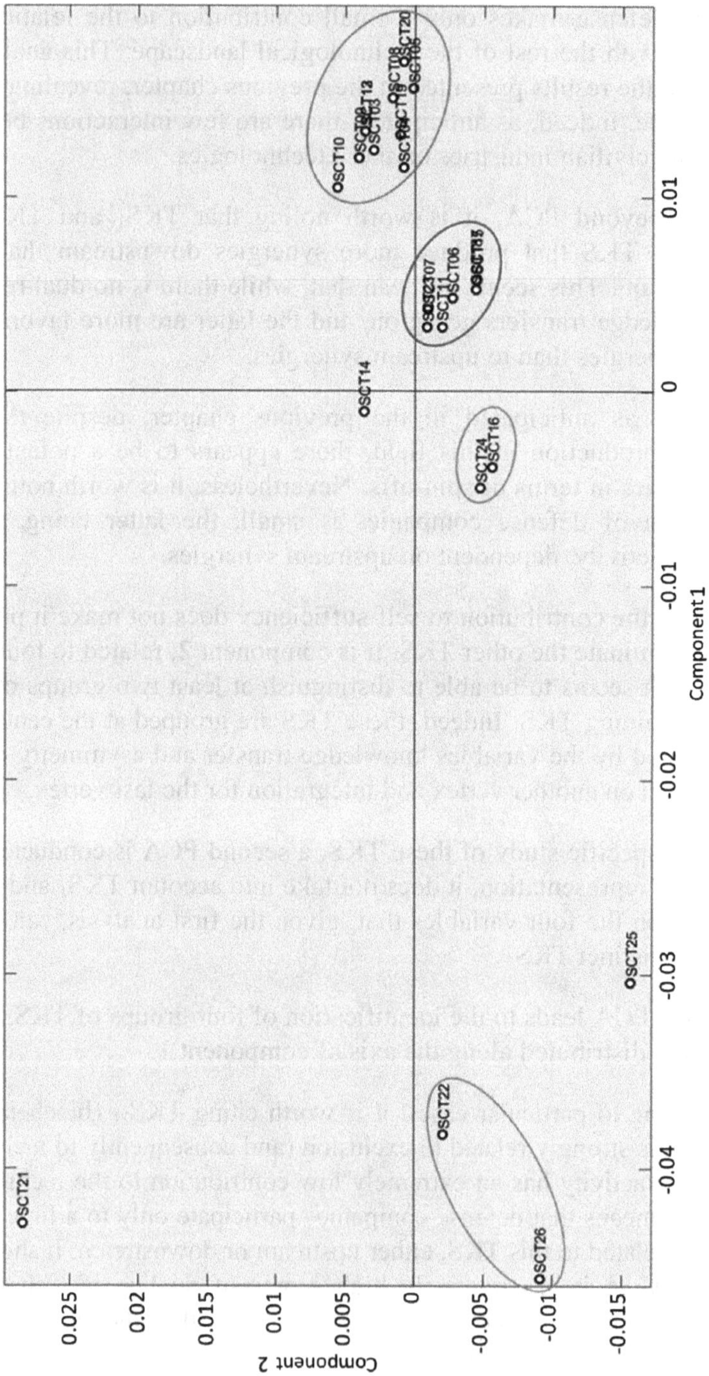

Figure 6.9. *PCA on the scores of influence of 24 TKS with unrestrained dual potential. For a color version of this figure, see www.iste.co.uk/meunier/innovation.zip*

Another particular case is that exemplified by TKS_{22} and TKS_{26} (light signals and metals), which are marked by a strong contribution of defense to asymmetry and self-sufficiency, similar to TKS_{25} (combustion engine) to a smaller extent. All these TKS share the fact that their integration is loosely related to defense companies. This means that the latter participate to a small extent in the synergies that are present both upstream and downstream of the production of knowledge related to this TKS. Overall, the previous chapter showed that these TKS were characterized by low scores of duality related to their internal structure. TKS_{26} and TKS_{22} were among the less dual, while TKS_{25} was characterized by a stronger duality of architectural knowledge, but belonged to the profile of duality of industrial production marked by low duality. It appears that this new analysis is consistent with that of the previous chapter and, due to the low involvement of the defense companies in the integration in the rest of the technological universe, confirms the weakness of the dual potential of these TKS. Indeed, taking part in the synergies upstream and downstream of a TKS means that defense is positioned either as a link in a chain, which explains the position of TKS_{26} and TKS_{22}, and to a smaller extent that of TKS_{25}, or as a set that operates independently of the rest of the structure, similarly to TKS_{21}. Finally, it is worth noting that, as predicted in Chapter 5, TKS_{26} is one of the few TKS that are not central to defense, but whose upstream synergies are higher than downstream synergies. The profile of this TKS appears to be that of a TKS related to spin-ins.

Finally, the dual potential in terms of knowledge flow seems to be marginal for these TKS. On the one hand, TKS_{21}, which concerns biochemistry, seems to develop in autarky in the defense industries; this is certainly explained by a very specific use of this knowledge by defense companies. Even though this knowledge is not the most significant (synergetic) for these companies, the latter are forced to master it independently of the companies that use them traditionally. On the one hand, while TKS_{26}, TKS_{22} and TKS_{25} are loosely related with the rest of the structure for defense companies, they are more strongly marked by spin-offs or spin-ins than by a mutual relation with the rest of the knowledge structure; this does not correspond to the definition of duality retained for this work. At a more in-depth consideration, TKS_{22} and TKS_{25} depend overall more strongly on upstream synergies than they contribute to downstream synergies, while the reverse is true for TKS_{26}. On the other hand, the defense contribution is not consistent with TKS_{26} and TKS_{22}, while it is consistent with TKS_{25}. This means that, for TKS_{26} and TKS_{22}, defense tends to act contrary to the global tendency, favoring spin-ins for the first and spin-offs for the second. For the last TKS, the contribution of defense is consistent with that of the rest of the structure, favoring spin-ins rather than spin-offs.

This TKS profile shows an unbalanced influence, which does not exclude a certain collaboration with the rest of the technological landscape. It exists and this collaboration is very likely oriented toward knowledge transfers rather than toward dual joint production.

Second, the other groups of TKS are spread along the main axis and they are consequently distributed depending on the scores of defense contribution to insertion, from the lowest on the left to the highest on the right. First come the TKS marked by orange circles (16 and 24), followed by those marked by red circles (6, 7, 11, 15, 17, 18 and 23) and finally by TKS marked by blue circles (3, 4, 5, 8, 9, 10, 12, 13, 19 and 20). It is worth noting that this analysis is valid for the defense companies taken as a whole, while an individual study may indicate more diverse situations.

TKS_{16} and TKS_{24} (vehicle and metal working) belong, respectively, to profile 3 of internal duality of "industrial production" and to profile 4 of "marginal" internal duality. These two profiles group the TKS with extremely generic technologies, but whose dual potential is weakened due to their low importance in the defense industries. It is certainly for this reason that the participation of defense companies as a whole to their integration in the global technological landscape is relatively low. Their profile in terms of flow is similar to the one presented in the previous chapter and it is related to a marginal dual influence.

The last two groups illustrate TKS of profile 1 with "mastered" internal duality potential and of profile 2 with "emerging" duality with a distribution of TKS that is close to that observed in the previous chapter. TKS_3, TKS_5, TKS_9 and TKS_{10}, marked by aeronautics (aircraft engines, communication systems, drones and defense drones) and whose duality is "mastered", are all located in the group for which the defense industries contribute the most to integration, similar to TKS_{19} and TKS_{20} (electronics and sensors) for which duality was qualified as "emerging" in the previous chapter. Only TKS_{12} (tires), which is part of this group, was perceived as a TKS with lower dual potential.

Moreover, the other TKS of emerging duality, TKS_{15}, TKS_{17} and TKS_{18}, and whose technologies are related to the electric and autonomous car, are in the second group, for which defense plays an important role in the technological integration in the global landscape. This group is completed by TKS_6 and TKS_7 whose dual potential is "mastered", due to their link with aeronautics; it is certainly due to the increasing predominance of the automotive field in the guidance systems that TKS_6 is not part of the first group. Finally, TKS_{11} and TKS_{23} (vehicle refining and equipment) complete this group, although their dual potential appeared weak compared to the previous analysis.

Finally, these two groups of TKS show an established dual influence that could be qualified as "mature" when they are more integrated, given that the concerned technologies are very heavily marked by aeronautics.

In the context of this analysis of influence, TKS_4 related to the defense vehicle is once again a specific case. Indeed, while in the previous chapter it was characterized by a low dual potential related to the internal structuring of its knowledge, it appears that the defense knowledge environment strongly participates in its integration. Once again, this can be explained by its very generic composition except for one technology, which is very damaging to its dual potential in Chapter 5, but which, concerning the influence, is not sufficient to compensate the strong integration of TKS related to other technologies.

Finally, TKS_{14} related to electrical systems has a specific profile. Indeed, its scores of influence are close to the mean in all the fields; it consequently occupies a central place in the figure, while its self-sufficiency score is very low; this shows the relatively low predominance of defense in this TKS. It consequently appears that its dual influence is neutral.

Therefore this analysis globally confirms the one presented in the previous chapter, while revealing several unexpected positions. Aeronautics technologies are those for which the defense companies have the highest involvement both in their internal structuring and in their integration in the global landscape. The control of the dual potential of these technologies is the highest. Moreover, a set of TKS associated with the electric or autonomous car seems to follow the same diagram at a slightly lower level. These technologies are partly also aeronautics technologies, particularly required for drone development, but they are also present in other technological fields of defense companies related, for example, to smart vehicles or to systems of systems. This analysis shows a calibration of TKS depending on the more or less significant control of ingoing and outgoing flows, which favors to a greater or lesser extent the dual exploitation of TKS.

This analysis of the contribution of defense to the technological flow evidences three challenges:

– the first challenge of this contribution of defense industries to the influence of a TKS is related to the control of the internal flows of a TKS and it is the contribution to self-sufficiency that reveals it. It is with regard to this challenge that it clearly appears that, for the first two TKS, defense plays a predominant role, which confirms their non-dual nature;

– the second challenge, certainly the most interesting in the context of duality, is the one related to the role played by defense in the control of both ingoing and outgoing flows of a TKS. It is associated with the scores for the contribution to the integration of TKS in the global technological landscape. When it is strong, this integration shows that the defense industries are involved both in the upstream and downstream synergies of a TKS. This involvement favors the joint technological production in the TKS, as it enables a "commonality" of knowledge and therefore a cognitive proximity with both defense and civilian partners. Sharing the same knowledge base both upstream and downstream, defense is more easily integrated in the global landscape. This is how a highly integrated TKS reflects a "controlled flow duality". The scores obtained here are overall consistent with the scores of internal duality and they show that an internal duality is often reflected by a duality of knowledge flow;

– the challenge of the orientation of flows is the last challenge of this analysis. It is apprehended through the scores for contribution to asymmetry. This score enables a better perception of the equilibrium between the technologies that play a role upstream or downstream of the TKS and the manner in which defense companies contribute to this equilibrium. It seems that this challenge can also be apprehended in terms of securing the technological supply for key technologies in the defense knowledge environment that also have a strong strategic interest.

Beyond the measures related to the contribution of the defense domains as a whole, which give an indication on the dual potential, it is worth taking a detailed look at the companies that play a significant role in this influence.

To address this question, the contribution of all the companies was calculated for all the TKS according to the model presented in the previous section. The companies were considered as civilian since no part of their turnover is associated with this domain in our data. On the other hand, the companies having a defense activity were considered as civilian and defense in proportion to their turnover. This makes it possible to rank their involvement in one or another of these domains.

The indicators relevant for the measurement of the contribution of companies to the influence of a TKS are those with respect to the three above-mentioned challenges: self-sufficiency, integration and asymmetry. The results are not detailed in this work, but three examples are given in order to show the diversity of company profiles.

Indeed, since the situation of each company is by definition a specific case with respect to these TKS, it appears excessive to draw conclusions on the role of companies without associating this with a monographic work on the company in question. This constitutes one of the major axes to extend this work. Nevertheless, the mean rankings offer several paths of reflection:

– Nexter: a non-dual company. Indeed, this small size company when compared to several giants in the domain seems to play a prominent role in the interdependences in TKS (self-sufficiency: sixth rank on average in the defense landscape). On the other hand, in line with its extremely low percentage of civilian activity (3%), it scarcely participates in the integration of these TKS in the global landscape. The very low duality of the strategy seems therefore in line with its technological profile;

– Raytheon: a company with a dual technological profile that chose a strategy rooted in defense. Raytheon features a technological profile which plays at the same time a major role in the defense domain (self-sufficiency: first rank on average in the defense landscape) and whose contribution to technological integration is also very strong (integration: sixth rank on average in the defense landscape). This position appears to be the reflection of a strategic choice. The company focused on the defense markets while due to its technological specialization it is closer to the field of electronic equipment, which is by definition strongly integrated in the global technological landscape (it is the industry integrating the most circularities);

– Alliant Techsystems: a company with dual technological profile and dual strategy. Alliant Techsystems appears, on the one hand, to be very important for the structuring of TKS, both in its defense component and in its civilian component (self-sufficiency: fifth rank on average in the defense landscape and eighth rank on average in the civilian landscape); on the other hand, Alliant Techsystems seems to play an important role in the technological integration of TKS as a company in the defense domain and as a company in the civilian domain (integration: first rank on average in the defense landscape and 78th rank on average in the civilian landscape). This seems to correspond to the strategy displayed by the group, which involves the harmonious cohabitation of the aerospatial part and of the armament part of its activity, an aspect that is reinforced after the merger with Orbital. A last interesting element of this case is that the company supplies synergies downstream to a greater extent than it is dependent on synergies upstream; this *a priori* confers it a certain technological autonomy.

6.4. Conclusion

Thanks to IGT tools, this chapter made it possible to show the interest of measuring the influence of a TKS for the study of duality. In this theoretical context, several indicators were proposed in relation to both the centrality of cohesion and the egocentricity of TKS.

The analysis of TKS made it possible to propose a new ranking of TKS depending on their dual potentials during the 2010–2012 period. This ranking proved consistent with the one presented in the previous chapter. It enabled pointing out the capacity of the defense knowledge environment to contribute to the dissemination of technologies such as guidance systems, civilian drones or the autonomous car. This demonstrates, using facts, a dual potential already identified in the previous chapter. As already mentioned in Chapter 4, repeating this type of analysis over several years would enable the definition of tendencies that could be useful not only to defense manufacturers for the definition of the dualization strategy, but also to public authorities in directing dual financing.

The results proved their relevance at the company level. Nevertheless, in order to be fully exploitable and to define and detail the recommendations, the latter should be completed by an analysis related to each domain of activity and for each company. The challenge taken on by this study was first of all to show the relevance of the tools in the measurement of the dual potential of companies.

General Conclusion

Since its introduction in the 1980s, duality has become a major preoccupation not only for researchers but also for manufacturers and public authorities. This concept refers to the complex relation between the civilian and defense domains, and more specifically to the links that can be established between actors in these two domains.

The problems related to these links in the technological production are multidimensional: sectorial, organizational, institutional and regulatory. They also concern, particularly when innovation is involved, matters related to technical or technological similarities between the two production environments. These similarities can be analyzed in various ways. Some focus on the technical characteristics of a system, others on the community participating in its elaboration, while still others choose the perspective of institutions.

In this study, dedicated to dual technological innovation, knowledge production, its dissemination and the cognitive proximities that structure the production of a given technological system are relevant inputs. This is how the dual potential of a technology is measured and the interactions between the defense and civilian domains are characterized.

Dual technological innovation is one of the components of duality that raises the question of collaborations between the defense and civilian domains throughout the process of innovation, knowledge elaboration and uses. This aspect of duality has a very specific importance as it enables an engagement with three challenges that defense actors and also civilian actors, inherent to the duality concept, must face.

The first challenge is related to the identification of the perimeter of dual technological innovation. Nowadays, there are many approaches to this subject, but none of them gathers a clear consensus. There are three advantages to the proposed approach. First of all, the approach in terms of innovation systems accounts for the importance of institutional constraints imposed on the innovation process, particularly in the field of defense. Furthermore, systemic framework reveals the complexity of interactions between many actors, which is often a characteristic of dual innovation process. Finally, it offers the possibility of building a framework of analysis the perimeter of which is not predefined.

The two other challenges are methodological and empirical. The first is related to the measurement of duality, as there are presently few tools that can quantify it. Finally, the last challenge resides in the influence of this duality on the innovation process as a whole. Given that technology is at the core of these two challenges and that knowledge often defines a technology in economics, this is how these challenges are addressed. The raw material for the empirical analysis is therefore constituted of these formal and tacit, individual or mutually designed pieces of knowledge. The study of knowledge production in the civilian and defense domains enabled the measurement of their capacity to jointly produce technologies whose characteristics are, if not identical, at least compatible.

While taking a certain number of usage precautions, the originality of this work in addressing these challenges resides in using patent data aggregated at company level. This knowledge-based approach has the advantage of being applicable to any type of technological innovation without *a priori* evaluation of its potential use. This opportunity to use quantitative data allows a distancing from traditional case studies that are normally employed when dealing with this subject. On the other hand, the patent is not an omniscient indicator of company innovation capacities. This is why this approach is a complementary solution to the analysis produced by the experts in technological domains and to monographic studies.

The foundations of the systemic approach to duality rely on a review of the theoretical and empirical literature concerning the technological relations between the civilian and defense domains. After having explored the various definitions of duality – identification of material or intangible supports of duality – the subject of various modalities of duality organization and "governance" was approached. Moreover, the discussion on the various scopes of innovation systems (national, regional or sectorial) enabled the definition of an original framework for dealing with duality.

This work combines these elements in order to propose the concept of dual innovation system (DIS), whose main point of interest is to offer a synthetic perspective on all the characteristics of technological duality, while underlining the complexity of interactions it generates. Indeed, for a specific technology, a DIS is a set of institutions in the defense and civilian domains that contribute to an innovation process in an institutional space constrained by the strategic challenges of defense innovation. It includes all the mechanisms for transfer and formal and informal cooperation that are involved throughout the innovation process; it delimits the dual diffusion potential of a technology in various domains; it underlines the necessity of building a technology-dependent perimeter at the core of this system.

In this context, the analysis then focused on the knowledge dissemination process. This process is particularly detailed, to the extent that it is presented as an essential element of the dual potential of technologies. To this purpose, the reader can refer to the literature on the economics of innovation, leading to an in-depth presentation of the concept of technological system. Considering the specific value assigned to knowledge as structuring element of these systems, the interest in studying how knowledge is disseminated at the scale of these technological systems was pointed out for the analysis of their duality.

This framework of analysis led to the definition of the concept of technological knowledge systems (TKS). Due to this concept, the analysis of technological artifacts can be freed. A TKS corresponds to all the pieces of knowledge that, closely interrelated, are at the origin of synergies in the technological production. This coherent set of knowledge (whether or not founded on scientific principles) associated with specific competences can be used to propose technical solutions that are then combined within one or more technological systems. The TKS is therefore particularly favorable to the analysis of duality, defense systems and their technical characteristics which are often protected as a more or less partial secret. Finally, as each TKS is part of its own innovation approach, each of them is associated with a DIS with a specific profile; this analysis is therefore fully consistent with the proposed framework of analysis.

The empirical analysis unfolds in three stages. First, the identification of TKS relies on tools from economic dominance theory (EDT) and on the concept of knowledge bases, which makes it possible to integrate in the analysis one part of the tacit knowledge employed by companies in order to interconnect component knowledge. The study of TKS made use of knowledge bases of the largest international companies. Thus, in selecting defense companies, tools from IGT make it possible to define 26 TKS specific to defense innovation and with diversified technological profiles.

While not directly specific to duality, the methodological contribution of this chapter was however a cornerstone of this work. Indeed, there is a double interest in the clustering method that it describes: on the one hand, this method can be used to calculate, for each of the two pole combinations, the synergies they generate, taking simultaneously into account the interdependences of these poles and the interdependences in the rest of the structure. Hence, a combination of two poles that is too damaging to the synergetic potential of the rest of the structure achieves a lower score of synergy than another combination that preserves more circularities in the rest of the structure. This makes it possible to assign the highest synergy scores to the combinations of the two most interdependent poles that do not break circularities in the complementary part. On the other hand, it enables a reasoning per layer, through partial subgraphs, which allows the definition of a perimeter that is relevant for the identification of TKSs.

Next in the analysis was an evaluation of the dual potential of 26 TKS. This evaluation used technological coherence theory, which provides tools for the analysis not only of knowledge as individual component but also of architectural knowledge that underlies the articulation of knowledge in TKS. The indicators enable the study of TKS coherence, meaning the way in which their pieces of knowledge are structured. The comparison of this coherence in the domain of defense and in the global knowledge environment with respect to five original indicators makes it possible to calculate cognitive proximities between the defense and civilian domains for each of the 26 TKS and to measure their dual potentials.

According to the empirical results obtained on the studied sample, 17 of the TKS have a significant dual potential. They have various profiles. Each profile is defined by a level of duality and specific knowledge structuring characteristics. Moreover, certain TKS simply show an absence of dual potential for various reasons (from too high defense specificity, limiting any civilian capacity, to specificities of architectural knowledge limiting possible collaborations beyond knowledge transfers).

The last stage expanded the dual analysis of TKS by studying the influence of knowledge both inside a TKS but also, and especially, between a TKS and the technologies related to it, and finally in the network including these technologies and referred to as an "egocentric network". This approach is itself in line with EDT and makes it possible to propose new tools issued from IGT. These tools measure the contribution of defense to these interdependences for a better understanding of the participation of TKS, from a dual perspective, to in structuring of knowledge production both in the defense knowledge environment and in the civilian knowledge environment.

From a more global perspective, there are three main results. The first is a theoretical one: it concerns the above-mentioned framework, which enables approaching technological duality from a systemic perspective. It is the DIS, completed by the TKS.

This theoretical framework shows that the duality of an innovation system depends on the technology that is at the core of this system. This is why each DIS depends on a set of knowledge that defines a technology. The concept of DIS is therefore completed by the concept of TKS. This is how each TKS gives rise to a specific DIS, or how, by defining the TKS as a function of the synergies observed in innovation production, it is possible to measure the dual potential of any technology without preconceptions on the duality of this technology. In other words, it is possible to identify the DIS of any technology.

The second major result is a methodological one, corresponding to the use of tools from mathematical graph theory to analyze duality. A set of new indicators were proposed. They concern, on the one hand, technological coherence theory and, on the other hand, EDT and are used for the measurement of the dual potential of TKS, and for their influence on the innovation process as a whole. This constitutes the third result. Showing not only the compatibility of these approaches but also their high complementarity in the analysis of technological duality, this study opens a new field of research. This shows that the quantitative methods resulting from graph theory and already proven in innovation economics or in the analysis of international trade are applicable to the study of duality, considering all the required precautions.

The third result is empirical, even operational. It is the proposal of a scale of duality built from original tools developed in the thesis. This scale, composed of five indicators relying on technological coherence theory, points out the existence of a *continuum* of duality. Indeed, the analysis indicates that only two TKS have no dual potential. But this does not mean that they exclusively concern the defense or the civilian domain. It is more specifically related to the fact that, for these systems, the potential for relations between the defense and the civilian domains is more similar to technological transfers than to collaboration between defense and civilian domains, which defines a dual innovation process. On the other hand, for all the other systems, it appears that there is systematically a certain similarity in how innovations are produced, which opens the door for a more or less significant duality along any of the studied dimensions. Providing evidence of this continuum of duality is therefore a major empirical result.

This work opens several perspectives. They can be distributed along two axes. First, there are perspectives directly linked to the study object. As previously noted, this DIS is intended to cover all the components of duality throughout the innovation process. But the empirical work focuses on the analysis of knowledge by adopting a global point of view. This could be extended, on the one hand, by investigating the other layers of a DIS related to development, production and to the markets of technological duality. On the other hand, a DIS in relation to a specific technology could also be studied by drawing its perimeter and studying the specific interactions between the civilian and defense domains that operate within it. These complementary approaches to DIS could specifically be used for addressing the subject of companies, for example.

The second perspective is related to tools. This work shows the relevance of mathematical graph theory in addressing questions related to production and particularly to knowledge dissemination. These preoccupations prove to be essential beyond duality. Many other domains related to the economic analysis of innovation geography, problems of industrial convergence or the innovation strategy of companies can be explored using these tools. They consequently open many perspectives for new developments, which can emerge both in the academic and in the operational domains.

References

Abernathy, W.J. (1978). *The Productivity Dilema: Roadblock to Innovation in the Automobile Industry*. Johns Hopkins University Press, Baltimore.

Abrams, D.S., Akcigit, U., Popadak, J. (2013). Patent value and citations: Creative destruction or defensive disruption. PIER Working Paper Archive, University of Pennsylvania.

Acosta, M., Coronado, D., Ferrandiz, E., Marin, M.R., Moreno, P.J. (2017). Patents and dual-use technology: An empirical study of the world's largest defence companies. *Def. Peace Econ.*, 1–19.

Acosta, M., Coronado, D., Marín, R. (2011). Potential dual use of military technology: Doses patents shed light on this process? *Def. Peace Econ.*, 22, 335–349.

Acosta, M., Coronado, D., Marín, R., Prats, P. (2013). Factors affecting the diffusion of patented military technology in the field of weapons and ammunition. *Scientometrics*, 94, 1–22.

Alic, J.A. (1994). The dual use of technology: Concepts and policies. *Technol. Soc.*, 16, 155–172.

Alic, J.A., Branscomb, L.M., Brooks, H., Epstein, G.L., Carter, A.B. (1992). *Beyond Spinoff: Military and Commercial Technologies in a Changing World*. Harvard Business Press, Brighton.

Amable, B. (2003). Les systèmes d'innovation. In *Encyclopédie de l'innovation*, Mustar, P., Penan, H. (eds). Economica, Paris, 367–382.

Ansoff, H.I. (1957). Strategies for diversification. *Harv. Bus. Rev.*, 35, 113–124.

Ansoff, H.I. (1965). *Corporate Strategy: Business Policy for Growth and Expansion*. McGraw-Hill, New York.

Arrow, K. (1962). Economic welfare and the allocation of resources for invention. In *The Rate and Direction of Inventive Activity*, Nelson, R.R. (ed.). Princeton University Press, Princeton, 609–625.

Asheim, B.T., Coenen, L. (2005). Knowledge bases and regional innovation systems: Comparing Nordic clusters. *Res. Policy*, 34, 1173–1190.

Autant-Bernard, C., Massard, N. (2000). Scientific interactions, geographic spillovers and innovation an empirical study on the French case. ERSA Conference Paper. European Regional Science Association, Barcelona.

Autant-Bernard, C., Massard, N., Cowan, R. (2014). Editors' introduction to spatial knowledge networks: Structure, driving forces and innovative performances. *Ann. Reg. Sci.*, 53, 315–323.

Avadikyan, A., Cohendet, P. (2005). L'émergence d'une économie de la défense fondée sur la connaissance : quelques leçons tirées des réformes au Royaume-Uni. *Revue d'économie industrielle*, 112, 65–82.

Ayerbe, C., Lazaric, N., Callois, M., Mitkova, L. (2012). Nouveaux enjeux d'organisation de la propriété intellectuelle dans les industries complexes. Une discussion à partir du cas Thales. *Revue d'économie industrielle*, 1(137), 9–42.

Ayerbe, C., Lazaric, N., Callois, M., Mitkova, L. (2014). The new challenges of organizing intellectual property in complex industries: A discussion based on the case of Thales. *Technovation*, 34, 232–241.

Azulay, I., Lerner, M., Tishler, A. (2002). Converting military technology through corporate entrepreneurship. *Res. Policy*, 31, 419–435.

Bainée, J. (2013). Conditions d'émergence et de diffusion de l'automobile électrique : une analyse en termes de "bien-système territorialisé". PhD Thesis, Pantheon-Sorbonne University Paris 1.

Bavelas, A. (1948). A mathematical model for group structures. *Hum. Organ.*, 7, 16–30.

Belin, J. (2015). La R&D des entreprises de défense dans le système national d'innovation français. *Déf. Ind*, 3, 1–3.

Belin, J., Guille, M. (2008). R&D et innovation en France: quel financement pour les entreprises de la Défense ? *Innovations*, 28, 33–59.

Bellais, R. (2005). Recherche et défense, vers un nouveau partenariat ? *Innovations*, 21, 145.

Bellais, R. (2014). *The Evolving Boundaries of Defence: An Assessment of Recent Shifts in Defence Activities*. Emerald Group Publishing Limited, Bingley.

Bellais, R., Guichard, R. (2006). Defense innovation, technology transfer and public policy. *Def. Peace Econ.*, 17, 273–286.

Berge, C. (1958). *La théorie des graphes*. Dunod, Paris.

Bergek, A., Hekkert, M., Jacobsson, S. (2008a). Functions in innovation systems: A framework for analysing energy system dynamics and identifying goals for system-building activities by entrepreneurs and policymakers. In *Innovations for a Low Carbon Economy: Economic, Institutional and Management Approaches*, Foxon, T.J., Köhler, J. (eds). Elgar Publishing, Cheltenham, 79–111.

Bergek, A., Jacobsson, S., Carlsson, B., Lindmark, S., Rickne, A. (2008b). Analyzing the functional dynamics of technological innovation systems: A scheme of analysis. *Res. Policy*, 37, 407–429.

Bergek, A., Jacobsson, S., Hekkert, M., Smith, K. (2010). Functionality of innovation systems as a rationale for and guide to innovation policy. Working document, IMIT/RIDE, 117–146.

Besancenot, D., Vranceanu, R. (2006). European defence firms: The information barrier on private finance. *Def. Peace Econ.*, 17, 23–36.

Bijker, W.E. (2010). How is technology made? – That is the question! *Camb. J. Econ.*, 34, 63–76.

Bijker, W.E., Hughes, T.P., Pinch, T., Douglas, D.G. (2012). *The Social Construction of Technological Systems: New Directions in the Sociology and History of Technology*. MIT Press Cambridge, Massachusetts.

Bonacich, P., Lloyd, P. (2001). Eigenvector-like measures of centrality for asymmetric relations. *Soc. Netw.*, 23, 191–201.

Bonomo, J., Lowell, J.F., Pinder, J., Webb, K.W., Saul, J., Cannon, P., McCombs, J.S., Adamson, D.M. (1998). *Monitoring and Controlling the International Transfer of Technology* [Online]. Available at: https://www.rand.org/pubs/monograph_reports/MR979.html [Accessed 7 August 2019].

Bouvier-Patron, P. (1994). L'application des concepts de *lock-in* et de "barrières à la mobilité" à une théorie des réseaux d'entreprise. *Rev. Fr. d'économie*, 9(1), 205–232.

Bouvier-Patron, P. (2015). FabLab et extension de la forme réseau: vers une nouvelle dynamique industrielle? *Innovations*, 2(47), 165–188.

Braddon, D. (1999). Commercial applications of military R&D: U.S. and EU programs compared. Thesis, University of the West of England, Bristol.

Bresnahan, T. (2010). General Purpose Technologies. In *Handbook of the Economics of Innovation,* Bronwyn, H.H., Rosenberg, N. (eds). Elsevier, Oxford, 761–791.

Buesa, M. (2001). Controlling the international exchanges of armaments and dual. *Def. Peace Econ.*, 12, 439–464.

Callon, M. (1991). Réseaux technico-économiques et irréversibilités. In *Les figures de l'irréversibilité en économie*, Boyer, R., Chavance, J., Godard, O. (eds). Editions de l'Ecole des hautes études en sciences sociales, Paris, 195–230.

Callon, M., Laredo, P., Rabeharisoa, V., Gonard, T., Leray, T. (1992). The management and evaluation of technological programs and the dynamics of techno-economic networks: The case of the AFME. *Res. Policy*, 21, 215–236.

Cantner, U., Pyka, A. (2001). Classifying technology policy from an evolutionary perspective. *Res. Policy*, 30, 759–775.

Carlsson, B., Jacobsson, S., Holmén, M., Rickne, A. (2002). Innovation systems: Analytical and methodological issues. *Res. Policy*, 31, 233–245.

Carlsson, B., Stankiewicz, R. (1991). On the nature, function and composition of technological systems. *J. Evol. Econ.*, 1, 93–118.

Cartwright, D., Harary, F., Norman, R. (1965). *Structural Models: An Introduction to the Theory of Directed Graphs*. Wiley, New York.

Cecere, G., Corrocher, N., Gossart, C., Ozman, M. (2014). Technological pervasiveness and variety of innovators in Green ICT: A patent-based analysis. *Res. Policy*, 43, 1827–1839.

Chakrabarti, A.K., Anyanwu, C.L. (1993). Defense R&D, technology, and economic performance: A longitudinal analysis of the U.S. experience. *IEEE Trans. Eng. Manag.*, 40, 136–145.

Chakrabarti, A.K., Dror, I., Eakabuse, N. (1993). Interorganizational transfer of knowledge: an analysis of patent citations of a defense firm. *IEEE Trans. Eng. Manag.*, 40, 91–94.

Chandler Jr., A.D. (1962, 1998). *Strategy and Structure: Chapters in the History of the American Industrial Enterprise*. MIT Press Cambridge, Cambridge.

Chesnais, F. (1993). The French national system of innovation. In *National Innovation Systems: A Comparative Analysis*, Nelson, R.R. (ed.). Oxford University Press, Oxford, 192–229.

Chesnais, F., Serfati, C. (1992). *L'armement en France: genèse, ampleur et coût d'une industrie*. Nathan, Paris.

Chinworth, M.W. (2000a). Country Survey XIII: Japan's security posture and defense industry prospects. *Def. Peace Econ.*, 11, 369–401.

Chinworth, M.W. (2000b). *Perception Gaps: An Assessment of Dual-Use Technology Models in Japan and the United States*. Cranfield University, Silsoe.

Chu, A.C., Lai, C.-C. (2012). On the growth and welfare effects of defense R&D. *J. Public Econ. Theory*, 14, 473–492.

Cohen, G. (1997). Cohérence technologique, aspects structurel et temporel: application au programme spatial europeen. PhD Thesis, University of Strasbourg 1.

Cohen, W.M., Levinthal, D.A. (1990). Absorptive capacity: A new perspective on learning and innovation, administrative science quarterly. *Technology, Organizations, and Innovation*, 35(1), 128–152.

Cohen, W.M., Nelson, R.R., Walsh, J.P. (2002). Links and impacts: The influence of public research on industrial R&D. *Manag. Sci.*

Cohendet, P., Gaffard, J.-L. (2010). Coordonner autant qu'inciter pour connaître, Working document, HAL.

Cooke, P., Gomez Uranga, M., Etxebarria, G. (1997). Regional innovation systems: Institutional and organisational dimensions. *Res. Policy*, 26, 475–491.

Cournot, A.A. (1847). *De l'origine et des limites de la correspondance entre l'algèbre et la géométrie*. Hachette, Paris.

Cowan, R., Foray, D. (1995). Quandaries in the economics of dual technologies and spillovers from military to civilian research and development. *Res. Policy*, 24, 851–868.

Cowan, R., Foray, D. (1997). The economics of codification and the diffusion of knowledge. *Ind. Corp. Change*, 6, 595–622.

Curnow, R.C., Moring, G.G. (1968). "Project Sappho": A study in industrial innovation. *Futures*, 1, 82–90.

Daguzan, J. (2001). Technologies duales et défense, entre politique et management. *Armement-Rech. Civ. Rech. Def.*, 76, 142–148.

David, P.A. (2004). Understanding the emergence of "open science" institutions: Functionalist economics in historical context. *Ind. Corp. Change*, 13, 571–589.

De Bandt, J. (2002). L'émergence du nouveau système technique ou socio-technique. *Rev. d'Économie Ind.*, 100, 9–38.

Defourny, J., Thorbecke, E. (1984). Structural path analysis and multiplier decomposition within a social accounting matrix framework. *Econ. J.*, 94, 111–136.

Depeyre, C. (2013). Boeing Boeing: la dualité civil-militaire source d'un rebond stratégique dans l'ère post-guerre froide. *Entrep. Hist.*, 73, 58–74.

Depeyre, C., Dumez, H. (2010). The role of architectural players in coopetition: The case of the US defense industry – Google Research. In *Coopetition: Winning Strategies for the 21st Century*. Yami, S., Castaldo, S., Battista Dagnino, G., Le Roy, F. (eds). Edward Elgar Publishing, Northampton.

Dernis, H., Dosso, M., Hervás, F., Millot, V., Squicciarini, M., Vezzani, A. (2015). World corporate top R&D investors: Innovation and IP bundles. Document, European Union/OECD.

Dernis, H., Khan, M. (2004). Triadic patent families methodology, OECD working paper.

Deyle, H.-G., Grupp, H. (2005). Commuters and the regional assignment of innovative activities: A methodological patent study of German districts. *Res. Policy*, 34, 221–234.

Dibiaggio, L., Meschi, P.X. (2010). *Le management dans l'économie de la connaissance*. Pearson Education, Paris.

Doloreux, D., Bitard, P. (2005). Les systèmes régionaux d'innovation: discussion critique. *Géographie Économie Société*, 7, 21–36.

Dombrowski, P.J., Gholz, E., Ross, A.L. (2002). Military Transformation and the Defense Industry after Next: The Defense Industrial Implications of Network-Centric Warfare. U.S. Naval War College, Newport.

Dosi, G. (1982). Technological paradigms and technological trajectories: A suggested interpretation of the determinants and directions of technical change. *Res. Policy*, 11, 147–162.

Dosi, G. (1988). Sources, procedures, and microeconomic effects of innovation. *J. Econ. Lit.*, 1120–1171.

Dosi, G. (2009). Economic theory to the understanding of a knowledge-based economy. *Econ. Impact Knowl.*, 123, 123–130.

Dosi, G., Marengo, L., Pasquali, C. (2006). How much should society fuel the greed of innovators? *Res. Policy*, 35, 1110–1121.

Dosi, G., Nelson, R.R. (2010). Technical change and industrial dynamics as evolutionary processes. In *Handbook of the Economics of Innovation*, Hall, B.H., Rosenberg, N. (eds). Elsevier, Oxford, 51–127.

Droff, J. (2013). Technological change and disruptive trends in the support of defense systems in France. *J. Innov. Econ.*, 12, 79.

Edquist, C. (2001). The systems of innovation approach and innovation policy: An account of the state of the art. *DRUID Conference*, Aalborg, 12–15.

Edquist, C. (ed.) (1997). *Systems of Innovation: Technologies, Institutions, and Organizations*. Pinter, London.

El Younsi, H., Lebert, D., Meunier, F.-X., Zyla, C. (2015). Exploration, exploitation et cohérence technologique. *Économique Appliquée*, 68, 187–204.

Elidrissi, D., Hauch, V. (2008). Systèmes régionaux d'innovation: superpositions et articulations: l'exemple de Sophia-Antipolis. *Rev. Sci. Gest.*, 233, 59.

Elzen, B., Enserink, B., Smit, W.A. (1996). Socio-technical networks: How a technology studies approach may help to solve problems related to technical change. *Soc. Stud. Sci.*, 26, 95–141.

Elzen, B., Geels, F.W., Green, K. (eds) (2004). *System Innovation and the Transition to Sustainability: Theory, Evidence and Policy.* Edward Elgar Publishing, Cheltenham.

Fan, J.P., Lang, L.H. (2000). The measurement of relatedness: An application to corporate diversification. *J. Bus.*, 73, 629–660.

Farjoun, M. (1994). Beyond industry boundaries: Human expertise, diversification and resource-related industry groups. *Organ. Sci.*, 5, 185–199.

Fauchart, E. (2003). On knowledge sharing patterns among rival firms: the case of knowledge on safety. *DRUID Summer Conference*, Copenhagen.

Fauchart, E., Keilbach, M. (2009). Testing a model of exploration and exploitation as innovation strategies. *Small Bus. Econ.*, 33, 257–272.

Fink, C., Hamdan-Livramento, I., Raffo, J. (2015). Rapport 2015 sur la propriété intellectuelle dans le monde. Report, OMPI, Geneva.

Fiott, D. (2014). The three effects of dual-use: Firms, capabilities, and governance. *ISSUE Briefs*, 21, 1–4.

Flament, C., Pinard, M., Breton, R., Fontaine, F. (1963). *Applications of Graph Theory to Group Structure*. Prentice Hall, Upper Saddle River.

Flamm, K. (1988). *Creating the Computer: Government, Industry, and High Technology*. Brookings Institution Press, Washington.

Fleming, L., Sorenson, O. (2001). Technology as a complex adaptive system: Evidence from patent data. *Res. Policy*, 30, 1019–1039.

Foray, D. (1990). Recherche et technologie militaires: la remise en cause d'un modèle? *Rev. d'Économie Ind.*, 53, 99–114.

Foray, D., Guichard, R. (2001). Le PEA: nouvel outil de politique technologique et de gestion de l'innovation de défense dans un environnement turbulent [Online]. Available at: https://hal.archives-ouvertes.fr/hal-00292963/document.

Foss, N.J., Christensen, J.F. (2001). A market-process approach to corporate coherence. *Manag. Decis. Econ.*, 22, 213–226.

Freeman, C. (1988). Main objectives and epistémological considerations. In *Technical Change and Economic Theory*. Dosi, G., Freeman, C., Nelson, R., Silverberg, G., Soete, L. (eds). Sant'Anna School of Advanced Studies, Pise.

Freeman, C. (1991). Networks of innovators: A synthesis of research issues. *Res. Policy*, 20, 499–514.

Freeman, C., Soete, L. (1997). *The Economics of Industrial Innovation*. Psychology Press, Hove.

Freeman, L.C. (2004). *The Development of Social Network Analysis*. ΣP Empirical Press, Vancouver.

Friedkin, N.E. (1991). Theoretical foundations for centrality measures. *Am. J. Sociol.*, 6, 1478–1504.

Gagnepain, J.-J. (2001). Recherches publiques civile et de défense. *Armement-Rech. Civ. Rech. Def.*, 76, 25–29.

Galbraith, C.S., DeNoble, A.F., Ehrlich, S.B. (2004). "Spin-in" technology transfer for small R&D bio-technology firms: The case of bio-defense. *J. Technol. Transf.*, 29, 377–382.

Gallié, E.-P., Mérindol, V. (2015). Quand la quantité de brevets ne va pas de pair avec la qualité: l'exemple du secteur de l'Aéronautique et de la Défense. *Collection Résultats et recherches*, 3, 1–13.

Gallo, J. (2006). Information et pouvoir dans les organisations: un essai de quantification par la théorie des graphes d'influence. Pantheon-Sorbonne University Paris 1.

Gansler, J.S. (1989). *Affording Defense*. MIT Press, Cambridge.

Gholz, E. (2002). America's innovation advantage: systems integration in the U.S. defense industry. American Political Science Association, Boston.

Gille, B. (1978). *Histoires des techniques: techniques et civilisation, technique et sciences*. Gallimard, Paris.

Gorz, A. (2003). *L'immatériel: connaissance, valeur et capital*. Galilée, Paris.

Goyal, V.K., Lehn, K., Racic, S. (2002). Growth opportunities and corporate debt policy: the case of the U.S. defense industry. *J. Financ. Econ.*, 64, 35–59.

Guichard, R. (2004a). Éléments pour un repositionnement de la R&D de défense au sein du système d'innovation français. *Rev. d'Économie Ind.*, 108, 7–20

Guichard, R. (2004b). Quelles modalités pour une politique duale efficace en France? *Innovations*, 19, 37.

Guichard, R., Heisbourg, F. (2004). *Recherche militaire: vers un nouveau modèle de gestion?* Economica, Paris.

Guillou, S., Lazaric, N., Longhi, C., Rochhia, S. (2009). The French defence industry in the knowledge management era: A historical overview and evidence from empirical data. *Res. Policy*, 38, 170–180.

Gummett, P., Reppy, J. (eds). (1988). *The Relations between Defence and Civil Technologies*. Springer, The Netherlands.

Gutman, F. (2001). Une dualité nécessaire. *Armement-Rech. Civ. Rech. Def.*, 67, 10–16.

Hall, B.H., Jaffe, A.B., Trajtenberg, M. (2005). Market value and patent citations. *RAND J. Econ.*, 36(1), 16–38.

Ham, R.M., Linden, G., Appleyard, M.M. (1998). The evolving role of semiconductor consortia in the United States and Japan. *Calif. Manage. Rev.*, 41, 137–163.

Harary, F., Norman, R.Z. (1953). *Graph Theory as a Mathematical Model in Social Science.* Institute for Social Research, Cambridge.

Henderson, R., Jaffe, A.B., Trajtenberg, M. (1998). Universities as a source of commercial technology: A detailed analysis of university patenting, 1965–1988. *Rev. Econ. Stat.*, 80, 119–127.

Henderson, R.M., Clark, K.B. (1990). Architectural innovation: The reconfiguration of existing product technologies and the failure of established firms. *Adm. Sci. Q.*, 35, 9–30

Hobday, M. (1998). Product complexity, innovation and industrial organisation. *Res. Policy*, 26, 689–710.

Hobday, M., Davies, A., Prencipe, A. (2005). Systems integration: A core capability of the modern corporation. *Ind. Corp. Change*, 14, 1109–1143.

Hobday, M., Rush, H., Tidd, J. (2000). Innovation in complex products and system. *Research Policy*, 29(7–8), 793–804.

Jaffe, A.B. (2000). The US patent system in transition: Policy innovation and the innovation process. *Res. Policy*, 29, 531–557.

Jaffe, A.B., (1986). Technological opportunity and spillovers of R&D: Evidence from firms' patents, profits, and market value. *Am. Econ. Rev.*, 76, 984–1001.

Jaffe, A.B., Trajtenberg, M. (1996). Flows of knowledge from universities and federal laboratories: Modeling the flow of patent citations over time and across institutional and geographic boundaries. *Proc. Natl. Acad. Sci. USA*, 93, 12671–12677.

Jaffe, A.B., Trajtenberg, M. (2002). *Patents, Citations, and Innovations: A Window on the Knowledge Economy.* MIT Press, Cambridge.

Jaffe, A.B., Trajtenberg, M., Henderson, R. (1993). Geographic localization of knowledge spillovers as evidenced by patent citations. *Q.J. Econ.*, 108, 577–598.

Kline, S.J., Rosenberg, N. (1986). An overview of innovation. Posit. Sum Strategy Harnessing Technol. *Econ. Growth*, 14, 640.

Krafft, J., Quatraro, F., Saviottti, P.-P. (2011). The Knowledge Base Evolution in Biotechnology: A Social Network Analysis. *Economics of Innovation and New Technology*, 20(5), 445–475.

Kuhlmann, S. (2001). Future governance of innovation policy in Europe – three scenarios. *Res. Policy, Innovations in European and US innovation Policy*, 30, 953–976.

Kulve (te), H., Smit, W.A. (2003). Civilian-military co-operation strategies in developing new technologies. *Res. Policy*, 32, 955–970.

Lafon, A. (2001). L'ONERA: un acteur et un intégrateur de la recherche duale. *Armement-Rech. Civ. Rech. Def.*, 76, 119–124.

Lantner, R. (1972). Recherche sur l'interprétation du déterminant d'une matrice *input-output*. *Rev. D'économie Polit.*, 82, 435–442.

Lantner, R. (1974). *Théorie de la dominance économique*. Dunod, Paris.

Lantner, R., Lebert, D. (2013a). Structural analysis: The amplification by loops and circuits in the representative graphs of square matrices. *International Conference on Matrix Analysis and Applications*, Konya.

Lantner, R., Lebert, D. (2013b). Dominance, dependence and interdependence in linear structures. A theoretical model and an application to the international trade flows. Working document, Pantheon-Sorbonne University Paris 1.

Lantner, R., Lebert, D. (2015). Dominance et amplification des influences dans les structures linéaires. *Économique Appliquée*, 68, 143–165.

Lapierre, G. (2001). Similitudes et particularités de la recherche civile et de défense dans le domaine des communications acoustiques sous-marines. *Armement-Rech. Civ. Rech. Def.*, 76, 83–92.

Lazaric, N., Mérindol, V., Rochhia, S. (2011). Changes in the French Defence Innovation System: New roles and capabilities for the Government Agency for Defence. *Ind. Innov.*, 18, 509–530.

Le Goff, R., Carluer, F. (2002). NTIC et apprentissage multimodal localisé: vers la constitution d'un "Espace Serviciel"? *Économie Appliquée*, 3, 135–171.

Leavitt, H.J. (1951). Some effects of certain communication patterns on group performance. *J. Abnorm. Soc. Psychol.*, 46, 38.

Lebert, D. (2016). Théorie de la dominance économique et flux intra- et inter-territoriaux de connaissances technologiques. *Innovations*, 50, 43.

Lebert, D., Goff, R.L., Meunier, F.-X., Zyla, C. (2016). Théorie de la dominance économique et dynamiques cognitives des territoires. *Séminaires du Centre de recherche en gestion*. École polytechnique, Palaiseau.

Lebert, D., Meunier, F.-X. (2017). Introverted or extroverted? Profiles of regional technological connectedness in Europe. *WEAI 92nd Annual Conference*, San Diego.

Lebert, D., Younsi, H.E. (2015). Théorie de la dominance économique: indicateurs structuraux sur les relations interafricaines. *Économique Appliquée*, 68, 167–186.

Lequeux, F. (2002). Concurrence et effets de dominance économique dans l'industrie multimédia. PhD Thesis, Pantheon-Sorbonne University Paris 1.

Levin, R.C., Cohen, W.M., Mowery, D.C. (1985). R&D appropriability, opportunity, and market structure: New evidence on some Schumpeterian hypotheses. *Am. Econ. Rev.*, 75, 20–24.

Leydesdorff, L., Alkemade, F., Heimeriks, G., Hoekstra, R. (2015). Patents as instruments for exploring innovation dynamics: Geographic and technological perspectives on "photovoltaic cells". *Scientometrics*, 102, 629–651.

Lichtenberg, F.R. (1995). Economics of defense R&D. *Handb. Def. Econ.*, 1, 431–457.

Lu, W.-M., Kweh, Q.L., Nourani, M., Huang, F.-W. (2015). Evaluating the efficiency of dual-use technology development programs from the R&D and socio-economic perspectives. *Omega*, 62, 82–92.

Luce, R.D., Perry, A.D. (1949). A method of matrix analysis of group structure. *Psychometrika*, 14, 95–116.

Lundvall, B.-Å. (1985). *Product Innovation and User-Producer Interaction.* Aalborg University Press, Aalborg.

Lundvall, B.-Å. (1992). *National Innovation System: Towards a Theory of Innovation and Interactive Learning.* Pinter, London.

Lundvall, B.-Å. (2010). *National Systems of Innovation: Toward a Theory of Innovation and Interactive Learning.* Anthem Press, London.

MacKenzie, D.A. (1993). *Inventing Accuracy: A Historical Sociology of Nuclear Missile Guidance.* MIT Press, Cambridge.

MacKenzie, D.A., Wajcman, J. (eds). (1999). *The Social Shaping of Technology*, Open University Press, Buckingham.

Malerba, F. (2002). Sectoral systems of innovation and production. *Res. Policy*, 31, 247–264.

Mansfield, E. (1998). Academic research and industrial innovation: An update of empirical findings. *Res. Policy*, 26, 773–776.

Mansfield, E., Schwartz, M., Wagner, S. (1981). Imitation costs and patents: An empirical study. *Econ. J.*, 91, 907–918.

March, J.G. (1991). Exploration and exploitation in organizational learning. *Organ. Sci.*, 2, 71–87.

Markard, J., Hekkert, M., Jacobsson, S. (2015). The technological innovation systems framework: Response to six criticisms. *Environ. Innov. Soc. Transit.*, 16, 76–86.

Markard, J., Truffer, B. (2008). Technological innovation systems and the multi-level perspective: Towards an integrated framework. *Res. Policy*, 37, 596–615.

Massard, N., Mehier, C. (2009). Proximity and innovation through an "accessibility to knowledge". *Lens. Reg. Stud.*, 43, 77–88.

Massard, N., Torre, A., Crevoisier, O. (2004). Proximité géographique et innovation. In *Économie de Proximités*, Pecqueur, B., Zimmermann, J.B. (eds). Hermes-Lavoisier, Paris.

Meier, O., Hunger, I. (2014). Between control and cooperation: Dual-use, technology transfers and the non-proliferation of weapons of mass destruction. Master's Thesis, University of Hamburg.

Mérindol, V. (2004). R&D de défense et coordination civile-militaire. In *L'innovation et l'économie contemporaine: espaces cognitifs et territoriaux*, Uzunidis, D. (ed.). De Boeck Supérieur, Brussels, 85–113.

Mérindol, V. (2005). La défense dans les réseaux d'innovation: une analyse en termes de compétences. *Rev. d'Économie Ind.*, 112, 45–64.

Mérindol, V. (2010). New approaches for military innovation in knowledge-based economics: An inquiry into the new role of defence in innovation processes [Online]. Available at: http://www.cerna.mines-paristech.fr/Donnees/data04/470-merindol-submit-2-LRP-v27.pdf.

Mérindol, V. (2014). Gouvernance de l'innovation: une analyse de la cohérence des dispositifs de coordination à travers la gestion des connaissances. PhD Thesis, University of Strasbourg 1.

Mérindol, V., Fortune, E. (2009). Analyse des informations disponibles dans la base Patstat. *OST – Observatoire des sciences et des techniques*, 1, 1–16.

Mérindol, V., Versailles, D.W. (2007). Explanations of the triptych government/industry/academic. In *Management of Technology: New Directions in Technology Management*, Sherif, M.H., Khalil, T.M. (eds). Elsevier, Oxford, 137–155.

Mérindol, V., Versailles, D.W. (2010). Dual-use as knowledge-oriented policy: France during the 1990-2000s. *Int. J. Technol. Manag.*, 50, 80–98.

Mérindol, V., Versailles, D.W. (2015a). La dualité dans la stratégie des entreprises. *Ecodef*, 70, 1–6.

Mérindol, V., Versailles, D.W. (2015b). La cohérence technologies-produits au sein des firmes multi-technologiques: le rôle clé des portefeuilles de business models. *XXIVe Conférence internationale de management stratégique*, Paris, France.

Meunier, F.-X. (2019). Construction of an operational concept of technological military/civilian duality. *J. Innov. Econ.*, 29(159), 159–182.

Meunier, F.-X., Zyla, C. (2016). Firm growth and knowledge flows: Comparative analysis between defence and civil areas. *J. Innov. Econ. Manag.*, 20, 89–108.

Ministre de la défense (2006). Projet de loi de finance 2006, programme 191. Report, French Ministry of Defense. Available at: http://alize.finances.gouv.fr/budget/plf 2006/bleus/pdf/DBGPGMPGM191.pdf.

Molas-Gallart, J. (1997). Which way to go? Defence technology and the diversity of "dual-use" technology transfer. *Res. Policy*, 26, 367–385.

Molas-Gallart, J. (1998). Defence procurement as an industrial policy tool: The Spanish experience. *Def. Peace Econ.*, 9, 63–81.

Molas-Gallart, J., Sinclair, T. (1999). From technology generation to technology transfer: The concept and reality of the "dual-use technology centres". *Technovation*, 19, 661–671.

Molas-Gallart, J., Tang, P. (2006). Ownership matters: Intellectual property, privatization and innovation. *Res. Policy*, 35, 200–212.

Montgomery, C.A. (1994). Corporate diversification. *J. Econ. Perspect.*, 8, 163–178.

Moraillon, H. (2001). Dualité de la recherche aéronautique: mythe ou réalité? *Armement-Rech. Civ. Rech. Def.*, 76, 113–118.

Moura, S. (2011). L'État dans le financement de la R&D militaire des entreprises. *Ecodef*, 54, 1–4.

Mowery, D.C. (2009). National security and national innovation systems. *J. Technol. Transf.*, 34, 455.

Mowery, D.C. (2010). Military R&D and innovation. In *Handbook of the Economics of Innovation*, Hall, B.H., Rosenberg, N. (eds). Elsevier, Oxford, 1219–1256.

Mowery, D.C., Rosenberg, N. (1991). *Technology and the Pursuit of Economic Growth*. Cambridge University Press, Cambridge.

Nasiriyar, M., Nesta, L., Dibiaggio, L. (2013). The moderating role of the complementary nature of technological resources in the diversification-performance relationship. *Ind. Corp. Change*, 23, 1357–1380.

Nelson, R.R. (1992). National innovation systems: A retrospective on a study. *Industrial and Corporate Change*, 1(2), 347–374.

Nelson, R.R., Winter, S.G. (1975). Growth theory from an evolutionary perspective: The differential productivity puzzle. *Am. Econ. Rev.*, 65(2), 338–344.

Nesta, L., Saviotti, P.-P. (2005). Coherence of the knowledge base and the firm's innovative performance: Evidence from the U.S. pharmaceutical industry. *J. Ind. Econ.*, 53, 123–142.

Nesta, L., Saviotti, P.-P. (2006). Firm knowledge and market value in biotechnology. *Ind. Corp. Change*, 15, 625–652.

Niosi, J. (2002). National systems of innovations are "x-efficient" (and x-effective): Why some are slow learners. *Res. Policy*, 31, 291–302.

OECD (2005). Oslo Manual. OECD, Paris.

Olsson, O. (2000). Knowledge as a set in idea space: An epistemological view on growth. *J. Econ. Growth*, 5, 253–275.

Penrose, E.T. (1959). *The Theory of the Growth of the Firm*. Sharpe, New York.

Perroux, F. (1948). Esquisse d'une théorie de l'économie dominante. *Économie Appliquée*, 1, 243–300.

Perroux, F. (1973). L'effet d'entraînement: de l'analyse au repérage quantitatif. *Économie Appliquée*, 7, 307–320.

Perroux, F. (1994). *Pouvoir et économie généralisée*. PUG, Grenoble.

Pinch, T.J., Bijker, W.E. (1984). The social construction of facts and artefacts: Or how the sociology of science and the sociology of technology might benefit each other. *Soc. Stud. Sci.*, 14, 399–441.

Piscitello, L. (2000). Relatedness and coherence in technological and product diversification of the world's largest firms. *Struct. Change Econ. Dyn.*, 11, 295–315.

Piscitello, L. (2005). Corporate diversification, coherence and firm innovative performance. *Rev. d'Économie Ind.*, 110, 127–148.

Polanyi, M. (1983). *The Tacit Dimension*. University of Chicago Press, Chicago.

Ponsard, C. (1967). Les graphes de transfert et l'analyse économique des systèmes interrégionaux (suite). *Rev. Économique*, 18, 543–575.

Ponsard, C. (1968). De l'influence de paramètres singuliers sur le comportement d'un système linéaire de flux interrégionaux. *Revue d'économie politique*, 78(4), 567–605.

Porter, M.E. (1985). *The Competitive Advantage: Creating and Sustaining Superior Performance*. Free Press, New York.

Powell, W.W., Giannella, E. (2010). Collective invention and inventor networks. In *Handbook of the Economics of Innovation*, Hall, B.H., Rosenberg, N. (eds). Elsevier, Oxford, 575–605.

Prencipe, A. (1997). Technological competencies and product's evolutionary dynamics: A case study from the aero-engine industry. *Res. Policy*, 25, 1261–1276.

Prencipe, A. (2000). Breadth and depth of technological capabilities in CoPS: The case of the aircraft engine control system. *Res. Policy*, 29, 895–911.

Quenzer, A. (2001). La dualité: ses fluctuations et son nouveau souffle. *Armement-Rech. Civ. Rech. Def.*, 76, 42–47.

Reed, M.I. (2001). Organization, trust and control: A realist analysis. *Organ. Stud.*, 22, 201–228.

Robins, J., Wiersema, M.F. (1995). A resource-based approach to the multibusiness firm: Empirical analysis of portfolio interrelationships and corporate financial performance. *Strateg. Manag. J.*, 16, 277–299.

Rondi, L., Vannoni, D. (2005). Are EU leading firms returning to core business? Evidence on refocusing and relatedness in a period of market integration. *Rev. Ind. Organ.*, 27, 125–145.

Rosenberg, N. (1976). *Perspectives on Technology.* Cambridge University Press, Cambridge.

Rumelt, R.P. (1974). *Strategy, Structure, and Economic Performance.* Harvard University Press, Cambridge.

Sachwald, F. (1999). Defence industry restructuring: The end of an economic exception. IFRI, Paris.

Salancik, G.R. (1986). An index of subgroup influence in dependency networks. *Adm. Sci. Q.*, 31, 194–211.

Sapolsky, H.M. (2003). Inventing systems integration. In *The Business of System Integration*, Davies, A., Hobday, M. (eds). Oxford University Press, Oxford, 15–34.

Schumpeter, J. (1911). *Théorie de l'évolution économique: recherches sur le profit, le crédit, l'intérêt et le cycle de la conjoncture.* Dalloz, Paris.

Serfati, C. (2005). Défense et politique technologique: quelques questions en débat. *Innovations*, 21, 21–41.

Serfati, C. (2008). Le rôle de l'innovation de Défense dans le système national d'innovation de la France. *Innovations*, 28, 61.

Sharif, N. (2006). Emergence and development of the National Innovation Systems concept. *Res. Policy*, 35, 745–766.

Smith, K. (2000). Innovation as a systemic phenomenon: Rethinking the role of policy. *Enterp. Innov. Manag. Stud.*, 1, 73–102.

Sorenson, O., Fleming, L. (2004). Science and the diffusion of knowledge. *Res. Policy*, 33, 1615–1634.

Storper, M. (1995). Regional technology coalitions an essential dimension of national technology policy. *Res. Policy*, 24, 895–911.

Stowsky, J. (2004). Secrets to shield or share? New dilemmas for military R&D policy in the digital age. *Res. Policy*, 33, 257–269.

Teece, D.J. (1986). Profiting from technological innovation: Implications for integration, collaboration, licensing and public policy. *Res. Policy*, 15, 285–305.

Teece, D.J., Rumelt, R., Dosi, G., Winter, S. (1994). Understanding corporate coherence. *J. Econ. Behav. Organ.*, 23, 1–30.

Trajtenberg, M. (1990). A penny for your quotes: Patent citations and the value of innovations. *RAND J. Econ.*, 21, 172–187.

Trajtenberg, M. (2006). Defense R&D in the anti-terrorist era. *Def. Peace Econ.*, 17, 177–199.

Tucker, J.B. (1994). Dilemmas of a dual-use technology: Toxins in medicine and warfare. *Polit. Life Sci.*, 3(1), 51–62.

Ulrich, K. (1995). The role of product architecture in the manufacturing firm. *Res. Policy*, 24, 419–440.

US Congress (1990). Arming our allies: Cooperation and competition in defense technology. Office of Technology Assessment, Washington, DC.

Utterback, J.M., Abernathy, W.J. (1975). A dynamic model of process and product innovation. *Omega*, 3(6), 424–441.

Uzunidis, D., Bailly, M.A. (2005). Politiques de recherche et innovation militaire: Schumpeter *versus* Smith aux États-Unis et en Europe. *Innovations*, 21, 43.

Versailles, D., Mérindol, V. (2014). *La dualité dans les entreprises de défense*. ESG Management School, Paris.

Verspagen, B. (2004). Structural change and technology: A long view. *Rev. Économique*, 55, 1099.

Von Hippel, E. (1987). Cooperation between rivals: Informal know-how trading. *Res. Policy*, 157–175.

Winter, S. (1998). Knowledge and competence as strategic assets. *Strateg. Manag. Intellect. Cap.*, 165–187.

Index

A, C, D

E, F, G

I, K, L

M, N, P

R, S, T

Other titles from

iSTE

in

Innovation, Entrepreneurship and Management

2020

ANDREOSSO-O'CALLAGHAN Bernadette, DZEVER Sam, JAUSSAUD Jacques, TAYLOR Robert
Sustainable Development and Energy Transition in Europe and Asia (Innovation and Technology Set – Volume 9)

BEN SLIMANE Sonia, M'HENNI Hatem
Entrepreneurship and Development: Realities and Future Prospects (Smart Innovation Set – Volume 30)

CHOUTEAU Marianne, FOREST Joëlle, NGUYEN Céline
Innovation for Society: The P.S.I. Approach (Smart Innovation Set – Volume 28)

CORON Clotilde
Quantifying Human Resources: Uses and Analysis (Technological Changes and Human Resources Set – Volume 2)

CORON Clotilde, GILBERT Patrick
Technological Change (Technological Changes and Human Resources Set – Volume 1)

CERDIN Jean-Luc, PERETTI Jean-Marie
The Success of Apprenticeships: Views of Stakeholders on Training and Learning
(Human Resources Management Set – Volume 3)

DELCHET-COCHET Karen
Circular Economy: From Waste Reduction to Value Creation
(Economic Growth Set – Volume 2)

DIDAY Edwin, GUAN Rong, SAPORTA Gilbert, WANG Huiwen
Advances in Data Science
(Big Data, Artificial Intelligence and Data Analysis Set – Volume 4)

DOS SANTOS PAULINO Victor
Innovation Trends in the Space Industry
(Smart Innovation Set – Volume 25)

GUILHON Bernard
Venture Capital and the Financing of Innovation
(Innovation Between Risk and Reward Set – Volume 6)

LATOUCHE Pascal
Open Innovation: Human Set-up
(Innovation and Technology Set – Volume 10)

MAKRIDES Andreas, KARAGRIGORIOU Alex, SKIADAS Christos H.
Data Analysis and Applications 3: Computational, Classification, Financial, Statistical and Stochastic Methods
(Big Data, Artificial Intelligence and Data Analysis Set – Volume 5)
Data Analysis and Applications 4: Financial Data Analysis and Methods
(Big Data, Artificial Intelligence and Data Analysis Set – Volume 6)

MASSOTTE Pierre, CORSI Patrick
Complex Decision-Making in Economy and Finance

MICHAUD Thomas
Science Fiction and Innovation Design (Innovation in Engineering and Technology Set – Volume 6)

MONINO Jean-Louis
Data Control: Major Challenge for the Digital Society
(Smart Innovation Set – Volume 29)

MORLAT Clément
Sustainable Productive System: Eco-development versus Sustainable Development
(Smart Innovation Set – Volume 26)

SAULAIS Pierre, ERMINE Jean-Louis
Knowledge Management in Innovative Companies 2: Understanding and Deploying a KM Plan within a Learning Organization
(Smart Innovation Set – Volume 27)

2019

AMENDOLA Mario, GAFFARD Jean-Luc
Disorder and Public Concern Around Globalization

BARBAROUX Pierre
Disruptive Technology and Defence Innovation Ecosystems
(Innovation in Engineering and Technology Set – Volume 5)

DOU Henri, JUILLET Alain, CLERC Philippe
Strategic Intelligence for the Future 1: A New Strategic and Operational Approach
Strategic Intelligence for the Future 2: A New Information Function Approach

FRIKHA Azza
Measurement in Marketing: Operationalization of Latent Constructs

FRIMOUSSE Soufyane
Innovation and Agility in the Digital Age
(Human Resources Management Set – Volume 2)

GAY Claudine, SZOSTAK Bérangère L.
Innovation and Creativity in SMEs: Challenges, Evolutions and Prospects
(Smart Innovation Set – Volume 21)

GORIA Stéphane, HUMBERT Pierre, ROUSSEL Benoît
Information, Knowledge and Agile Creativity
(Smart Innovation Set – Volume 22)

HELLER David
Investment Decision-making Using Optional Models
(Economic Growth Set – Volume 2)

HELLER David, DE CHADIRAC Sylvain, HALAOUI Lana, JOUVET Camille
The Emergence of Start-ups
(Economic Growth Set – Volume 1)

HÉRAUD Jean-Alain, KERR Fiona, BURGER-HELMCHEN Thierry
Creative Management of Complex Systems
(Smart Innovation Set – Volume 19)

LATOUCHE Pascal
Open Innovation: Corporate Incubator
(Innovation and Technology Set – Volume 7)

LEHMANN Paul-Jacques
The Future of the Euro Currency

LEIGNEL Jean-Louis, MÉNAGER Emmanuel, YABLONSKY Serge
Sustainable Enterprise Performance: A Comprehensive Evaluation Method

LIÈVRE Pascal, AUBRY Monique, GAREL Gilles
Management of Extreme Situations: From Polar Expeditions to Exploration-Oriented Organizations

MILLOT Michel
Embarrassment of Product Choices 2: Towards a Society of Well-being

N'GOALA Gilles, PEZ-PÉRARD Virginie, PRIM-ALLAZ Isabelle
Augmented Customer Strategy: CRM in the Digital Age

NIKOLOVA Blagovesta
The RRI Challenge: Responsibilization in a State of Tension with Market Regulation
(Innovation and Responsibility Set – Volume 3)

PELLEGRIN-BOUCHER Estelle, ROY Pierre
Innovation in the Cultural and Creative Industries
(Innovation and Technology Set – Volume 8)

PRIOLON Joël
Financial Markets for Commodities

QUINIOU Matthieu
Blockchain: The Advent of Disintermediation

RAVIX Joël-Thomas, DESCHAMPS Marc
Innovation and Industrial Policies
(Innovation between Risk and Reward Set – Volume 5)

ROGER Alain, VINOT Didier
Skills Management: New Applications, New Questions
(Human Resources Management Set – Volume 1)

SAULAIS Pierre, ERMINE Jean-Louis
Knowledge Management in Innovative Companies 1: Understanding and Deploying a KM Plan within a Learning Organization
(Smart Innovation Set – Volume 23)

SERVAJEAN-HILST Romaric
Co-innovation Dynamics: The Management of Client-Supplier Interactions for Open Innovation
(Smart Innovation Set – Volume 20)

SKIADAS Christos H., BOZEMAN James R.
Data Analysis and Applications 1: Clustering and Regression, Modeling-estimating, Forecasting and Data Mining
(Big Data, Artificial Intelligence and Data Analysis Set – Volume 2)
Data Analysis and Applications 2: Utilization of Results in Europe and Other Topics
(Big Data, Artificial Intelligence and Data Analysis Set – Volume 3)

UZUNIDIS Dimitri
Systemic Innovation: Entrepreneurial Strategies and Market Dynamics

VIGEZZI Michel
World Industrialization: Shared Inventions, Competitive Innovations and Social Dynamics
(Smart Innovation Set – Volume 24)

2018

BURKHARDT Kirsten
Private Equity Firms: Their Role in the Formation of Strategic Alliances

CALLENS Stéphane
Creative Globalization
(Smart Innovation Set – Volume 16)

CASADELLA Vanessa
Innovation Systems in Emerging Economies: MINT – Mexico, Indonesia, Nigeria, Turkey
(Smart Innovation Set – Volume 18)

CHOUTEAU Marianne, FOREST Joëlle, NGUYEN Céline
Science, Technology and Innovation Culture
(Innovation in Engineering and Technology Set – Volume 3)

CORLOSQUET-HABART Marine, JANSSEN Jacques
Big Data for Insurance Companies
(Big Data, Artificial Intelligence and Data Analysis Set – Volume 1)

CROS Françoise
Innovation and Society
(Smart Innovation Set – Volume 15)

DEBREF Romain
Environmental Innovation and Ecodesign: Certainties and Controversies
(Smart Innovation Set – Volume 17)

DOMINGUEZ Noémie
SME Internationalization Strategies: Innovation to Conquer New Markets

ERMINE Jean-Louis
Knowledge Management: The Creative Loop
(Innovation and Technology Set – Volume 5)

GILBERT Patrick, BOBADILLA Natalia, GASTALDI Lise,
LE BOULAIRE Martine, LELEBINA Olga
Innovation, Research and Development Management

IBRAHIMI Mohammed
Mergers & Acquisitions: Theory, Strategy, Finance

LEMAÎTRE Denis
Training Engineers for Innovation

LÉVY Aldo, BEN BOUHENI Faten, AMMI Chantal
Financial Management: USGAAP and IFRS Standards
(Innovation and Technology Set – Volume 6)

MILLOT Michel
Embarrassment of Product Choices 1: How to Consume Differently

PANSERA Mario, OWEN Richard
Innovation and Development: The Politics at the Bottom of the Pyramid
(Innovation and Responsibility Set – Volume 2)

RICHEZ Yves
Corporate Talent Detection and Development

SACHETTI Philippe, ZUPPINGER Thibaud
New Technologies and Branding
(Innovation and Technology Set – Volume 4)

SAMIER Henri
Intuition, Creativity, Innovation

TEMPLE Ludovic, COMPAORÉ SAWADOGO Eveline M.F.W.
Innovation Processes in Agro-Ecological Transitions in Developing Countries
(Innovation in Engineering and Technology Set – Volume 2)

UZUNIDIS Dimitri
Collective Innovation Processes: Principles and Practices
(Innovation in Engineering and Technology Set – Volume 4)

VAN HOOREBEKE Delphine
The Management of Living Beings or Emo-management

2017

AÏT-EL-HADJ Smaïl
The Ongoing Technological System
(Smart Innovation Set – Volume 11)

BAUDRY Marc, DUMONT Béatrice
Patents: Prompting or Restricting Innovation?
(Smart Innovation Set – Volume 12)

BÉRARD Céline, TEYSSIER Christine
Risk Management: Lever for SME Development and Stakeholder Value Creation

CHALENÇON Ludivine
Location Strategies and Value Creation of International Mergers and Acquisitions

CHAUVEL Danièle, BORZILLO Stefano
The Innovative Company: An Ill-defined Object
(Innovation between Risk and Reward Set – Volume 1)

CORSI Patrick
Going Past Limits To Growth

D'ANDRIA Aude, GABARRET Inés
Building 21st Century Entrepreneurship
(Innovation and Technology Set – Volume 2)

DAIDJ Nabyla
Cooperation, Coopetition and Innovation
(Innovation and Technology Set – Volume 3)

FERNEZ-WALCH Sandrine
The Multiple Facets of Innovation Project Management
(Innovation between Risk and Reward Set – Volume 4)

FOREST Joëlle
Creative Rationality and Innovation
(Smart Innovation Set – Volume 14)

GUILHON Bernard
Innovation and Production Ecosystems
(Innovation between Risk and Reward Set – Volume 2)

HAMMOUDI Abdelhakim, DAIDJ Nabyla
Game Theory Approach to Managerial Strategies and Value Creation
(Diverse and Global Perspectives on Value Creation Set – Volume 3)

LALLEMENT Rémi
Intellectual Property and Innovation Protection: New Practices and New Policy Issues
(Innovation between Risk and Reward Set – Volume 3)

LAPERCHE Blandine
Enterprise Knowledge Capital
(Smart Innovation Set – Volume 13)

LEBERT Didier, EL YOUNSI Hafida
International Specialization Dynamics
(Smart Innovation Set – Volume 9)

MAESSCHALCK Marc
Reflexive Governance for Research and Innovative Knowledge
(Responsible Research and Innovation Set – Volume 6)

MASSOTTE Pierre
Ethics in Social Networking and Business 1: Theory, Practice and Current Recommendations
Ethics in Social Networking and Business 2: The Future and Changing Paradigms

MASSOTTE Pierre, CORSI Patrick
Smart Decisions in Complex Systems

MEDINA Mercedes, HERRERO Mónica, URGELLÉS Alicia
Current and Emerging Issues in the Audiovisual Industry
(Diverse and Global Perspectives on Value Creation Set – Volume 1)

MICHAUD Thomas
Innovation, Between Science and Science Fiction
(Smart Innovation Set – Volume 10)

PELLÉ Sophie
Business, Innovation and Responsibility
(Responsible Research and Innovation Set – Volume 7)

SAVIGNAC Emmanuelle
The Gamification of Work: The Use of Games in the Workplace

SUGAHARA Satoshi, DAIDJ Nabyla, USHIO Sumitaka
Value Creation in Management Accounting and Strategic Management: An Integrated Approach
(Diverse and Global Perspectives on Value Creation Set –Volume 2)

UZUNIDIS Dimitri, SAULAIS Pierre
Innovation Engines: Entrepreneurs and Enterprises in a Turbulent World
(Innovation in Engineering and Technology Set – Volume 1)

2016

BARBAROUX Pierre, ATTOUR Amel, SCHENK Eric
Knowledge Management and Innovation
(Smart Innovation Set – Volume 6)

BEN BOUHENI Faten, AMMI Chantal, LEVY Aldo
Banking Governance, Performance And Risk-Taking: Conventional Banks Vs Islamic Banks

BOUTILLIER Sophie, CARRÉ Denis, LEVRATTO Nadine
Entrepreneurial Ecosystems (Smart Innovation Set – Volume 2)

BOUTILLIER Sophie, UZUNIDIS Dimitri
The Entrepreneur (Smart Innovation Set – Volume 8)

BOUVARD Patricia, SUZANNE Hervé
Collective Intelligence Development in Business

GALLAUD Delphine, LAPERCHE Blandine
Circular Economy, Industrial Ecology and Short Supply Chains
(Smart Innovation Set – Volume 4)

GUERRIER Claudine
Security and Privacy in the Digital Era
(Innovation and Technology Set – Volume 1)

MEGHOUAR Hicham
Corporate Takeover Targets

MONINO Jean-Louis, SEDKAOUI Soraya
Big Data, Open Data and Data Development
(Smart Innovation Set – Volume 3)

MOREL Laure, LE ROUX Serge
Fab Labs: Innovative User
(Smart Innovation Set – Volume 5)

PICARD Fabienne, TANGUY Corinne
Innovations and Techno-ecological Transition
(Smart Innovation Set – Volume 7)

2015

CASADELLA Vanessa, LIU Zeting, DIMITRI Uzunidis
Innovation Capabilities and Economic Development in Open Economies
(Smart Innovation Set – Volume 1)

CORSI Patrick, MORIN Dominique
Sequencing Apple's DNA

CORSI Patrick, NEAU Erwan
Innovation Capability Maturity Model

FAIVRE-TAVIGNOT Bénédicte
Social Business and Base of the Pyramid

GODÉ Cécile
Team Coordination in Extreme Environments

MAILLARD Pierre
Competitive Quality and Innovation

MASSOTTE Pierre, CORSI Patrick
Operationalizing Sustainability

MASSOTTE Pierre, CORSI Patrick
Sustainability Calling

2014

DUBÉ Jean, LEGROS Diègo
Spatial Econometrics Using Microdata

LESCA Humbert, LESCA Nicolas
Strategic Decisions and Weak Signals

2013

HABART-CORLOSQUET Marine, JANSSEN Jacques, MANCA Raimondo
VaR Methodology for Non-Gaussian Finance

2012

DAL PONT Jean-Pierre
Process Engineering and Industrial Management

MAILLARD Pierre
Competitive Quality Strategies

POMEROL Jean-Charles
Decision-Making and Action

SZYLAR Christian
UCITS Handbook

2011

LESCA Nicolas
Environmental Scanning and Sustainable Development

LESCA Nicolas, LESCA Humbert
Weak Signals for Strategic Intelligence: Anticipation Tool for Managers

MERCIER-LAURENT Eunika
Innovation Ecosystems

2010

SZYLAR Christian
Risk Management under UCITS III/IV

2009

COHEN Corine
Business Intelligence

ZANINETTI Jean-Marc
Sustainable Development in the USA

2008

CORSI Patrick, DULIEU Mike
The Marketing of Technology Intensive Products and Services

DZEVER Sam, JAUSSAUD Jacques, ANDREOSSO Bernadette
Evolving Corporate Structures and Cultures in Asia: Impact of Globalization

2007

AMMI Chantal
Global Consumer Behavior

2006

BOUGHZALA Imed, ERMINE Jean-Louis
Trends in Enterprise Knowledge Management

CORSI Patrick *et al.*
Innovation Engineering: the Power of Intangible Networks

Printed in the USA/Agawam, MA
September 16, 2026

910661.023